Faithful
and
Fractured

"I've enjoyed being called to pastoral leadership and have felt privileged to help a new generation of pastors into the vocation. But let's face it: church can be demanding, difficult, and even toxic for those who try to lead. The research reported and skillfully interpreted in *Faithful and Fractured* can be of great help to those of us who oversee pastors and to pastors themselves. It offers tested, proven guidance for us to remain faithful even when we are fractured by the vocation to which God has called us."

—**Will Willimon**, Duke Divinity School; United Methodist bishop, retired; author of *Pastor: The Theology and Practice of Ordained Leadership*

"There are plenty of books outlining how difficult the work of ministry is and the toll it takes on the men and women who do it. There are far fewer resources that point to what can be done to reverse the damage. *Faithful and Fractured* honestly assesses the problem and then goes on to break new ground, describing practical ways that clergy can build positive mental health to not only survive ministry but also flourish while doing it."

—**Matt Miofsky**, lead pastor of The Gathering; author of *Happy? What It Is and How to Find It*

"An invaluable resource for clergy and for all who care for them, especially their therapists, spiritual directors, and judicatory leaders. This book should be required reading for every seminary student. May the wisdom that is reflected in these pages become a way of life for pastors in the years ahead."

—**Elaine Heath**, Duke Divinity School

"Pastoring is a dangerous, glorious journey. Drawing on extensive research on the lives of working pastors, Proeschold-Bell and Byassee offer a life-giving path for pastors to become fully alive. Follow the deep and practical wisdom of this book and watch your life and ministry flourish."

—**Ken Shigematsu**, pastor of Tenth Church, Vancouver, British Columbia; author of *God in My Everything*

"Bravo! *Faithful and Fractured* is as important as it is urgent. Christian ministry is a high calling and a gift, yet it is beset by profound challenges and difficulties. The rigorous work of the Clergy Health Initiative, supported generously by The Duke Endowment, provides significant quantitative and qualitative data on which to base new strategies and actions. The future of ministry will be much brighter and more life giving if we pay attention to this beautifully crafted, substantive book."

—**L. Gregory Jones**, Duke Divinity School

Faithful
and
Fractured

Responding to the
CLERGY HEALTH CRISIS

Rae Jean Proeschold-Bell
and Jason Byassee

Baker Academic
a division of Baker Publishing Group
Grand Rapids, Michigan

© 2018 by Rae Jean Proeschold-Bell and Jason Byassee

Published by Baker Academic
a division of Baker Publishing Group
PO Box 6287, Grand Rapids, MI 49516-6287
www.bakeracademic.com

Printed in the United States of America

Library of Congress Cataloging-in-Publication Data
Names: Proeschold-Bell, Rae Jean, author. | Byassee, Jason, author.
Title: Faithful and fractured : responding to the clergy health crisis / Rae Jean Proeschold-Bell and Jason Byassee.
Description: Grand Rapids, MI : Baker Publishing Group, [2018] | Includes bibliographical references.
Identifiers: LCCN 2017051464 | ISBN 9780801098833 (pbk. : alk. paper)
Subjects: LCSH: Clergy—Health and hygiene.
Classification: LCC BV4397.5 .P76 2018 | DDC 253/.2—dc23
LC record available at https://lccn.loc.gov/2017051464

Scripture quotations are from the New Revised Standard Version of the Bible, copyright © 1989, by the Division of Christian Education of the National Council of the Churches of Christ in the United States of America. Used by permission. All rights reserved.

Cover image: The Japanese art of kintsugi transforms broken ceramic vessels into beautiful and unique works of art using gold. The term "kintsugi life" highlights how you can employ this metaphor in your own life.

18   19   20   21   22   23   24   7   6   5   4   3   2   1

From Rae Jean

I dedicate this book to the United Methodist Church pastors of North Carolina, who have constantly inspired and taught me.

I also dedicate this book to Robb Webb and Kristen Richardson-Frick, who are passionately committed to the United Methodist Church and who care deeply for the health of pastors.

From Jason

This book is for pastors and for those who care about pastors. I dedicate my portion of it to one of the latter group—Susan—whose elegance and kindness and desire for holiness made her a new mother for me.

Contents

Illustrations

Unless otherwise noted, all data in figures comes from surveys completed in 2016 by full-time church-appointed pastors.

Tables

Preface

The Birth of the Duke Clergy Health Initiative

Ten years: that's how long I (Rae Jean) have been studying the health of clergy. Prior to this project, I had not once considered how clergy care for themselves. I had been studying health issues, like HIV, that are held up by society as public health concerns, and my work was funded by the federal government. Although the National Institutes of Health funds research on some occupations, clergy isn't one of them. But in 2007, a friend of mine was hired to work on a new grant awarded by The Duke Endowment to Duke Divinity School. The project goals were to understand and improve the holistic health of United Methodist clergy in North Carolina. My friend asked if I would work as a part-time researcher for the project.

My first instinct was to say no. I knew nothing about clergy. More importantly, my work was devoted to health inequalities, and I doubted that clergy could be that unhealthy because, after all, they generally are educated and have health insurance. But as a researcher, I've learned it's best to get all the information and then decide, rather than to rely on assumptions.

I soon learned that clergy were crying out for help. Clergy would attend conferences together and be astounded by how much stress they dealt with, how many funerals they officiated for, and how many of them were overweight. Talk about stress and burnout was common. Their health insurance costs were astronomical, making it impossible for some churches to pay for a full-time pastor with health benefits. United Methodist bishop Lawrence McCleskey said at a meeting hosted by The Duke Endowment, "If we don't get insurance right for clergy, there won't be a church left to strengthen."[1] This statement garnered the attention of program officers at The Duke Endowment, which has a program focused on strengthening the rural church. When The Duke Endowment gave leaders from one United Methodist district funds to improve the health of their clergy, leaders from other districts raised an outcry, saying that *their* clergy needed the help just as much. This ultimately led The Duke Endowment to create a grant for the Duke Clergy Health Initiative.

As a community psychologist, I found this groundswell of interest compelling. However, clergy health was a departure from my typical work, and I really might have walked away had it not been for what I perceived as a lack of science behind these observations about clergy health. Of course clergy were gaining weight—that was true of individuals across the United States. And of course clergy health insurance was becoming more expensive—everyone's was! Before we decided clergy were a special case, I thought we ought to have systematic data. Later, I learned that there was in fact data behind The Duke Endowment's decision—reports showed clergy submitting more health care claims than the general population.[2]

So I put one toe in the water, and soon my whole soul followed. The Duke Clergy Health Initiative, stewarded by David Toole and eventually staffed by an extraordinary group of twenty-six wellness advocates, program implementers, data collectors, and staff, set out to understand the health of United Methodist clergy. We began by conducting thirteen focus groups so we could hear from clergy in their own words. The quotations in this book come from clergy focus groups held between 2008 and 2010 to understand ministry life and well-being from the perspective of pastors. Some quotes also come from clergy interviews held in 2014 and 2015 to understand positive mental health and burnout among clergy.

Percentages and other numeric data in this book come from the biennial surveys (described in the following paragraphs), in which all United Methodist Church (UMC) clergy in North Carolina were invited to participate; these were held in 2008, 2010, 2012, 2014, and 2016. Most of the analyses for this book use 2016 data from clergy with current appointments (in other words, not retired clergy or those working outside of the UMC). We conducted most analyses selecting for clergy with full-time or part-time appointments to churches, and for those analyses the sample size is usually 1,105, although sometimes responses are missing for a few clergy. We limit some analyses to

1. L. McClesky, communicated at a meeting of The Duke Endowment, 2006.
2. Frenk et al., "Psychotropic Medication Claims"; Meador et al., "Church Benefits Association Survey."

full-time church-appointed clergy (i.e., excluding part-time pastors), with a usual sample size of 852, although again, sometimes a few responses are missing. In one or two places, we report findings using survey data from before 2016 because either the question was not included on the 2016 survey or we compared the clergy data to other population data and wanted to keep the years of data collection comparable.

For each of these studies, clergy gave explicit consent to share their data, whether the data was a verbal quotation or a survey response. We promised to share their data only in ways that would not allow any single individual to be identified.

In 2008 we also conducted a survey of all United Methodist clergy in North Carolina.[3] This survey was remarkable in two respects. First, all currently appointed United Methodist clergy in the state were invited to participate. I argued against this approach—we researchers are used to sampling, and I didn't think we needed to hear from eighteen hundred clergy. But the two United Methodist bishops in North Carolina told me they would only endorse the survey if everyone was included. I mentioned already that I knew nothing about clergy, and this was lesson one: the United Methodist Church is a connectional ministry, meaning inclusion is paramount, even for something as tedious as taking a survey.

The second remarkable aspect of the survey was the high degree to which clergy participated. I learned a second lesson: clergy were really worried about their health and the health of their clergy brothers and sisters. They also knew that their responses would inform a health intervention designed specifically for them. Their response rate was an unheard-of 95 percent.[4] And the clergy didn't stop there—but neither did we. We made the survey longitudinal and repeated it in 2010, 2012, 2014, and 2016, and each survey wave had a great response rate. This is the only existing self-reported longitudinal data set of clergy health, which allows us to see how individual clergy do over time.

In addition, we used these surveys and focus groups to design a holistic health program tailored to clergy. This program, Spirited Life, aimed to improve pastors' overall health—their minds, bodies, and spirits. During focus

3. We have published many articles from the 2008 survey that describe its methods. See, for example, Proeschold-Bell et al., "Using Effort-Reward Imbalance Theory." The Duke Clergy Health Initiative website provides a less detailed description and offers numerous findings in accessible formats at http://clergyhealthinitiative.org.

4. In research, the higher your response rate is, the less biased your findings likely are. For example, if we had a much lower response rate, we might worry that sicker clergy hadn't participated and that our findings would show clergy as healthier than they really are. The wonderful thing about a 95 percent response rate is that it allows us not to worry about whether our findings are biased in one direction or another—the data are essentially complete.

group meetings, pastors reported that "self-care" sounds "selfish";[5] we therefore thought it important to start Spirited Life with a theological grounding.
Participants first attended a workshop in which we cared for them, offering
them a chance to be in the pews while other pastors gave sermons and served
communion. The content of the sermons connected theology and health, often
with a focus on incarnation. In one sermon, Rev. Ed Moore showed an image
of the jars at Cana and compared those jars to pastors' bodies. If a pastor's
jar is broken, it is harder to fill to the brim with the water about to be changed
to wine. If the jar has integrity, however, it can hold God's grace much better.
This initial workshop also included time to articulate personal health goals;
we asked pastors to set goals themselves in order to encourage their own
agency. We then supported pastors through health coaching for an extended
period of time (two years) so they could make a behavior change, slip up, and
still have the support of a health coach to get back at it.[6] Two years was also
enough time to work on more than one goal, if desired. For interested pastors,
we facilitated their participation in an online weight-loss and healthy-eating
program and in stress-reduction programs. Because it's hard to stay engaged in
healthy behaviors for a long time, we used additional workshops and a small
grant to reengage pastors across the span of those two years.

Spirited Life was innovative in its long time frame and its combination
of weight-loss and stress-management programming. We were all eager to
find out if it made a difference in clergy health. Through rigorous research,
we learned that Spirited Life led to clinically meaningful (and statistically
significant) improvements for weight, waist circumference, blood pressure,
and HDL cholesterol.[7] These physical health results endured across the two-
year intervention, whereas most programs don't sustain results past one year.
These results were also impressive in that other programs tend to target one
specific outcome (such as blood pressure) and only enroll people highly motivated to improve it. By contrast, we enrolled all who responded and let them
choose their health goals, and we still found significant improvements in the
outcomes we measured.

To be clear, the significant improvements we found were in *physical* outcomes. Spirited Life did not improve depression or stress symptoms. A big
motivation for this book was my frustration that Spirited Life didn't help
pastors' mental health. I took this failure personally and worked together
with our team to seek a more fruitful way forward, which ultimately led us

5. Proeschold-Bell et al., "Theoretical Model."
6. Proeschold-Bell et al., "Randomized Multiple Baseline Design."
7. Proeschold-Bell et al., "Two-Year Holistic Health and Stress Intervention."

to the field of positive mental health—the focus of chapters 6 and 7 in this book. In addition, spread throughout the book are lessons we learned about providing programs to clergy and the concepts related to pastors' lives and behavior change that we consider essential.

If you've picked up this book and are a clergy person, I'm delighted by that. The findings and tentative solutions in this book are meant for you—I had you in mind the whole time I was writing. Likewise, if you are reading this book as someone who cares about clergy—either because you help run their health insurance program or because you teach them leadership skills or because you want to see congregations thrive into the future—know that I wrote with you also in mind.

Even though most of my knowledge is about United Methodist clergy, I hope that clergy across many denominations and faiths will read this book. Clergy face similar issues, even when theology differs. Studies on the work of diverse clergy show great similarities in terms of job demands, roles, and how clergy spend their time.[8] These studies cover mainline Protestant and other Christian clergy, as well as Catholic priests, and they occurred in the United States, the United Kingdom, Hong Kong, Australia, and New Zealand. It is true, though, that the clergy health issues in this book are most relevant to conditions in high-income countries. More research still needs to be done on clergy health in low- and middle-income countries.

You will see in chapter 1 that findings indicating health problems for United Methodist clergy also hint at a larger problem among clergy more broadly. Episcopal, Unitarian, Presbyterian, and Lutheran denominations are among those who see distressing signals in their health insurance and claims data. Even though we draw on data from United Methodists (the largest of the "mainline" denominations in the United States), these findings are broadly relevant.

Reading this book won't require you to slog through research findings without a theological voice. Recognizing my limitations, I sought a theologian to offer a religious perspective throughout the book. I am grateful to Jason Byassee for joining me in this endeavor and for deepening my thinking, and hopefully yours, about clergy health.

Our two voices will alternate like the dialogue Jason and I truly had while working on this book. Most of Jason's insights take shape within the "Behind the Pulpit" sections, in which he sometimes offers theological grounding and

8. Carroll, *God's Potters*; Dewe, "New Zealand Ministers of Religion"; Frame and Shehan, "Work and Well-Being in the Two-Person Career"; Gleason, "Perception of Stress among Clergy and Their Spouses"; Hang-Yue, Foley, and Loi, "Work Role Stressors and Turnover Intentions"; Kay, "Role Conflict and British Pentecostal Ministers"; Kuhne and Donaldson, "Balancing Ministry and Management"; Noller, "Clergy Marriages."

other times provides examples of pastors' experiences. These examples are true, although in order to protect pastors' identities, he has changed names and details and has merged multiple pastors' and parishioners' experiences. You'll also hear Jason's voice in some tables, lists, and sidebars throughout the book. We hope you'll find our dialogue both informative and applicable to your own circumstances.

Behind the Pulpit
Why Share These Findings?

I (Jason) am interested in this project because of the gospel's promise. Irenaeus says "the glory of God is a human being fully alive."[9] I'm part of a denomination with pastors who are remarkably unhealthy and thus less alive. That means we are not living the fully alive life that Irenaeus describes as the way of discipleship. To shift the image, we are fractured in a number of ways. Paul says we hold the treasure of grace in "earthen vessels," a charmingly modest image. But if those vessels are nothing but shards on the floor, we receive no grace, nor can we pass any on to others. Rae Jean's work documents these fractures clearly. So where's the problem *in our gospel*? How is the thing that is supposed to make us fully alive actually making less of us?

I've seen it go the other way too. Sometimes folks *get it*, and life with Jesus becomes the most alive sort of life there is. Sometimes even we clergy make progress toward better health. A buddy and I lumbered our way to finishing a marathon a few years back. With another set of friends at my church, I ran a half marathon to raise money for a ministry in our church. I've lost thirty pounds before putting forty back on, so I know the greater energy that comes from the former, the misery from the latter. And I believe Jesus is Lord over all life—including every bite we take (and don't take). Christianity has always been bound up with holy feasting and holy fasting on the way to fullness of life with God.

As a theologian, I will try to flesh out some concepts theologically, like "call" and "control" and "work." I will also bring to bear my experience as a pastor who has participated in surveys and studies like these alongside my peers. Rae Jean collects the data and interprets it; I offer some theological and pastoral shading along the way.

One of Christ's historic roles is that of healer, making the cosmos and all creatures fully well, as he shows through his ministry in first-century Galilee and Judea. Christians have founded hospitals and clinics ever since,

---

9. *Against Heresies* 4.20.7, in *Irenaeus of Lyons*, 153.

demonstrating God's claim to be Lord even over disease and its distortion of human flourishing. The church has a strong history of caring for folks' physical health. But we have been more nervous about helping with mental health. Antidepressant medication was recently recommended to a clergy friend. She balked—perhaps thinking that if she were spiritually and mentally stronger, she wouldn't need it. The psychiatrist said, "You know most of your colleagues are on antidepressants, right?" The doctor may have overstated this, but he was giving this pastor (and caregiver) permission to accept care, allowing her to keep serving Jesus's church. My dad is a psychologist, so I grew up surrounded by mental health professionals. Though clergy and their churches have not always integrated the wisdom of mental health professionals into their lives, I would like to see this become integral to clergy and congregation health. I want to see my pastor colleagues more whole, more fully alive. I think life with Jesus is the best sort of life there is. And I want more of that life "that really is life" as Paul puts it (1 Tim. 6:19), for all of us, in pursuit together.

What to Expect

There is a true crisis in clergy physical health. We believe it stems from the stressors pastors face today and the expectations other people have of pastors, paired with pastors' expectations of themselves. In this book, we look at what it means to be called to holy work and how the deep sense that your work is sacred makes you more likely to sacrifice (even if unconsciously) your well-being. We also look at the external expectations. It is the combination of the two that sets the stage—for some clergy at least—for depression and stress.

To drive home to you the dire state of clergy physical health, we share robust numbers on what we know of pastors' physical health problems. We also make sense of the history of clergy health and why it's wrong to think that clergy used to be physically fit but aren't today.

In the final three chapters, we take you with us into the world of positive mental health—a world we wish we had known about sooner and one we think holds great promise for the promotion of mental health *and* physical health. The benefits of positive mental health hold for clergy and nonclergy alike, and in chapter 6 we delve into the science behind positive emotions. We then let pastors speak in their own words through quotes culled from interviews with ordinary pastors who have high positive mental health and are, by all accounts, flourishing. Their recommendations for sustaining positive mental health in ministry are the heart of chapter 7. Finally, we end by envisioning the future of ministry and suggesting what is possible now, in this very moment.

We know most of you don't have the resources or the calling to design clergy health programs. Even so, we hope that someone who reads this book does just that! For you, we've included an appendix with the gold nuggets from our experiences in designing integrated physical-mental-spiritual programs for clergy. We share our hard-learned lessons in the hope of benefiting others who, like us, create programs to improve clergy health.

Taken together, the chapters in this book should inform individual clergy striving to be strong ministers across the years; lay leaders aspiring to improve the environment of their churches; clergy supervisors interested in fostering a cadre of strong clergy; and maybe even program developers seeking to design programs to promote the physical and mental health of clergy, which will benefit us all.

1

Creatures Doing
the Creator's Work

Twelve-hour workday. Three committee meetings. One breakfast meeting and one lunch meeting. Working with the Music Director to tweak the sound system in the Fellowship Hall for Sunday youth worship. Working with the Associate Pastor on Confirmation Sunday plans. At least three dozen emails and one dozen phone calls. Various conversations with folks about new members, revamped websites, capital campaigns, session retreats, NEXT Church, Sunday school classes and one member who asked how my family is adjusting to the move. *Honestly, I get to do this for a living. How awesome is that?*

Steven Lindsley, Facebook post (May 7, 2014)

Ah, a day in the life of a pastor. Despite public perception, pastors do so much more than write and deliver Sunday's sermon. You likely know this already, or else you wouldn't have picked up this book. However, it's worth taking a minute to examine the content of a pastor's day, beyond its essential busyness.

The day is long. This particular pastor is writing a Facebook post during his first weeks at a new church, at the end of a twelve-hour workday (and you have to wonder, is posting about ministry life essentially doing more work?). This pastor broke bread while working, with both breakfast and lunch occurring during work meetings. It's unclear whether he ever got a break during the day or was able to have dinner with his family, but let's hope that he did.[1] The one dozen phone calls suggest frequent interruptions and a lot of work with people. Working with the associate pastor suggests a supervisory relationship, indicating that this pastor needs to have managerial and delegation skills. But perhaps most notable is the range of activities that fall within a single day, from attracting new members to raising money to communicating using the web to—almost laughably—tweaking the sound system!

This pastor spent his day moving from one different task to another, quite likely at a pace set by others, with interruptions, and with little opportunity to see a particular project or decision through to completion. This pastor also drew on diverse skill sets throughout the day. Studies have shown that toggling between tasks that involve different skill sets can result in a particular kind of stressor termed "task switching." In fact, toggling from task to task can be harder on someone than doing the same very stressful task all day—because the very act of changing gears costs mental resources and can slow a person down and lead to errors.[2]

Figure 1.1
Feelings of Unpredictability

"My daily activities from week to week are unpredictable."

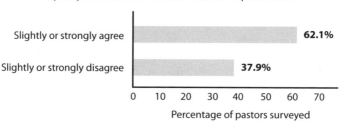

Percentage of pastors surveyed

Responses are from 2016 surveys of full-time church-appointed pastors.

This pastor had a very long day. He did not mention driving, but pastors who serve in rural areas often make long drives in order to do things like visit parishioners in hospitals. Also, this pastor did *not* mention preparing his sermon for Sunday, but I'm sure he thought about it and maybe even worried about it. As we heard in one clergy focus group, "Sunday always comes right on time"—even if you're not ready for it!

1. Darling, Hill, and McWey, "Understanding Stress and Quality of Life for Clergy and Clergy Spouses"; Wells et al., "Relationship between Work-Related Stress and Boundary-Related Stress."
2. Monsell, "Task Switching."

For this pastor, this particular day did not involve any crises, but it is quite in the nature of clergy work to require adjustment and readjustment as new priorities arise. Sometimes these new priorities mean performing a funeral during a full week when Sunday's sermon isn't ready yet. Other times, new priorities can come in the form of parishioners in crisis. Studies have shown that, among people in the United States seeking help for a serious mental illness, nearly a quarter approach clergy as their first line of professional support.[3]

Although 74.8 percent of full-time church-appointed pastors reported that they don't mind advance scheduling, 25.2 percent slightly or strongly agreed with the statement, "I do not like to make appointments too far in advance because I do not know what might come up."

Even though this pastor's day was lengthy, long hours in and of themselves do not seem to be a problem for the mental health of clergy. The weeks of Advent that lead into Christmas and the observances during Holy Week, leading into Easter, may be among the busiest times of the year for pastors, but pastors see work during those seasons as essential—core to their calling—and because they carry such great meaning, those times of the year are not the most stressful for clergy. In fact, in looking at our survey data, there was no relationship between the number of hours worked per week and depression or anxiety. Working long hours when one is energized in ministry is not necessarily a problem.

What does seem to be a problem is when pastors feel like they can't ever take a break from ministry work or when they feel guilty for not doing enough.[4] Our survey data give us an idea of how common these pressures are among clergy. Pastors working in poor areas, whether rural or urban, face extra pressure from the economic stagnation, resource-deprived schools, and lack of hope for the future experienced by their parishioners. The gospel message works well in such circumstances, but the toll on pastors is real.

When asked, "Over the past year, how guilty have you felt about not doing enough in your role as clergy?," 25.6 percent of full-time church-appointed pastors in 2016 indicated they felt moderately guilty, and 9.5 percent said they felt very or extremely guilty.

Consider also the numerous meetings each week for things like spiritual growth or building and maintaining the church. The pastor cannot possibly organize and attend all the events, and doing so might in fact undermine the church by undercutting the feeling of ownership of the members. Churches rely on parishioners—who are essentially

3. Wang, Berglund, and Kessler, "Patterns and Correlates."
4. Proeschold-Bell et al., "Using Effort-Reward Imbalance Theory."

Figure 1.2
Expectations for Availability

"How much of your time do you think church members
expect you to make available to them?"

Less than 40 hours a week — 2.0%
About 40 hours a week — 14.1%
Between 40 and 50 hours a week — 40.4%
Most of my time, including significant time beyond a 40+ hour work week, although a day off per week is generally acceptable — 37.1%
Nearly all of my time, with a day off not really feeling acceptable — 2.8%
All of my time, 24 hours a day, 7 days a week — 3.6%

0   10   20   30   40

Responses from full-time church-appointed clergy in 2016. In 2014, the responses
to "most," "nearly," and "all of my time" totaled to 6.5 percentage points higher;
interventions with NC clergy and congregations may be making a difference.

unpaid volunteers—to conduct much of this work.[5] The pastor has to notice who is good at what and develop the skills of volunteers. And the number of volunteers needed can be numerous: volunteers for the finance committee, building maintenance, hospitality events, childcare, helping the pastor develop a vision for the church, and many other tasks. In one focus group I led, a second-career pastor who used to work for a large company emphasized how hard it is to lead volunteers and, more generally, to work within the organizational structure of the United Methodist Church.

> In many small churches, there's a lot of stress. I came out of working in a company with a $7-million-dollar budget and a number of people that I was in charge of, and I did not have the pressure and stress that's on me in the ministry of three churches. You just have a control in industry that you don't have [in ministry]. If you had a disruptive individual that wasn't a team player, you could fire him! Your CEO . . . was readily down the hall and available for discussion about problems. Now, he's in Raleigh and he's not available. Your district managers are tied up in paperwork and everything else and not able to come to the churches or to the locations where you need them to help relieve that stress.

5. Carroll, *God's Potters*.

Pastors must be good leaders on small and large levels. They demonstrate leadership on a smaller level when they identify talented parishioners and work with them, and they demonstrate leadership on a larger level in where they choose to put their—and the church's—energy. On both levels, pastors are highly visible, and their work and actions (even those unrelated to work) are often judged.[6]

Behind the Pulpit
Rent-Free Living

Folks in the recovery community sometimes give out this sage advice: Don't let anyone live in your head rent-free. If they're not adding value to your life, kick them out of your thoughts. I wish it were that easy.

I got to know Beth early in my time as head pastor. Her presence brings to mind a different saying, this one from out on the Canadian prairie: be wary of whoever meets you at the train. That is, the first person welcoming you to the stop on the prairie is there for a reason. He or she wants something from you or is alienated from the rest of the community and wants to get to you first. So it was with Beth. She had great energy for starting ministries, had a heart for reaching the community, and came to worship like she was hooked up to a homing beacon. She was cheerful when she saw me, and when she hugged me, she smelled good—like being-close-to-grandma good.

Till she quit showing up for anything. A friend saw her and asked where she'd been: "I just can't do it right now," Beth said. Then I started hearing things from her friends. "Beth says you only care about the younger people." "Beth says you've wrecked her Sunday school class." "Beth says you're out of town too much." I was tempted to turn this last complaint around on her: "If you think I'm gone too much, you must like it when I'm here!" But logic was not what Beth was after. She was after hurtful story lines that could undermine me. That the story lines were mutually contradictory didn't matter any more than it matters for attack narratives in partisan politics. Folks eventually assume that where there's smoke there's fire. And Beth made plenty of smoke.

I tried going to her directly. We'd have a friendly visit, but no behavior change resulted. I tried sending notes. Sometimes these received thanks but no behavioral alteration. I tried asking her friends what was eating her. "Beth just gets that way," they said. But then I started wondering about these friends. Why

6. Lee and Iverson-Gilbert, "Demand, Support, and Perception."

were they listening to her? Why were they passing on these critiques if there wasn't a shred of truth in them?

Then the really damaging accusations started to fly. "Beth says your salary is x." The figure was some 60 percent more than I actually made. I wanted to reply, "I thought making money was no crime in this country," or, "I plan to make that one day, when I deserve it," but I didn't. I just said that Beth didn't know what she was talking about. And I told the askers what I actually made. In Methodist land you can find our salaries with a few clicks of a mouse. These salaries are public for reasons of accountability and history, and they have always been. In my case, as one of the higher paid people in the conference, this should have encouraged my fellow church folks to help keep me from the danger of wealth, about which John Wesley often preached. But here it was being used to suggest I was out of touch, elitist, overpaid, and not worth it. The bizarre accusations kept coming. I'd broken Beth's confidentiality. I'd run off all the old people. I'd also run off all the parents of young children. Again, these claims were impossible to square with the facts on the ground. But they were coming fast and furious.

I could guess at where this pain all came from in Beth's past, but that didn't matter. In terms of our church, I could see her point. The new members joining our church were disproportionately from my age group—parents with young kids. As they joined, it drastically changed the dynamics in the Sunday school class that Beth was teaching, and she missed the folks whose kids had been placed in another Sunday school class to accommodate growth. This was not planned by me or anybody else; it just happened (and has continued since I left—no credit for me!), but it affected her life and left her feeling unhappy. I had no idea Sunday school classes were competitive! Shows how naïve I was. In a strange, roundabout way, you could blame me for this, even though not a single dime was moved in the budget and no plan was made by the staff to make these things so.

One thing I actually *did* do was scratch the children's sermon from our liturgy. Children's sermons go on too long. They patronize the kids. They bore the adults. I did this after years of advocacy for the change by our children's minister, our children's ministry team, and our worship committee. The few people who wanted to keep the children's sermon weren't usually the children's sermon preachers. Those who peached the children's sermons did their best with a dated practice, worked hard at it, often produced good fruit from wretched soil, and seemed relieved, for the most part, by this decision. The complaints came from the children's sermon preachers' friends, who worried that the sermon-givers were being disrespected. We continued to have children come forward during worship—but they did so to lead. They blessed something or someone, laid hands on it for prayer, and took an active part in leading our worship. It was a great change, and I couldn't have thanked our children's minister more for suggesting it. But it *was* genuinely change, and it prompted the comment about my running off the parents of young kids. This demographic actually thanked me for the change (and the kids, frankly, didn't care either way, although they can tell when they're being used as a prop). It was the right thing to do, and doing the right but potentially costly thing is called leadership. I exercised it. And Beth resented it.

In the end, it turned out that I was safe from Beth's machinations. Sometimes she went too far in public, and when she did, it won me support. She would be so extreme that even her friends had conversations with me afterward and left feeling reassured, fortified, and newly confident in my leadership.

But what if that all hadn't been the case? What if we were in a smaller church and Beth's voice were louder, amplified in a smaller echo chamber? What if she had contributed a significant portion of the budget? What if she had been, frankly, more convincing? What if folks hadn't been inclined to give me the benefit of the doubt?

Even though things banked in my favor, Beth clearly got in my head. I'd recite emails I'd like to send her. I'd rehearse speeches I planned to give to her friends. I'd anticipate places her arguments would pop up in committee meetings and refute them in advance. I still do! Instead of strategizing how the church could creatively do ministry in our community, I was sparring with Beth in my mind.

I had a lot of the things one would imagine goes into being happy: a big church, a decent payday by church standards, lots of support, and an affirming congregation. And I felt stressed all the time. Some of this depends on one's internal motor—I've wrestled with anxiety and depression at various times in my life, something that can make me more prone to feel stress (Rae Jean discusses this more in chap. 3). Some of it is just the nature of the job—folks see someone in a visible position of power and naturally look for that person's flaws. I get it. This scrutiny comes with standing up in front of people and daring to speak of God. Sometimes their minds wander from my words: "He's gained weight." "He's more arrogant than I thought." "Wait, that's outrageous!" And naturally some of this comes from folks' own lives and has nothing to do with me.

But it does. I want people to be pleased with me. Too much so. It's one reason I went into this job. Jesse Helms, the late, staunchly conservative senator from North Carolina, used to joke that the other side could nominate one Mortimer Snerd to run against him and that guy would immediately have 45 percent of the vote.[7] He slept at night knowing that nearly half the electorate wanted him out. I could have 5 percent of people unhappy with me and it would ruin my day. This is, of course, ridiculous psychological math. I advise against it. But I could never figure out how to do the job without that sort of counting.

Another pastor friend said something wise: whatever you do in ministry, 10 percent of people will adore the ground you walk on, 10 percent of people will hate your guts and actively work for your ouster, and 80 percent of people will shake your hand, say "good sermon, preacher!" once a week, and not think about you again till the next time they turn up.

Our problem is often one of meaning. We go into ministry because we want to be part of Jesus's saving lives and of his coming kingdom, which will renew all things. And then we can't see how our jobs have anything to do with those things. Fill out these forms. Go to these meetings. Get gossiped about. Where's the drama we sought? The life-changing, earth-restoring avalanche of grace we wanted to be part of?

Stanley Hauerwas exaggerates only a little when he imagines a parishioner asking a pastor if he can pick up her son Johnny from school and take him to ball practice. The pastor has the time in the afternoon and can't think of a reason to say no. So he does it. He's well on his way to becoming a quivering mass of availability, to paraphrase Hauerwas.[8] We're not sure what ministry is for, so we act desperately nice in every circumstance, foisting our neediness and desire to please all comers. We went into ministry to change lives and society, and we end up being nibbled to death by ducks, as Hauerwas has been known to say.[9] That's not martyrdom. It's pathetic. No wonder so many ministers flame out with money or sex troubles when they don't eat themselves to death. These are signs of despair. A Catholic friend of mine nearly worked himself to death for his diocese. His bishop stopped his freneticism with these wise words: it's good to be a martyr but not to the bureaucracy.

What's the answer? A bigger gospel. One with a crucified Jew who rules the cosmos. One where resurrection changes all our systems of power and glory. One where we ministers are profoundly secondary because Christ and his church are first. A gospel big enough to take up a cross and follow Jesus is the answer to every human challenge. It has to be the answer here too. I was never quite able to keep the concerns about criticism out of my head, but I think part

---

7. "Conservative Icon Jesse Helms Dead at 86."

8. This story and phrasing is attributed to Stanley Hauerwas, Christian Ethics lectures (Duke Divinity School, Durham, NC, spring 1997).

9. This phrasing is attributed to Stanley Hauerwas, Christian Ethics lectures (Duke Divinity School, Durham, NC, spring 1997).

of the answer is walking alongside other people—clergy and parishioners—who are intent on focusing on the gospel and reminding us—yes, even us clergy—of the cross.

Clergy Work: Roles and Opportunities

Anecdotally among United Methodist Church (UMC) clergy, the most stressful seasons are (1) Charge Conference, which involves reporting church membership and financial numbers to the bishop and (2) the annual evaluation of the pastor by the church leaders. These are two times when UMC clergy are being judged, and I'm sure other Christian traditions have an analogue. Being judged creates a particularly difficult kind of stressor for clergy both because it is interpersonal in nature and because the judging is of the clergy person's work, which is sacred to them. Clergy want to do their absolute best in the work they are called by God to do, and falling short is stressful to them in a way that is less likely to be the case for people doing work they do not consider to be sacred. Being judged by congregants may also occur in a public way, which can be shaming and emotionally difficult. We will delve more into holy work in chapter 2.

Churches are led by many people, and that's intentional because it allows many people to do God's work. However, this can also lead to disagreements that can turn into battles. Consider first that pastors are paid by the church to lead the church. This situation itself is tricky—who has final decision-making power: the pastor or the church leaders? Or the bishop? Or even God?

Figure 1.3
Presence of Conflict

"Over the last six months, has there been any conflict in your primary congregation?"

No conflict that I'm aware of	20.0%
Some minor conflict	61.0%
Major conflict	10.1%
Major conflict with leaders or people leaving	8.9%

0   10   20   30   40   50   60   70

Responses are from 2016 surveys of full-time church-appointed pastors.

Also, when thinking about why work in the church may involve conflict, consider the diversity of the parishioners themselves and the differing opinions they may have on how a pastor's time is best spent. One parishioner may think that visiting parishioners who are too sick to come to church is paramount, whereas another may think that growing the church through focusing on the youth ministry is most important. These are matters of opinion in which no one is clearly right or wrong. With many directions possible, pastors can end up trying to focus on everything. As one pastor told us, "Every person sitting in the pew has a separate job description for our job. And when you put it all together, it's an impossible task. Part of our job is to help them understand what our real job entails and what their job entails as well."

The difficulty of a pastor's job description has also been written about by L. Gregory Jones, who likewise acknowledges that the sheer diversity of tasks and having essentially multiple bosses can make the work seem fragmented and undesirable.[10] He suggests that churches and pastors should reorient pastors' work to focus on the process—the process of bearing witness, building relationships, and fostering practices of faithful living—with their sole boss being God.

Lacking this theological perspective, MyPlan.com regularly publishes job descriptions to help students and professionals make career decisions. In the 2017 clergy job description, twenty-one tasks are listed and thirty-six skill sets presented.[11] Although many jobs have a similar number of tasks and skill sets required, the skills for clergy strike me as more diverse. The tasks include caregiving, interpretation and meaning-making, writing and public speaking, hiring and directing paid and unpaid staff, educating youth and adults, fundraising, making financial decisions, strategizing to grow, and organizing civic and interfaith events. In addition to working within their own organizations, clergy also work with the public.

Table 1.1 Skill Sets for Clergy

Importance (out of 100)	Skill Set (items here were chosen for their diversity from thirty-six listed)
83	Resolving conflicts and negotiating with others
78	Assisting and caring for others
78	Organizing, planning, and prioritizing work
77	Communicating with persons outside the organization

10. Jones, "Job Description."
11. "Clergy," O*NET 20.3 database.

77	Establishing and maintaining interpersonal relationships
74	Interpreting the meaning of information for others
74	Getting information
73	Making decisions and solving problems
72	Thinking creatively
70	Interacting with computers
69	Training and teaching others
68	Judging the qualities of things, services, or people
68	Communicating with supervisors, peers, or subordinates
65	Providing consultation and advice to others
64	Developing and building teams
60	Developing objectives and strategies
59	Coaching and developing others
58	Coordinating the work and activities of others
56	Performing administrative activities
51	Analyzing data or information
50	Selling or influencing others
48	Documenting/recording information
41	Monitoring and controlling resources

Source: http://www.myplan.com/careers/clergy/description-21-2011.00.html.

When the tasks and skills of clergy are laid out in a long list, it becomes apparent that the core work of ministry occurs between people—between the pastor and parishioners, between and among parishioners, between the pastor and community members, and every other sort of iteration. Even when everyone assumes good intent, ministry work is ripe for misunderstandings and differences of opinion, leading to potential conflict.

How does conflict arise among well-intentioned Christian people? What does conflict look like in a church, and how do pastors experience it? The answers to these questions are best described with a story from experience.

Behind the Pulpit
Navigating Conflict

During the four years that I was head pastor of a large church, the church did well. The church grew by some 15 percent, brought in more money each year and flipped big deficits into big surpluses, added a worshiping community, sent folks to seminary, and grew in depth and breadth of impact. I loved that church, and they seemed to love me.

Most of them anyway.

There were a few parishioners who kept me up at night and made me wonder how long I'd get to keep my post. Once I remember telling a buddy before a meeting that I expected to be heated, "They're coming after me with the long knives tonight."

Did I really mean it? That church leaders were coming to administrative council bent on slaying me? I think I did. I was that anxious. We pastors tend to be pleasers, as you may have heard. We thrive even more on folks' encouragement and approbation than most other humans. We pastors got enough pats on the head earlier in life for doing God stuff that we went to seminary and into church work. And then all of a sudden the place from which we've always gotten showers of encouragement becomes a place from which we get stinging, blistering, bilious criticism. It's like the inhaler that is supposed to keep you alive suddenly starts puffing sand into your lungs instead. Or needles.

Take that night when I was convinced the long knives were coming. We had a staff problem. I was new to this senior pastorate and only thirty-six years old, promoted above my "station" on the job ladder to a 1,300-member multisite church in a vibrant college town in the Appalachian Mountains. And I'd supervised exactly zero people before. None. Zilch. I knew how I liked being supervised from previous jobs and figured I'd do that. More importantly, I knew how I *didn't* like being supervised and figured I'd avoid that. I'd tell people the truth, look them in the eye, get to know their families, and encourage their flourishing in life and work, and together we'd set off on an adventure of church growth on the way to changing our community. We'd make up a merry band traveling together to churchly and social and financial bliss. The church grows and people think well of you. Your pay increases and ministry colleagues envy you. Your kids have what they want, you go on cool vacations, your spouse is happy, and everything hums in sync. (You may detect from my tone that not all my motivations were entirely holy.) I could do this supervision thing. How hard could it be? People generally like me, and I'm good at getting them to do what I want. It's why I landed a job like that in the first place.

So suddenly I was at the head of a table of a dozen staffers, each responsible for ministering to hundreds of people. I knew what it was like to sit in another seat around a table like that. You needed to turn up on time, be prepared for the meeting, be ready to advocate for resources for your ministry area, escape with as little extra work appended to your portfolio as possible (curse the words in every job description: "other duties as assigned"), and move on. But suddenly as a staff supervisor, my job was to get us all rowing in the same direction—not pulling against one another for attention and resources but pulling together in one direction, making one another better on the way to the whole being better. There's a reason skewerings of office culture like *The Office* and *Office Space* are so delicious: because it's much easier to be cynical about institutions trying to do what I had to do than it is to sit in that chair and actually do it well.

And I didn't always do it well. I was with a friend recently who was reporting on his institution's new executive: "He's fired a few people," he said. "And we don't really do that around here." I know what he meant. They're a small shop. Harmony is valued above all else. Firing someone is awful. In the church, you're commanded to love. We boil that down to being nice. And being fired is not nice. Ergo we fire no one. It's really, really hard to get fired in church. Because people in chairs like mine are often cowards. We want to be liked above all else, so we'd rather bear with subpar performance than take the heat that comes from firing someone. We're wrong to do this, as I hope you can tell my description here implies. "We're commanded to love people—not to employ them," a wise older friend says.

Lucky for me, as a proud member of the coward club, I never had to fire anyone. We set a new direction as a congregation—staff and lay leaders rowing together—and some were called to do other kinds of work elsewhere. Bless them—they've each done good ministry before and since moving on. But one narrative about the changes in our staff became particularly damaging for me. It was that I was running off the older members of the staff. This was demonstrably false. Our oldest and our youngest pastoral staffer both left of their own accord. Both had done great work at the church, and both went on to do great work elsewhere. But appearance is reality in politics and in church. And in this case, my own profile—my relative youth as a senior pastor—lent to this false appearance. I *was* change. I looked young, and it seemed like the folks I brought in were even younger. Again, it *seemed*. One replacement hire was decades older than the person who left, but it didn't matter. The grumbling began. "He doesn't like old people." People said I was only interested in the young people in our church. The elderly better get ready for a season of being ignored.

This was really dangerous. If the greatest generation folks are dishonored, everybody will be displeased. Who disses Grandma and gets away with it? Further, those folks give more than younger people. They often have more resources. They grew up in a time when giving to the church was relatively unquestioned as an institution. And they show up in greater numbers. If we were going to reach the new folks we all wanted to reach, and the young people that the general denomination had told us for years we *had* to reach, I needed the older folks' help. To have a wedge driven between them and me was not helpful to the mission.

And then I made things worse.

"What are you going to look for in Suzanne's replacement?" someone asked at the long-knife meeting, innocently enough. Forty-odd pairs of eyes looked at me. They were disproportionately older. Although we had more young members in the congregation, it takes new folks a while to trickle into leadership, and folks who've been in the church for years tend to suggest their friends and accept assignments themselves more readily. I started reeling off what we needed: someone hungry to serve, someone who could look after our older people, someone who could preach and lead and offer pastoral care. Then I said it.

"Somebody young."

This was preposterously stupid. I'd played right into the hands of the backhanded gossip about me. It would have been illegal to act upon; you can't discriminate based on age in your hiring. This person would have elder care among her responsibilities. It was ridiculous to prejudice the coming hire toward somebody young. I'm not sure what I was thinking. Enthusiasm is often associated with youth, but I should have known better. I know that I can find a trainload of sorry young people who quit putting their heart into their work years ago, not to mention a slew of older people who have spirits and work ethics that shame their younger peers.

I didn't even mean what I said. But I'd said it. And now it was out there, on the record (somebody was taking minutes), for folks to see and tell their friends. Way to dig your own grave, genius.

By the end of the meeting, some of the saints around the table had thrown me a lifeline. One sympathetic man said, "I'm sure you don't mean to limit us to young people." I looked at him—a lay leader I admired, whose approval I really wanted. No, needed. I could tell he was disappointed in me and trying to help me out. Another saint sitting by him had a daughter in pastoral ministry. He spoke up to say that she ministered effectively to the elderly as a twenty-something herself. "Maybe we need a young person with an old soul," someone else helpfully suggested. The meeting was not a total waste. In fact, they took my gauche comment and jujitsued it into something fruitful.

But there was also real damage done, and it was my fault. *And that's where stress comes from.* In this church I had every advantage one could wish for. The congregation had been led so well for so long that it could survive a lousy pastor. Perhaps that's part of why I was sent there. I had time to learn on the job leading a healthy church that needed no quick or instantaneous turnaround. Dozens of pastors in our conference would have given a significant bodily appendage to be appointed there. But I was sent instead. And there in public I said the stupidest thing imaginable. Maybe I'd heard once too often that the church has to have younger people or we'll die. Maybe I was just comfortable working with folks younger than me. Or maybe my own pride and ambition, my own desire for the wrong things (see my comments above about the sort of growth I longed for), some correct observations about what was holding us back, and some hackneyed thoughts about what would fix it, all mixed together to become dramatically unwise words. My sin, lack of experience, and anxiety hurt my efforts and made things worse.

Even so, I had supporters aplenty and growth to point to. Rotating leaders is natural—I had to find my own team. The folks who quit had their own patent issues, obvious to all observers. And the tussles with the staff gave way to genuine mutual respect and love and to the hiring of new staff that immediately made us all look better (just not always younger!). But imagine if I'd had fewer supporters, no growth, or lasting conflict—then what? And plenty of folks in much tougher appointments have one or more of those things. During those four years, I couldn't sleep at night, even though I often had significant protection from the denomination that never really had to mobilize on my behalf. What if there'd been none when the wolves circled?

I wasn't out of the woods yet, though. Sometimes people don't just *seem* to be after you; sometimes they really are! To paraphrase the joke about paranoid people: it's not paranoia when they really *are* out to get you.

Clergy Skills Meet the Real World

Ministry is complex. The people and circumstances that the pastor inherits in a specific church are important. As Jason illustrates, just one parishioner—even a parishioner out of sync with most of his peers—makes a difference. Also, in the midst of complex interpersonal relationships and leadership decisions, what goes on in the pastor's mind is incredibly important, and the company that he or she keeps in talking through these leadership decisions can change the trajectory of the church, whether during times of conflict or of calm.

With the constant presence of cell phones and ready access to email, parishioners likely expect pastors to be more reachable today than ever before. Clergy were surely available when a parishioner died a century ago, and they are today too. But now there may be additional expectations of easy and immediate access to pastors, even for less weighty events.

There is also a sense in the United States today that we all deserve to be heard, and yet there isn't clear etiquette around when and how we speak. I'm thinking in particular of my neighborhood listserv and how, due to the more anonymous nature of the posts, people can say terrible things that they would never say to someone's face in a conversation. Thoughts that before may have been suppressed are now voiced, quickly and in ways that can be rapidly spread to others. Pastors have always had to contend with rumors, but now those rumors can fly more quickly.

These challenges are not unique to clergy. However, one difference is that clergy have many different responsibilities involving many distinct skill sets, which opens pastors up to more expectations and more criticism, and also to a large number of people—very few of whom see the whole picture of the pastor's work. The other difference, as stated before but worth repeating, is that a pastor's work is sacred to both the pastor and the parishioners. No pastor I know wants to be seen as whining about his or her sacred work. At the same time, the work and its context are challenging. In spite of that challenge, or maybe because of it, many pastors would second the Facebook post included at the beginning of this chapter, which concluded, "Honestly, I get to do this for a living. How awesome is that?"

2

When Work Is Holy

Highs and Lows of Ministry Work

In 2006, over 4,500 people across the United States were asked a question as part of the General Social Survey: "On the whole, how satisfied are you with the work you do—would you say you are very satisfied (4), moderately satisfied (3), a little dissatisfied (2), or very dissatisfied (1)?" Researchers looked at the occupation of the respondents and came up with a number of interesting findings (see table 2.1).[1]

Wow—clergy topped the list! Clergy had the highest mean score and therefore the number one ranking, but the percentage of clergy who said they were very satisfied was far and above the highest at 87.2 percent, compared to only 80.1 percent of firefighters.[2]

Does this seem odd, given that in the previous chapter we laid out so many potentially stressful circumstances for clergy?

When I first learned of this number-one ranking, I dismissed it, thinking that clergy pretty much *have* to say they are satisfied with their job because they are called by God to do it. Saying you aren't very satisfied might be like snubbing God or being ungrateful. Also, it turns out that only sixty-eight clergy took the survey, and we don't know how representative they were of

1. Smith, "Job Satisfaction in the United States."
2. In case you are curious, the five occupations with the absolute lowest job satisfaction were cashiers, food preparers, expediters (who ensure deliveries happen on schedule), butchers, and furniture salespersons, with only 23 percent to 27 percent of people in those occupations indicating they were very satisfied. See Smith, "Job Satisfaction."

Table 2.1 United States Job Satisfaction Ratings

Rank	Occupation	Mean Score	Percent Very Satisfied
1	Clergy	3.79	87.2
2	Physical therapists	3.72	78.1
3	Firefighters	3.67	80.1
4	Education administrators	3.62	68.4
5	Painters, sculptors, related jobs	3.62	67.3
6	Teachers	3.61	69.2
7	Authors	3.61	74.2
8	Psychologists	3.59	66.9
9	Special education teachers	3.59	70.1
10	Operating engineers	3.56	64.1
11	Office supervisors	3.55	60.8
12	Security and financial services salespersons	3.55	65.4

clergy in general—perhaps they were all from one specific denomination, for example. So we have to take this number one satisfaction rating with a big grain of salt. I may have stopped thinking about it entirely, except that a lot of clergy researchers cite this finding, so it kept coming up.

Now, after several more years learning from our clergy survey and interview data, I think this number one satisfaction rating may have a lot of truth to it, but it only tells half the story. I suspect that clergy are satisfied with their work *and* experience many difficult situations on a routine basis. Clergy experience lots of satisfaction and maybe also lots of dissatisfaction, and those experiences don't average out into some middle ground; instead, clergy hold both the highs and the lows.

One study suggests that clergy are rather unique in the wide range of emotions they experience. Researchers at the University of Loyola, Maryland, gave Episcopalian priests a commonly used measure of positive and negative emotions.[3] Usually people indicate experiencing either a lot of positive emotions or a lot of negative emotions. In contrast, clergy indicated experiencing a lot of positive emotions *and* a lot of negative emotions. In other words, they hold in their world funerals *and* baptisms, and one doesn't wash the other out. Of course, clergy could also experience negative emotions around activities devoid of meaning, like administrative hassles, but for those who

3. Stewart-Sicking, "Subjective Well-Being."

do, it does not seem to cut into their overall satisfaction with their work when compared to other workers.

Clergy and Call

In the words of longtime pastor and author Eugene Peterson, "I've loved being a pastor, almost every minute of it. It's a difficult life because it's a demanding life. But the rewards are enormous—the rewards of being on the front line of seeing the gospel worked out in people's lives. I remain convinced that if you are called to it, being a pastor is the best life there is."[4]

Notice that Peterson uses the word "called." I agree that being called to one's work makes a difference in being satisfied with work. Looking again at the top twelve occupations, we can see several jobs that one might feel called to, including being a firefighter, a psychologist, or a teacher. Finding great meaning in your work, whatever it is, leads to better satisfaction at work and in life.

But being "called" has a very special meaning for clergy, and I think it's essential to understand what "call" means for clergy as we seek to understand their physical and mental health.[5]

Behind the Pulpit
Hearing the Call

The archetypal call story for Christians is the call of Moses from the burning bush (Exod. 3). While it's true that most ministers haven't had an experience quite like this one, we can't think about calling without reference to the bush, the flame, the sandals, the voice. Moses's experience makes sense of ours.

You can find the story in the biblical book of Exodus. Exodus tells the proto-typical story of Israel being called out from slavery. The story includes all the best attributes of the God whom Jews and Christians worship. This God hears the oppressed and sets them free. God opposes the proud and gives grace to the humble. Sorrow may last for a night, but joy comes in the morning. All our best moments are here. There are puzzles here too. Why did God let his people groan in slavery not merely for a night but for years, centuries even? Why does God let his people wander for so long, apparently directionless, suffering in the

4. Wood, "'The Best Life.'"
5. Niebuhr, *Purpose of the Church*.

meantime? We don't know. God's ways are not our ways, and we have no ability to discern whether and how God should have worked differently. All we have are these stories. We hope they are enough.

The Jews began as a people when God called Abram to leave his house and his land and his father's people to go to a new land that God would show him. Even though Abram was ancient and his wife Sarai barren, God would give them a son and would bless this offspring and make their descendants as numerous as the stars in the sky or the sand on the sea.

God appears unexpectedly to Abram and says, "You! You're going to have a kid."

"I can't have kids."

"Shut up! Your kid will have so many kids no one can count them, and the whole world will be blessed by them."

"OK."

"Oh and one more thing: leave your country and your family and go to a new land I will show you."

Abram went. And that wasn't the hardest thing he ever had to do—far from it (see "Isaac, sacrifice of"). But whatever happens from here on out, Israel has God's promise to bless Abraham's (following his name change in Genesis) descendants and all the world through them. And so the good news has continued ever since: God chooses one unlikely family through whom to bless the world. Now all of us unlikely, unpromising types have a God who, at great cost to himself, is determined to bless us and others through us.

Exodus also includes a calling. And the story doesn't start well. "Now a new [Pharaoh] arose over Egypt, who did not know Joseph" (Exod. 1:8)—a verse God's people often use to describe the ascent to power of someone who means us ill. This new Pharaoh notices that the Jews are too numerous. He could have a revolt on his hands. So he turns them into slaves. He tries to wipe them all out by murdering their sons. And right under his nose one Israelite boy, Moses, is delivered miraculously—pulled up out of the water from a reed basket where his desperate mother had put him in hopes of an escape. Pharaoh's own daughter lifts out the baby and takes pity on him, raising him as her own. God's people are intertwined with their taskmasters, their foreign oppressors, in a land that once provided deliverance for Joseph and blessing for his family. God's ways are intertwined with human sin and self-regard writ large and small.

Moses grows up in Pharaoh's house and sees Pharaoh's murderous policies firsthand (Exod. 2:11–15). An Egyptian is beating a Hebrew. Moses looks around, sees no one, and kills the Egyptian. The next day, two Israelites are arguing. Moses breaks up their dispute, and one asks if Moses means to kill him the way he'd killed the Egyptian the day before. Moses's murder is unveiled by his own people. The rabbis point out that Moses has an anger problem.[6] He didn't need to kill the Egyptian, but he lashed out in anger and went far past justice. Now he's paying for it. He flees to the wilderness, helps a band of women water-gatherers from Midian, and ends up with a wife and a job—herding sheep. He's a long way from the palace.

Seasoned pastors have always spied pastoral wisdom in these stories: the people we lead will turn on us, and we will turn on them. Power can be dangerous—especially if we're momentarily in our parishioners' good favor. Things can turn in an instant, and we can be on the run for our lives. And our entire lives are wrapped up in a promise from a God who calls old men and women to dream big dreams and put their lives on the line; a God who will do something staggering before our eyes and then depart the scene for centuries, leaving his people groaning under slavery; an unpredictable God who keeps his own counsel and clock and yet will show up in unlikely places—like one bush on one hillside on a day that was otherwise unremarkable.

Life in Midian started out so ordinary for Moses: working for his father-in-law in a profession not known for its cleanliness, its excitement, or its intellectual engagement. (I remember the first shepherd I met, in Israel, leading camels, wearing a Michael Jordan T-shirt and trying to sell me Michael Jackson cassettes. It wasn't romantic.)

One day there's a burning bush. The flames won't go out.

A command: take off your shoes. Go to Pharaoh and tell him to let my people go.

But I can't; I won't.

You can, and you will.

Well, who are you, for when they ask?

I'm "I AM." Now go.

And Moses went, and did. God resurrected his people from slavery in Egypt. And the world's not been the same since because every tyrant everywhere now has to wonder if a bush might light on fire and a washed-up refugee might come back and lead the people the tyrant oppresses to freedom. The God of the universe works on behalf of the oppressed. And his I AM is always in present tense. Moses endured a lot; his people endured more. But you can endure a lot when you're working for I AM and can remember the sight and smell of a fire that won't burn out and the voice saying, "You will go."

Millennia later, another call occurs when God speaks, this time to an unmarried Jewish teenager from the sticks.

You! You're going to have a kid.

But I am a kid.

6. Elper and Handelman, *Torah of the Mothers*.

Like I was saying, this kid will also be my kid. And all the world will be blessed through him.

OK.

Israel and the church have been trying, and usually failing, to emulate Abram's and Moses's and Mary's "OK" back to God ever since.

Most of our callings are far less dramatic. A nudge, a suggestion, a hint, an acceptance, an assignment. But we have these lively stories of a surprising God who turns up where and when he wants and calls all kinds of people who are just as disreputable as we are, a God who does astounding, world-changing things through them, like starting a nation to bless the world, ending Israel's slavery in Egypt, and birthing salvation itself.

Discerning a Call

The calling that clergy experience, on a practical level, involves a discernment process that may take years to unfold and generally consists of the confluence of three things.[7] The first is the urge to serve God through ministry. This feeling could alight through a specific incident, or it could evolve over a number of years. Second, the church must affirm the individual's personal sense of call to serve in ministry; this could occur through a pastor or parishioner identifying that person as a potential leader. Third, an individual who experiences the first two aspects of call must also believe that he or she can develop the skills needed to become an effective clergy person. Then the individual goes through a rigorous process of education and examination. By the time someone is ordained, he or she has almost always experienced all three aspects of being called.

Pastors' sense of their call to be clergy is not set in stone. At times, pastors are fairly certain that they have been called by God to be a pastor, and at other times, they doubt this call. Matt Bloom at the University of Notre Dame has conducted interviews with clergy in which he asked them to tell their call story. Then, during multiple follow-up interviews, he asked them to tell their call story again. He found that when all is well with the church a clergy person is pastoring, that person's memory of her original call story is stronger and more definite. However, when the church is struggling, the clergy person's memory of her call story is weaker.[8]

---

7. Campbell, "Call to Ordained Ministry."
8. Personal communication with Matt Bloom, January 4, 2017.

Figure 2.1
Feelings of Doubt

"In the last six months, how often have you doubted
that you are called by God to the ministry?"

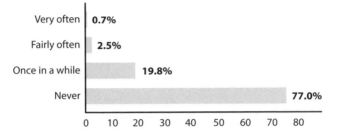

Figure 2.2
Thoughts of Leaving Ministry

"In the last six months, how often have you thought of
leaving pastoral ministry to enter a secular occupation?"

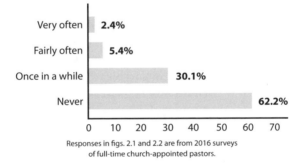

Responses in figs. 2.1 and 2.2 are from 2016 surveys
of full-time church-appointed pastors.

When Work Is Sacred

When a sense of call permeates the work of an already religious person, his or her work becomes personally sacred.[9] "Sacred" is defined as something that is set apart from ordinary things and has God at its heart. When something is personally sacred to you, it changes the way you act.

Ken Pargament, a longtime researcher of spiritual well-being and health who has studied how people sanctify aspects of their life, like marriage, has developed what he calls the sanctification theory. The theory he developed with Annette Mahoney is especially helpful to consider with clergy, who sanctify

9. Carroll, *God's Potters*.

their work.[10] Sanctification theory proposes that when someone gives sacred meaning to something, they exert substantial energy and time for it, fiercely protect it, experience strong emotions around it, draw on it as a resource, and experience desolation if it is lost.

Clergy define their work as sacred, so what are the implications of this for them? First, we expect pastors to experience stronger pulls to their work than do employees in other professions. Although anyone who feels called to a vocation can struggle with when to give lower priority to his or her work, this may be particularly challenging for clergy. After all, if your backdrop is burning bushes and having a child at age ninety, or if it's bumping into an angel with premarital plans for you and the maternity ward, who are you to turn down a relatively minor request like leaving vacation to perform a funeral?

In the first chapter, we considered the passion that drives people to become clergy in the first place but that can also be difficult to reconcile with mundane activities. We noted that pastors often aren't sure what ministry is for, which leads to attempts to please everyone and creates a circumstance Hauerwas calls being nibbled to death by ducks.[11]

When your work is sacred, sanctification theory suggests that you will exert extra energy to do it. Given how hard it often is to be sure of God's will, perhaps it is safer for clergy to say yes to requests than to say no. When work is sacred, clergy might end up with a default approach in which everything is equally important, meaning that they are more likely to overwork and, at the same time, less likely to take care of their own physical and mental health.

When we ran a health intervention for clergy, we found that clergy needed to be given permission to take care of themselves over and over again. It seemed they were defaulting to saying yes to everything and taking care of everyone except themselves, even after they decided to change this pattern. I believe it is essential for clergy supervisors, lay leaders, and parishioners to

> **"Even if I scheduled to go to the gym at four in the afternoon,** if someone walks into my office at three fifty, I have a really hard time pulling away and saying, 'You know what? I can't deal with you right now. I know the gym is only open until six, and I really do have to go now.' And of course I'll stay for an hour and just shoot the breeze."
>
> *Note:* Quotations in this chapter come from pastor focus groups.

10. Pargament and Mahoney, "Sacred Matters."
11. Wording attributed to Stanley Hauerwas, Christian Ethics lectures (Duke Divinity School, Durham, NC, spring 1997).

give permission—repeatedly—for pastors to spend time on themselves. It may also help to clarify a church's priorities and publicly recognize that the pastor can't give every task top priority.

Another implication of doing sacred work is that the stakes of perceived failure are higher for clergy than for other workers.[12] The converse may also be true: perceived success may be more meaningful to clergy. It therefore seems likely that clergy will experience extremes of both positive and negative emotions when engaging in their vocation—partly because their work exposes them to the full emotional spectrum that their parishioners encounter but also because clergy are emotionally invested in the work that is sacred to them.

With this emotional investment, criticism from parishioners may be extra potent for clergy.[13] Of course, there needs to be a way to give constructive criticism to all church members, including pastors, but given how powerfully clergy might take that criticism, a few guidelines could help.

> **"I have a lot of support. I** have three mothers [i.e., three parishioners who act like mothers to him]. I'm a part-time local pastor. And I have three mothers that I basically have to show my three-month doctor's report to make sure that I've got my blood sugar under control, that my weight is OK, that I'm riding my bike my six hours a week and doing the things that I need to do. They encourage me to take *more* time off, to be away more. They know that I take care of my wife, who is disabled. And I don't keep office hours. . . . They know where to reach me, and they know that I am going to be available. . . . And they quiz me, making sure [I take care of myself]."

Behind the Pulpit
Giving and Taking Criticism

How do we deliver criticism to our pastors?

My temptation is to answer, "Don't." Pope John XXIII, who summoned the Second Vatican Council, summed up much churchly wisdom on leadership this way: "Overlook much. Correct a little."[14] God overlooks our sins and only occasionally corrects us. So should our approach be.

But correct us God does, even if occasionally. And we ministers are sinners no less than anyone else—usually more. We're just inclined to be pleasers. So correction hurts us and our fragile egos more. Never mind this. In our heart of hearts we want the church to thrive, and we need to perceive criticism as

12. Meek et al., "Maintaining Personal Resiliency."
13. Proeschold-Bell et al., "Using Effort-Reward Imbalance Theory."
14. Pope John XXIII, *Overlook Much.*

a desire to love. You don't criticize something you don't care about you just move on. There is something from God in every criticism, however hidden and however unwelcome. We ministers need to learn to see criticism as an unwelcome gift. Of course it hurts more than hearing praise does. But it's vastly more likely to make us, and the whole congregation, better.

Just don't do it in the handshake line after church, OK?

I'm imagining trenchant criticism from someone I love. I'd prefer to hear it delivered surrounded by praise (fragile ego and all). I'd love to hear it offered over a meal someone else is buying. And I'd love to hear it in the context of the parish's mission. What is God trying to accomplish through us? How is this problem holding back that mission? And what is something tangible I can actually do to get out of God's and the church's way? What is something that will make me a better minister and the church a better local instantiation of the body of Christ?

No matter how it's delivered, the criticism may still hurt, but it'll be necessary, and I'll need to get over the hurt. I remember two or three times someone approached me this way, and I'll never forget it—I've tried to incorporate what they said ever since. Before you confront me or another clergy person this way, pray. Pray afterward too. Ask others to pray with you. Encourage a lot; correct a little. Whatever you say, I might not like it. But I'll be better for it. And so will all of us together.

When you are corrected, sometimes it'll be done like this. Other times it won't. Our culture is descending to a level of barbarity where we scream first and ask questions later (I blame cable news). Folks are becoming conditioned to act this way. When parishioners come after you, sometimes it'll feel like 90 percent nonsense. Fine. Take the 10 percent that's not and do something about it. You don't have to respond to everything. Overlook a lot; correct a little. They'll feel heard and honored that you responded to the 10 percent. And even if it's surrounded by nonsense, their criticism likely contains something helpful. Seize that helpful bit as a strange, unwelcome gift and dive into doing better. Be like the Syrophoenician woman who heard a harsh criticism from none other than Jesus himself in Mark 7:25–30 (can you imagine?). She perseveres and receives the healing she seeks for her daughter. Martin Luther points out the obvious: Jesus says no to her. Yet, Luther says, there is a yes *hidden in the no*.[15] She persists until she finds it. So we should do with criticism, however harsh—even a no from our Lord. Push through it and find the yes that's also there. And you'll be blessed, the dead will be raised, and the kingdom will come.

OK, maybe not quite, but you'll be better at what you do. And that's something.

---

15. Althaus, *Theology of Martin Luther*, 32.

When There's Too Much Holy Work to Do

When several demands are competing for your attention, especially demands that you consider important, it's easy to feel anxious. Anxiety is just one of many symptoms of stress. In an early attempt to measure stress among clergy, we encountered a tension that pastors experience in deciding how to manage their workload.

Pastors answered the ten questions of the Perceived Stress Scale, which measures appraisals of stress and has been used in hundreds of articles and translated into twenty-five languages.[16] When most of our survey respondents gave unexpected responses, we interviewed twelve pastors and asked them to walk us through their thinking on each of the stress questions.[17] We found that clergy think about *control* differently than people who don't have a Christian framework.

For example, one question asks, "In the last month, how often have you felt that things were going your way?" The pastors we interviewed said things like, "'God's way' should always supersede 'my way'" or that the goal was not for things to go the pastor's way but for her to do "what is best for Christ and his ministry in the world." As such, things could be stressful for a pastor and still be going the pastor's way because they were going God's way.

Another Perceived Stress Scale question asks, "In the last month, how often have you felt that you were unable to control the important things in your life?" Half the pastors we interviewed described lack of personal control as normal, both inside and outside of their work. The examples they gave included lack of control over church leadership decisions, being appointed to a different church, parishioners' problems, and their own health issues. One pastor stated that even when things seemed under control, they usually were not.

Most of the pastors we interviewed described accepting lack of control through their Christian faith. One pastor detailed how she had given control of her life over to God. She said that when she felt out of control, she asked herself, "How can I best manage this to allow God to do what God does?" Another pastor reported "coming to terms" with his lack of control, while yet another said his "need to control" was diminished because he trusted God. He believed it was healthy to relinquish control and indicated that he was more at peace when he did so.

In contrast, two pastors we interviewed indicated that giving up control was harder than some make it out to be. One said, "Clergy want and like control. You are supposed to feel peace because God is in control. Pastors are well

---

16. Cohen, Kamarck, and Mermelstein, "Global Measure of Perceived Stress."
17. Blouin and Proeschold-Bell, "Measuring Stress in a Clergy Population."

trained from a theological perspective to say that they have no control. Still, *people* want pastors to be in control." Another pastor said she struggled with wanting to control things that she should not. She said that as she learned to accept her lack of control, it provided emotional relief for her, and she attributed this acceptance to strong faith and greater maturity.

What does balancing your workload look like when you give control over to God? How does giving control to God help a pastor decide what to focus on or when a certain amount of work is enough for a day? When is handing over control peaceful, and when is it anxiety-provoking? A large secular literature suggests that having control decreases stress symptoms, whereas being out of control increases stress symptoms.[18] However, what if as a pastor—or a devout Christian—you determine that you're OK with you not being in control and with God being in control instead?

When Abram, Moses, and Mary were called by God, they gladly yielded control of their lives—and it didn't always turn out altogether well for them. Yet their surrender of agency brought about God's saving work through them. Research suggests that having control over your life calms you and prevents stress. But is control what Christians should strive for? And if not, what does giving control to God look like today?

Behind the Pulpit
Control versus Power

Some studies of happiness suggest that a high degree of control is essential to a flourishing life.[19] This makes sense, in a way. Folks who have had no control or agency, who have had their ability to flourish commandeered by others who are more powerful, can attest that a little control over one's life is a profound good. To have a bodily function "out of control" or behavior "out of control" or spending "out of control" is terrifying.

And yet, in Christian terms, control is not an unmitigated good. Israel wants a king. Why? Because other nations have kings and because those nations have secure borders (some of the time), a standing army for which they commandeer sons, crops, herds, and the Israelites' very lives. God knew the people of Israel would trust their king rather than their God, but God granted this dubious form of control—and hardly a single Israelite king used it well.

---

18. Krause and Stryker, "Stress and Well-Being."
19. Seeman, "Personal Control."

Jesus asked disciples to follow him. Where? By what means? For how long? None of these questions were raised, let alone answered. Discipleship is a matter of surrendering control to an Other who we think will handle it better than we could. So Christians practice relinquishing control as well. What was it someone wise said? "If you want to make God laugh, make a plan." Life is remarkably, fearfully out of our hands. We still plan, prepare, work, strive hard. And we leave the result to One infinitely more capable than we are, One who also loves us immeasurably more than we can imagine.

Work-Related Burnout in Clergy

As much as we would like to think that clergy are forever invigorated by the work of being a pastor, that isn't a realistic expectation. As noted in the first chapter, clergy experience lots of challenges from societal trends and the highly interpersonal nature of ministry work. These challenges range from shrinking budgets to parishioners who are more interested in appearances than holiness to promoting unity within the church body.

If you're not invigorated by your work, it is possible that you are burned out. Work-related burnout is conceptualized as three things: emotional exhaustion, depersonalization, and lack of personal accomplishment.[20] Burnout has been studied across thousands of people using the Maslach Burnout Inventory, a measure that provides cut-off scores for low, moderate, and high levels of each of the three kinds of burnout.[21]

Three components of work-related burnout are as follows:

Emotional exhaustion: Feeling strained as your emotional resources become depleted

Depersonalization: Becoming detached from, and cynical toward, the people you serve

Lack of personal accomplishment: Having doubts about how much you accomplish

In their responses to this burnout measure on our surveys (see fig. 2.3), 15.3 percent of clergy scored in the high burnout range for emotional exhaustion. Fewer clergy (12.4 percent) experienced high levels of depersonalization—that is, feeling distanced from or hardened against the needs of parishioners. This makes sense. Because empathy is a core value of clergy, pastors likely try especially hard not to view individuals cynically.

20. Maslach, "Burnout."
21. Maslach, Jackson, and Leiter, *Maslach Burnout Inventory Manual.*

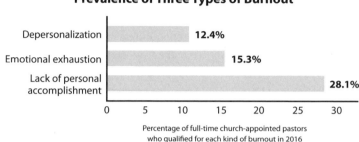

Figure 2.3
Prevalence of Three Types of Burnout

Percentage of full-time church-appointed pastors
who qualified for each kind of burnout in 2016

Perhaps of greatest concern is the finding that 28.1 percent of clergy scored in the high burnout range for feeling like they aren't working effectively or accomplishing much. Jason tells me that it's very hard for pastors to measure their accomplishments since their most important accomplishments are things like giving someone hope when they're at their lowest, or inspiring someone to do something enterprising that helps many people—or inspiring them just to listen, which ends up helping one person. Effectiveness in ministry is hard to measure, although many denominations track what can be counted, like annual giving, church attendance, and baptisms. While important, these numbers don't get at the essence of living life by Jesus's example. I liken it to trying to measure the work of teachers, which is generally done through test scores. Test scores tell you something, but they don't tell you the whole picture, and they certainly don't tell you when a teacher has lit in a student a lifelong love of learning.

Clergy Burnout Compared to Burnout in Other Caregivers

In our clergy surveys, 4 percent of clergy gave responses that qualified them for high levels of burnout in all three areas. By contrast, 30 percent of clergy gave responses qualifying them for low levels of burnout across the areas. Overall, this seems to be good news. Nearly one-third of clergy have simultaneously low levels of emotional exhaustion, depersonalization, and lack of accomplishment!

To put this 30 percent figure in context, we need to know what other kinds of employee groups experience in terms of burnout. My colleagues Christopher Adams, Holly Hough, and others compared the experience of burnout among clergy to that of other caregivers.[22] They scoured the literature to find

22. Adams et al., "Clergy Burnout."

all the available published research that used the Maslach Burnout Inventory with people in specific occupations. For examples of employees whose work involves emotional labor and intense interactions with people, they chose social workers, teachers, and counselors, and for employees who experience unpredictable schedules and are exposed to trauma, they chose police officers and emergency personnel. Comparatively, they found that, across the three kinds of burnout, clergy exhibit

- less burnout than police officers and emergency personnel;
- similar burnout to social workers and teachers; and
- worse burnout than counselors.

These findings suggest that, while clergy may have something to learn from counselors in controlling burnout, overall they are doing extremely well. In fact, given that many clergy are on call 24/7 without easy backup systems, clergy are doing remarkably well in preventing burnout and may actually be exemplars for those in other occupations.

How do clergy do it? In chapter 4 we describe how pastors manage their stress, which may help prevent feelings of emotional exhaustion. But first, in the next chapter we discuss another challenge clergy face: depression. Burnout and depression are different; feelings of burnout are specific to one's work and don't necessarily spill over into other areas of life. For example, a teacher can be emotionally exhausted at work and still feel energy in her family relationships. Depression, on the other hand, has been described as feeling empty, hopeless, worthless, and exhausted in everything.[23] We present data on what percentage of clergy experience depression, the things associated with depression in clergy, and concrete suggestions to help prevent or alleviate depression for pastors.

23. "About Specific Symptoms," 2013, http://www.allaboutdepression.com/dia_12.html.

3

Slowed Down and Overwhelmed

Clergy and Depressive Symptoms

Now that we understand something of the pressures on clergy and how sacred work makes it more likely that someone will ignore their health, let's turn to the data on the health of clergy. Are these pressures creating fractured health? Are clergy ignoring their mental and physical health? Even if they aren't ignoring their health, do they—and the people who support them—need to do more, and what can they do?

Let's start with depression. The intention of this book is to point toward clergy being fully alive and achieving positive mental health, but we cannot get to that point by sugarcoating the high rates of depressive symptoms that my team and others have found among clergy. Understanding what's going on may help prevent those symptoms.

Understanding Depression and Depressive Symptoms

Defining and diagnosing depression is harder than you might think, given how ingrained the word is in our dialogue ("That's depressing!"). Because there isn't a biological test for depression, we can't always definitively conclude that someone does or does not have it.[1] The causes of depression are also

1. This is true right now, but there has been some success in using blood tests to identify low levels of several markers that map onto depression and also differentiate people who were

diverse and to some extent unknown; people can be depressed due to difficult life events, or for biological reasons only (which feels like "no reason"),
or a combination of both.[2] Two people who experience the same life events
won't necessarily both suffer from depression, and even someone who feels
depressed at one time might not feel depressed during similar circumstances
in the future. Yet despite this lack of precision, depression is all too real and
can take a serious toll on those experiencing it. People experiencing depression
are less likely to follow through on medical advice,[3] more likely to experience
strain in their relationships,[4] and more likely to miss work and be less productive while at work.[5]

Until we understand the biology of depression better, mental health professionals have agreed to diagnose depression based on symptoms. These
professionals consider the number of symptoms, how severe those symptoms
are, and how long they've lasted. Some depressive symptoms are more physiological in nature, such as difficulty sleeping, low energy, and loss of appetite.
Other depressive symptoms seem more emotional or mental in nature, like
feeling guilty or worthless or having trouble concentrating.[6]

People's experiences are complicated. While it's hard enough for professionals to diagnose depression in a person, it's even harder to do so accurately
using a few survey questions. Depression survey screenings ask people whether,
and to what extent, they have experienced any of a list of symptoms in the
past two weeks. This approach successfully identifies the majority of people
with clinical depression, but it isn't a perfect approach. For some, screenings
like this won't work. Depression screenings may miss people with persistent
depression symptoms who haven't experienced many symptoms over the past
two weeks. Or they may falsely identify people as depressed because their
symptoms are not considered in context—for example, when someone has
experienced a death in the family, which may cause the symptoms of depression to appear but doesn't necessarily indicate the presence of a mental illness.

Despite all the difficulties of measuring depression with a survey, depression
is a serious condition. It affects a person's physical health, job performance,
and ability to thrive. It can make everything—and for pastors this includes
the church—feel challenging, hopeless, exhausting, and constantly irritating.

---

not responsive to cognitive behavioral therapy. More work needs to be done here. Redei et al.,
"Blood Transcriptomic Biomarkers."

2. Kinderman et al., "Psychological Processes."
3. DiMatteo, Lepper, and Croghan, "Depression Is a Risk Factor."
4. Rehman et al., "Actor-Partner Effects."
5. Beck et al., "Severity of Depression."
6. "Depression," National Institute of Mental Health.

Given these limitations, we can consider depression measured on surveys in two ways. We can count the number of symptoms frequently experienced as a measure of "depressive symptoms," or we can create a cut-off point and say, as is done in the measure we use, that anyone who scores ten or higher (out of twenty-seven) has crossed a threshold of enough symptoms to be considered "depressed."[7]

This distinction between depressive symptoms and depression is important. It is possible to have depressive symptoms without having clinical depression. Depressive symptoms slow you down, so even if you're experiencing them at levels that wouldn't qualify for a diagnosis, they can be a problem.[8] However, if the symptoms are so many or become so strong that you're feeling overwhelmed, it's time for assessment—you may qualify for clinical depression and need treatment.

"There were some days I struggled because I was so upset . . . and I feel so lonely. And other pastors must go through this too. You know, you're leaving your church . . . and you've got a personnel committee that can't wait for you to get out. And you've got these demands being put on you. . . . I didn't want to just leave and not give them notice. . . . I was so concerned about everybody else that I'm the one [who] feels so lonely and frustrated and anxious about everything. . . . And I don't have the spouse to come home and console me, and my child's gone too. It's just lonely."

Depressive Symptoms and Depression among Clergy

Figure 3.1 shows the percentage of pastors reporting various depressive symptoms for seven or more days out of the past two weeks, which is frequent enough to be considered a problem. The most common symptoms clergy experience are problems with energy (16.0 percent), eating (14.4 percent), and sleep (13.9 percent). More than one symptom can occur at any given time; the more symptoms someone experiences, the harder it is to participate fully in life.

When we shift from depressive symptoms as reported by clergy to a yes-or-no, depression-or-not scoring system, unfortunately, no researcher has ever reported good news. In 2002 and 2005, Sarah Knox and her colleagues included a depression screener[9] on two surveys of US Roman Catholic clergy and found the depression rates to be 20 percent and 18 percent.[10] While I

7. Kroenke, Spitzer, and Williams, "The Patient Health Questionnaire-9."
8. See, for example, Beck et al., "Severity of Depression."
9. Center for Epidemiologic Studies Depression Scale, which is different from the Patient Health Questionnaire-9 that we use in our studies. This may explain why the depression rates we find are lower.
10. Knox, Virginia, and Lombardo, "Depression and Anxiety in Roman Catholic Secular Clergy"; Knox et al., "Depression and Contributors to Vocational Satisfaction."

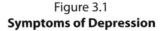

Figure 3.1
Symptoms of Depression

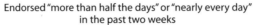

Endorsed "more than half the days" or "nearly every day"
in the past two weeks

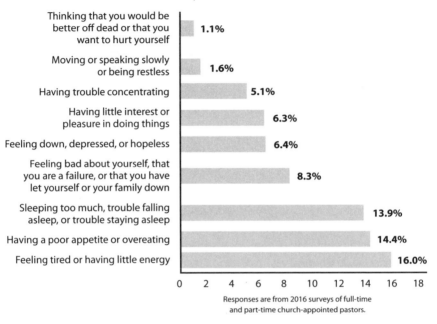

Responses are from 2016 surveys of full-time
and part-time church-appointed pastors.

worry that these rates are higher than is actually the case, there is nonetheless a major problem with depression in clergy.[11]

In 2008, we at the Clergy Health Initiative were able to go a step further by creating a study that allowed for direct comparison of clergy responses to those from a nationally representative US sample.[12] What's more, the good clergy of North Carolina participated in our study at an amazing level—95 percent of them responded. This is particularly important when studying depression because oftentimes people who are depressed bow out of life's extras, such as doing surveys, making it look like fewer people have depression than really do. We were grateful not to have that problem.[13]

11. These studies had response rates of 45 and 64 percent, respectively, which aren't terrible for survey research but still leave the findings open to bias. The clergy who chose not to take the survey may be more or less depressed than those who chose to.

12. The National Health and Nutrition Examination Survey (HANES) was the US comparison. To read this study see Proeschold-Bell et al., "Using Effort-Reward Imbalance Theory."

13. The national comparison sample was from the National Health and Nutrition Examination Survey, which had a 2008 response rate of 75 percent, which is also considered excellent for this kind of research.

With the help of Laurie Pratt, a researcher at the US Centers for Disease Control and Prevention who had access to comparable national depression data, we were able to make a fair comparison between clergy and the general US population. We used the same measure and cut-off score that she did. She had data from in-person interviews; we had data from phone interviews (one-third of the UMC clergy in North Carolina in 2008 were asked to respond to the survey items over the phone as an interview). She was able to consider age and gender, and so were we.

As you can see in the graph (fig. 3.2), 8.7 percent of clergy, compared to 5.5 percent of US adults, qualified for moderate depression or higher. In addition to being statistically significant, this is a striking difference. This measure of depression assesses symptoms for the past two weeks. You can therefore interpret the findings to mean that in the past two weeks, almost 9 percent of UMC clergy answered the items in a way that would qualify them for moderate or severe depression. In addition, this figure of 8.7 percent is probably conservative because those clergy had to be willing to admit to depressive symptoms to a live interviewer over the phone. While this 8.7 percent from phone interviews is the best comparison to the 5.5 percent of US adults, I believe our self-administered survey responses more. Responses indicated that 11.1 percent of the clergy qualified for depression.

We would like the following point to stand out to bishops, clergy supervisors, and personnel committees: we can assume it is common for clergy to become depressed at some point during their ministerial career, with 11.1 percent of clergy indicating high levels of depression symptoms in the past two weeks. Pastors experiencing depression should be pointed to treatment, but unless their case of depression continues unremittingly or is debilitating,

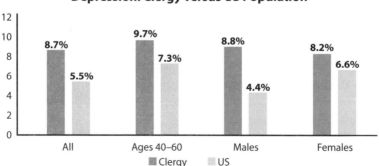

Figure 3.2
Depression: Clergy versus US Population

Depression prevalence rates in 2008 among all UMC clergy in NC compared to a representative sample from the United States.

it should not factor into decisions on church appointments. Even then, it shouldn't be a black mark, because a mental illness, like depression, changes.

Also, experiencing suffering oneself is no hindrance to serving fellow sufferers—quite the opposite in fact. In *The Wounded Healer*, Henri Nouwen makes the argument that being in touch with our own pain grants us gifts with which to help God heal others.[14] There are vast swaths of the Psalms, Lamentations, and the Prophets that only make sense if one knows a bit about despair.

Although depression may be more common for clergy than for other people, depression is also quite common in general. The World Health Organization ranks depression as the leading cause of disability, with worldwide estimates of 350 million people having experienced depression in the past year.[15]

In terms of depression at specific ages, Laurie Pratt and I looked at depression in the most common clergy age group: forty to sixty. There too clergy outpaced the US general population, with a depression rate of 9.7 percent versus 7.3 percent.

"One thing that I have learned about myself in the last nine years is that I actually deal with depression. It's not an episodic depression but a depression that is there. And I thought that it was something that I could dismiss and I didn't need any help with it. But I take medicine for it. And I don't tell anybody about it. . . . It surprised me that if I look at my family history, I can see that my dad probably had some of those traits. . . . But I never thought of myself as a depressed person, you know? [The medicine] I take seems to give me more energy, which is a good thing. . . . Sometimes I have a desire to share that, but I don't. . . . I think sometimes those kinds of things define who you are, and I don't want to be defined by that. . . . So I accepted it to the point that I take medicine, [but] I'm not sure I've accepted it fully."

Figure 3.2 also displays surprising gender differences. I was expecting that both male and female clergy would have higher depression rates than the general population, because I was already aware of the finding that clergy have overall higher depression rates. But I was not prepared for male clergy to have a depression rate consistent with that of female clergy or for male clergy to have a rate twice that of US males in general (8.8 percent vs. 4.4 percent). Nationally and internationally, women generally have higher rates of depression than men.[16] It's very interesting that this pattern is not true for clergy. Insurance committee staff for clergy should rejoice with this news;

14. Nouwen, *Wounded Healer*.
15. Marcus et al., "Depression."
16. Andrade et al., "Epidemiology of Major Depressive Episodes."

as denominations welcome more and more female clergy, these data suggest they should not worry that health claims related to depression will increase.

But what is going on that so many male clergy are depressed, compared to US men more broadly? Could it be that men who enter ministry are predisposed to depression in some way? One thing we know about depression is that the highest rate of depression for Americans (9.3 percent) occurs between the ages of 18 and 25.[17] We also know that people who have a diagnosis of major depressive disorder at an early age are more likely to experience one or more recurrences during their lives.[18] Is it possible that depressed young men seek healing in the church? As a response to depression, this would be quite healthy! And then could it be, with more time spent in the church, some portion of these young men with prior depression are noticed as having gifts in ministry and are encouraged to consider ministerial careers—more so than young men who don't have depression and therefore didn't seek healing in the church in the same numbers? Or is it possible that young men with depression who seek solace in the church have a different church experience and feel more called than young men who don't seek solace in the church for depression? We don't know, but any of these scenarios could explain the higher depression rates among male clergy.[19]

I often catch myself assuming that pastoral work is the cause of all the findings from the clergy data I work with, because after all, the one thing in common in the data is that all respondents are clergy. But ministry work does not necessarily cause the outcomes. Clergy people lived many years before entering ministry, and experiences during those years may have shaped them just as much, perhaps even more, than their time in ministry.

What would have happened to the mental health of clergy had they entered a different profession? Is it possible that working in ministry is *protective* against depression? Yes, clergy have high depression rates, but maybe those rates would be even higher if clergy weren't engaged in work that they find meaningful.

Fortunately, a high percentage of clergy in our surveys report getting therapy (see fig. 3.3). Among active, church-appointed pastors, we found that 44 percent had seen a therapist at some point in their lives and that 18 percent had seen a therapist in the past year. At the same time, there is still a gap in who could benefit from therapy and who's receiving it. Of the pastors who had

17. "Major Depression among Adults," National Institute of Mental Health.
18. Burcusa and Iacono, "Risk for Recurrence in Depression."
19. It may also be that males who are clergy respond differently to surveys than do males who are not clergy. Perhaps clergy males are more in tune with or willing to articulate their feelings.

Figure 3.3
Types of Therapists Most Recently Seen

Responses are from full-time and part-time church-appointed clergy in 2016 who saw "a mental
health professional for treatment of depression, anxiety, or stress" in the past year.

scores qualifying for depression, 56 percent of female pastors and 39 percent
of male pastors had seen a therapist in the past year.

Seeking therapy is an excellent way for pastors to receive support in dealing
with depression and depressive symptoms—and even the normal challenges
of clergy life. As Jason points out, though, sometimes our pain can serve as
a window into God's own suffering and the suffering of others.

Behind the Pulpit
Don't Waste Your Pain

I was once on a mission trip to a village in Honduras where nearly all the men
had left for the United States, and many who stayed behind were particularly
prone to suicide. Our medical provider was a nurse practitioner whose own
family had immigrated from Latin America to the United States and done well
financially. He said, "I can't help most of these people."

"Why?"

"Most of them are just depressed," he said. "I give them some Tylenol and
send them home."

We nodded gravely. I wish we'd objected. We were on a *church* mission
trip. We had massive resources with us to help: between the covers of our own
Bibles. Of course according to the medical disciplines that train our health care
providers, we didn't have the apparatus to treat serious long-term depression:
medication with time to experiment in finding the right cocktail for the specific

patient and psychotherapy with multiple repeat visits. This was a place with just Tylenol. But the massive success of such medical treatments has made us think medications can cure everything. They cannot. Our own Scriptures speak forcibly to the maladies we call "depression" in ways that biblical people have largely forgotten.

The first malady the Bible can cure is the folk belief that faith is a shield against harm. The Bible has as its central character a man tortured to death. Faith is no promise of safety—quite the reverse. And Jesus's crucifixion is no accident. All of Israel's Scripture is fulfilled in the man on the cross. All of the New Testament points toward the one whose suffering heals. Folk Christianity is replete with false promises that God "will not send you more than you can handle." Actually, God's own son got quite a bit more than he could handle. As Dostoevsky once put the point, the torture of one little girl can find no adequate compensation in the entire cosmos.[20] Undeserved suffering is at the heart of our Bible—which is good, because undeserved suffering is at the heart of our lives.

Another place a biblical mind wanders in thinking about suffering is, of course, the book of Job. "I loathe my life," Job says, in the sort of statement that seems to avoid needlepoint pillow covers and greeting cards (10:1). Elsewhere Job curses his very existence, even his conception, "Let the day perish in which I was born, / and the night that said, / 'A man-child is conceived'" (3:3). Job is chapter after chapter of lament. The ancient and medieval church loved it. Today's church? Not so much. A church reading its Bible well would wail with Job at least once in a while. I never hear it.

Kathryn Greene-McCreight's remarkable book *Darkness Is My Only Companion* takes its title from Psalm 88, the only psalm we have that *ends* on a discordant note.[21] Countless psalms *contain* a note of despair—they just tend not to end there. Their arc bends upward, so that by the end the psalmist is saying "hallelujah" all over again, and so are the people of God ever since. Psalm 88's despair over the author's lack of friends makes it, ironically, a surprising friend: a psalm that genuinely refuses to be consoled. The NRSV reads, "You have caused friend and neighbor to shun me; / my companions are in darkness," and the psalm ends. I once heard a musical version of this in which the final note was intentionally jarring, discordant—suggesting that we shouldn't try to smooth out what God has left jagged.

If you struggle with depression, if you can raise your head and energy enough to read, you'll discover you are far from alone. Greene-McCreight's book is a

20. Based on the story told in Dostoevsky, *Brothers Karamazov*, 241–42.
21. Greene-McCreight, *Darkness Is My Only Companion*.

worthy entry in the long canon of religious masters who have faced the darkness, somehow lived, and managed to tell the tale beautifully. There are modern
classics in this genre, such as C. S. Lewis's *A Grief Observed*, about the death of
his wife, or Nicholas Wolterstorff's *Lament for a Son* and Richard Lischer's *Stations of the Heart*, about the death of each's son. There are ancient entries into
the canon as well. Dante's great *Inferno* begins with a traveler lost in a thick
wood. He progresses through the layers of hell, purgatory, and heaven before
at last emerging "once more to see the stars."[22] The country called *grief* is well
travelled. That we so rarely signal this in church is a sign that we don't trust God
to be with us in the darkness. When my church in North Carolina announced
a "blue Christmas" service for those suffering from grief over the past year, only
ten or fifteen people attended, even though we regularly had seven hundred on
a given Sunday. Nobody wants to turn up and publicly announce they are in
pain. Others don't want to come and be with those in pain—as though grief is
contagious.

We have perhaps confused several quite different things here. There is a difference between clinical depression and the ordinary travails of being a pastor,
or a person. Greene-McCreight's book focuses on depression as a mental illness
in the technical sense, of the sort we realized we couldn't treat in the village in
Honduras. She endured hospitalization, electroconvulsive therapy, and endless
varieties of drug cocktails, and she became well, and wrote to tell us about finding God in the experience. Passages of Scripture came alive for her that had not
before—including descriptions of the psalmist neck-deep in the muck, betrayed
by friends and family, in despair over a God who does not answer. Like the disciples in the boat, she found herself praying to Jesus, "Do you not care that we
are perishing?" (Mark 4:38). And she discovered that God, indeed, hides God's
self (Isa. 45:15). Blaise Pascal, the great seventeenth-century French thinker,
spoke of those who think God is altogether present and of those who think God
is altogether absent, and he split the difference.[23] What we notice when we pursue God is the presence . . . of an absence. God does not rush to our side when
we despair, like a butler to his boss. God does not numb the pain like a narcotic.
God often does not even grant us the encouragement of knowing God exists or
cares. In the end, Greene-McCreight clung to the promises of a God even more
present when we feel God's absence than when we feel God's presence. She
prayed the prayers of the church. She trusted people's prayers for her. She clung
to lines of the liturgy like a life raft. She realized that philosophical certainty—"I
think therefore I am"—saves no lives. No, no, no. With truths from the Bible in

22. Dante, *Inferno*, 383.
23. Pascal, *Pensées*, 449, quoted in Greene-McCreight, *Darkness Is My Only Companion*, 120.

mind, she prayed, "I am loved by God, therefore I am." And she emerged again to see the stars.

One difficulty in our Christian tradition is that we believe in a good God. If you don't, you're not surprised that terrible things happen. But we do. Then the question comes, whence evil? If God could stop it, why doesn't God do that? The best answer is "I don't know." Greene-McCreight lets herself ponder whether there is a relationship between her sin and her suffering.[24] She doesn't want to sever the relationship entirely. Positing a relationship is better than imagining that suffering is meaningless. The second answer to the question of why God allows evil, after "I don't know," is this: God himself enters into evil. Becomes flesh. Is born. Weeps. Is abandoned, tortured. Dies. Is laid in a tomb.

Philosophical accounts of the "problem of evil" point out that the problem cannot be solved. Congratulations. But Christian speech about the problem of evil includes a God who is counted among the most extreme sufferers. And he does so for us.

We may even speak tentatively of God bringing good out of evil. Perhaps one of the reasons God hides himself, as Isaiah suggests, is that an experience of God's absence can bring us to long for God's presence more deeply. From the valley one can stand in awe of great things, whereas from a peak one can barely even see great things.[25] Suffering can increase our empathy with others who suffer. This isn't automatic—those who suffer can become isolated, self-absorbed, bitter. Or they can recognize that the great sea of suffering is one in which most of humanity also swims.

Seeking to help other sufferers has been one of the major pastoral responses to suffering over the past few generations. Henri Nouwen put words to it with his book *The Wounded Healer*. Understandably, most of us just want suffering to go away. Often people marry or pursue ordination or take on other great feats in an effort to fill the great loneliness at the heart of their being. It never works. The wound is permanent. It can never be closed, and asking something or someone to close it—whether a person or a ministry or anything at all—will fail. But if we notice the great gaping hole in our soul, if we tend to it and admire it, we can come to see it like the Grand Canyon—as a place of awe-inspiring beauty.

If we ministers have anything to offer another person, it is usually mediated through our pain. This doesn't mean turning the pulpit into an opportunity to avoid paying therapists—we have to work out our personal pain on our own, not in our sermons or pastoral care. But if we're aware of where and how it hurts in

24. Greene-McCreight, *Darkness Is My Only Companion*, 102–11.

25. The phrase is from G. K. Chesterton, the great English journalist and religious writer (1874–1936). I borrow it here from Z. Eswine's fantastic book *Spurgeon's Sorrows*.

us and how we've traveled spiritually in response to that hurt, we can help others in response to theirs. We can even—and this is dangerous—come to see the hurt as a sort of strange gift. Richard Rohr gets at this theme with his great book, aptly titled *Everything Belongs*. There is a place in the ecology of our souls for the worst pain. Not as something God inflicts in order to bring about good—that would be a terribly clumsy version of God. Not as something that we pull through like spiritual heroes, Marines, Green Berets in collars, emboldened by Friedrich Nietzsche's "whatever doesn't kill me makes me stronger."[26] No—pain is a source of grace the way darkness is the precursor to God's "let there be light." God is so good and creative that God can make a universe from dirt and life from a grave. What can God do with our pain?

I offer this position with some hesitation, and I would not offer it at all if I weren't supported by one of the great reflectors on the holocaust, Viktor Frankl. In his book *Man's Search for Meaning*, largely about his experience in the Nazi death camps, Frankl concludes that his fellow psychoanalysts are wrong. Human life is not a search for pleasure, as Sigmund Freud premised. It is not based on power, as Alfred Adler and Nietzsche and others said. Human life is fundamentally a search for meaning. Frankl observed that those who found meaning in their suffering, despite whatever the vile intentions of its inflictors were, disproportionately survived. Those who did not find meaning, whose hope gave out, were more quickly among those who died. This finding is far from expected. Many who perished longed to live. The point is to explain how anybody at all lived. And the answer is the meaning they took from their suffering. Frankl himself imagined a warm lecture hall, upholstered seats, and himself at a podium reflecting on what his experience teaches about humanity. While his body was in agony, starved, worked near to death, wearing rags, stricken with typhus, his mind had a glimpse of something profoundly meaningful, life-giving, yet to come. "The one who has a Why to live for can bear almost any How."[27] This is not to diminish the suffering of six million murdered—far from it. It is to say that living for a meaningful purpose, *sub specie aeternitatis* (in light of eternity), as Frankl puts it, is a powerful, nearly deathless way to live.

This is all a little dramatic for most pastors, isn't it? Comparing the Nazi extermination camps to email chains that criticize your preaching or youth group kids bullying your children or even serious depression. But Frankl draws just these kinds of parallels. He even founded a kind of psychotherapy, logotherapy,

26. Nietzsche's words, paraphrased here, are a reference to the philosopher's "higher health," owing to illness, "one which is made stronger by whatever does not kill it" (*Portable Nietzsche*, 680).

27. Nietzsche, quoted in Frankl, *Man's Search for Meaning*, 73.

to help sufferers coax meaning out of their experiences without minimizing any-one's pain.

I'm struck, from my own experience in the parish, by the truth of this. Real pain stems from lack of meaning. I could withstand nearly anything if I knew there was a payoff. Criticism got to me because it seemed mean, point-less, tawdry. I've melted like an insecure preteen at small-spirited comments reported through the gossip mill. And yet folks on the side of the angels have courageously faced slashed tires, crosses burned in yards, put-downs of family members, public disrespect—all because they knew their side would eventu-ally win out. Even these troubles pale in comparison to Frankl's Nazi camp experiences.

Simple acts of kindness can also cure a surprising amount of grief. Frankl speaks eloquently of the grace of a piece of bread given by a fellow sufferer. It wasn't the calories so much, as life-giving as those were—it was the kindness. Frankl also speaks, almost unbelievably, of a Nazi commandant who offered kindness to prisoners, paying for medicine out of his own pocket. A group of Hungarian Jews hid the Nazi soldier after the war and negotiated with American forces for leniency for him.[28] Mary Doria Russell, the great novelist, quotes a Talmudic proverb that no tapestry is so dark that God has not included within it at least a thread of grace.[29] As a pastor I was struck that a tiny word or gesture of personal thoughtfulness could see me through a month of otherwise sleepless nights.

To go back to Rohr: what we do not transform, we transmit. We have to do something with our pain or we will inflict it on others. Frankl speaks of camp survivors who went around inflicting wanton cruelty on others. Who could blame them? Yet their experience doesn't make it right to hurt other people. Rohr again: "If we don't learn to mythologize our lives, inevitably we will pathologize them."[30] That is, if we do not gather up the shards of fractured things and make them into some new whole, they will do harm. For example, my mother was a lifelong alcohol abuser and drug addict until she died of an accidental over-dose at age fifty-six. She was embarrassing, a headache, a drag on life—until she was gone, and then I just missed her desperately. But I've always noticed descriptions of the church as a mother. My mother's absence made space for another sort of mother. I know what it's like to suffer with family members who are substance abusers, mentally ill, or both (and most families have one or more

28. Frankl, *Man's Search for Meaning*, 85.

29. Russell, *Thread of Grace*. See epigraph to Russell's work.

30. This Rohr adage and the one above I take from Rev. Dr. John Pentland, pastor of Hill-hurst United Church of Canada in Calgary, AB. See Rohr, "Transforming Our Pain"; *On the Threshold of Transformation*, 1.

such individuals). The wound will never go away. And I wouldn't want it to. That would mean my mother had gone away entirely. I've learned not to blame her—she had her own wounds, unmythologized. My wounds help me see whatever comes into my life as a strange gift. I want no more such strange gifts. One is enough! But I'm surprised to find myself glad for this wound, without which I wouldn't be what I am, offering whatever grace I can to others.

Finding meaning in life can lift someone who is suffering out of depression. Rae Jean has told me about a highly effective therapy called Behavioral Activation that uses meaning to fight depression. In it, you write down how you spend every hour of the day and then rate each hour's activity on how important and how meaningful it was. Grocery shopping may be important but not very meaningful, spending time with a grandchild may be both important and meaningful, and checking Facebook may be neither. Ultimately, you try to get rid of all unimportant and meaningless activities. And it's been shown to work, in the most rigorous studies and even with people who are experiencing poverty and homelessness.[31] I'm not saying it's easy—it's actually especially hard to feel something is meaningful when you are experiencing the hopeless fog of depression. But it's a powerful start.

Even when they believe their life has meaning, people with wounds can cycle in and out of depression. And even people without emotional wounds can experience depression for biological reasons. Although we don't know the origins of the great darkness that Mother Teresa experienced for decades, we do know she never stopped serving God.[32] It may be the same for pastors. Finding or holding on to the individual meaning of their lives can help prevent depression, and it may help treat depression. But deep belief in God alone does not make a pastor immune to depression. Thank God pastors have meaning.

Ministerial Work Conditions and Depression

Keeping in mind that depressed people may self-select into ministry at higher rates, it is still worth trying to see if clergy who are depressed experience different ministry conditions from clergy who aren't depressed. I can't talk in causal terms here—I can't definitively say, for example, that working at more than one church causes depression for the pastor—but I can report on the relationships and trends in the data.

31. Mazzuchelli, Kane, and Rees, "Behavioral Activation Treatments"; Daughters et al., "Effectiveness of a Brief Behavioral Treatment."
32. Mother Teresa, *Mother Teresa*, ed. Kolodiejchuk.

In searching for factors related to depression in clergy, I grouped them according to a popular occupational health theory called effort-reward imbalance theory.[33] It's a pretty straightforward theory: if the effort you put in is greater than the reward you get back, it will lead to emotional distress. The authors of this theory group the work demands (or "efforts") into those external to the person versus those internal to the person. For clergy, I grouped the demands and rewards in terms of external demands, internal demands, and rewards.

External demands

- *Job stress, especially demands and criticism from parishioners* (example survey items: "During the past year, how often have the people in your congregation made too many demands on you?" "During the past year, how often have the people in your congregation been critical of the things you have done?")
- *Life unpredictability* (e.g., "My daily activities from week to week are unpredictable.")
- *Social isolation* (e.g., "How socially isolated do you feel?")

Internal demands

- *Feeling guilty about not working enough* (e.g., "Over the past year, how guilty have you felt about not doing enough in your role as clergy?")
- *Doubting one's call* (e.g., "How often have you doubted that you are called by God to the ministry?" "How often have you thought about leaving pastoral ministry to enter a secular occupation?")

Rewards

- *Ministry satisfaction* (e.g., "What is your level of satisfaction with your overall effectiveness as a pastoral leader in this particular congregation?")
- *Low financial stress* (e.g., "How stressful is your current financial situation for you?")
- *Sense of control over next church job* (e.g., "For your next appointment to a charge, how much importance do you think will be given to your particular gifts and calling for ministry?" This question reflects the fact that in the UMC, bishops appoint pastors to churches. Other

33. Siegrist, "Adverse Health Effects."

denominations have their own form of stress over job stability and agency
in what comes next.)

The findings that played out for clergy are consistent with effort-reward
imbalance theory in almost every way.[34] Clergy with scores qualifying them for
depression reported higher demands (both extrinsic and intrinsic) and lower
rewards. The only exception was that there was no significant relationship between sense of control over one's next church appoint-
ment and depression, and I now think I was wrong
to ever think that control might be seen by clergy as
a reward. I try to live and learn, and here is one thing
I've learned: Christian clergy think differently about
"control" than a lot of secular research on control suggests. Many studies find that having greater perceived
control relates to better mental health.[35] In contrast,
through interviewing clergy I found that they try to
seek God's way and that they can feel unfaithful if
they try to wrench control their way.[36] It now makes
sense to me that questions about control—including
control over one's current and future employment—
can miss the intended point for clergy.

**These categories
demonstrated** the
strongest relationships
with depression for clergy:

- Critical congregants
- Too many demands
  from congregation
- Feeling guilty for not
  doing enough
- Life unpredictability
- Social isolation
- Financial stress

But back to the effort-reward imbalance theory.
One of the fun things about quantitative research is that you can put actual
numbers to certain findings and also point to where the strongest relationships lie. The strongest relationships with depression in clergy were job stress
and feeling guilty about not doing enough. Specifically, pastors who reported
feeling like people in their congregation had (1) put too many demands on
them or (2) been critical of them and things they had done were much more
likely to qualify for depression. There was a similarly large relationship with
depression among pastors who reported feeling guilty about not doing enough
in their role as clergy. Feeling guilty is sometimes considered a symptom of
depression itself.[37] However, for clergy, I wonder if guilt is bound up in the
sacred nature of their work. As described in the last chapter, when your work
is holy, you will devote more time and energy to it and experience desolation

34. Proeschold-Bell et al., "Using Effort-Reward Imbalance Theory."
35. See, for example, social learning theory and research on the psychological construct
of internal locus of control: Krause and Stryker, "Stress and Well-Being"; Seeman, "Personal
Control."
36. Blouin and Proeschold-Bell, "Measuring Stress in a Clergy Population."
37. "Depression," National Institute of Mental Health.

if it is lost or threatened.[38] This desolation may be showing up as depressive symptoms.

There were three other measures on our survey that also showed a strong, although slightly attenuated, relationship with depression. Pastors who scored higher on life unpredictability, social isolation, doubting their call, and financial stress were more likely to qualify for depression. Conversely, pastors who reported higher satisfaction in ministry were less likely to qualify for depression.

To some extent, these results could apply to people in any occupation. Criticism, life unpredictability, financial stress, and social isolation can trigger depression for many people—not just clergy.[39] And satisfaction with one's work may be protective against depression for many of us. However, conditions may be ripe for clergy to experience more of these risk factors at the same time, which would explain their above-average rates of depression. For example, pastors' visible role may open them up to criticism more often, and moving more often may increase the chances of feeling socially isolated. Before turning to possible solutions, let's hear Jason's perspective.

"Unfortunately, I usually don't handle negative emotion very well. I can [usually] handle the situation as it occurs very well, but then I'll allow it to sort of fester in my emotional being. . . . I take medication every day that helps me stay level. . . . I never had any depression before I was a pastor. None. I'm developing a better sense of allowing God to be the center instead of me being the center, and . . . that's helped me to cope with those things better."

Note: The pastor made this statement after describing a stressful and very personal experience with the church.

Behind the Pulpit
Making Meaning in a Mean World

Pastoral work can be truly depressing, and not necessarily because of confronting grief with parishioners, since that's something pastors find meaning in. Pastoral work can be depressing in part because of the hurtful words and actions that parishioners direct at pastors, seemingly forgetting that pastors are people too. And depression is no laughing matter. A beloved pastor I knew killed himself in his church office. A certain message was being sent to a congregation there. Not

38. Pargament and Mahoney, "Sacred Matters."
39. There's a chicken-and-egg problem here in which you can't always know what happens first. Being depressed can lead you to isolate yourself or to do poorer work and then be criticized. In this chapter, we've had to talk about relationships rather than causal factors because we don't have airtight science on causes, but one can imagine reciprocal relationships occurring.

only despair, as in most suicides, but also an implication that the church had some blame for this.

Churches can be hard places. Everyone is an expert on how pastors ought to do their jobs, and the louder mouthed among them make this public—and that's in healthy congregations. Unhealthy ones can be deadly. A friend of mine is under fire in his parish. Some folks have left, others are threatening to leave, and everything he's worked for is coming unraveled. He came home happy the other day. "What's wrong with you?" his spouse asked. He responded, "I think it's the first day on the job here where no one attacked me." And yet he's one of the most gifted, well-equipped, and faithfully serving pastors I know.

I recently went from pastor to parishioner when I started attending a thriving multisite megachurch in Vancouver. Thriving churches are rare in this highly secular city. And yet I found myself internally as critical as anybody ever was to me in my parish: This thing isn't right; that could be better; why are we doing the other thing? Critical assessment is a way of caring. I expect the church to be amazing, and when it falls short, I wish it were better. It's a short step from noticing things that could be better to voicing those things to church leadership, and another short step from that expression to a pastor feeling attacked. It's really hard to lead a group of people anywhere to do anything. Ever tried to organize a family reunion or a group vacation?

Ministers are sent places to lead, and leading often includes making changes. We know that the best things about the church will never change: Jesus, the Scriptures, and serving our community. But sometimes church folks get confused and think nothing should ever change: the carpet, the meeting times, or the worship style. Many lay people paying the church's bills—often older people— didn't ask for change. They'd rather things stay just the way they are, thank you. Their whole life has changed. They can't even go to the doctor or the hairdresser or the grocery store without feeling their age. At least church is one place where they don't ask me to sign in with an iPad or check out my own groceries or pay with some unfamiliar technology. Now this minister is telling us to change? Who does she think she is? Doesn't she know I stayed here when all my friends left, kept the place afloat, supported this church when it would have been more convenient to leave?

And leading, including making changes, can feel risky in an environment where fewer Americans go to church. With many mainline churches closing, the pressure to grow church congregations is very real. I remember when I was once sent on a downward spiral. It was when a flyer went out for a new church start in Durham. It was glossy. Expensive. And it apparently went to everyone in town. Its minister was well coifed, expensively dressed, had a soul patch, and his glasses looked like they cost more than my car. His church boasted thousands of attendees, fun for children, spectacular music, and a new campus.

Guys like this are trotted out at Methodist events all the time (and yes, they do tend to be guys). The heavy implication is that if we just do this, that, or the other, we could have a church like his. I wonder how many Methodist ministers have made a pilgrimage to some gigachurch with an oceanic parking lot to then come back to Possum Trot, USA, and try to implement what they saw. It's ridiculous. To compare ourselves unfavorably to other pastors is just one step away from doubting our call and feeling guilty for not doing enough—two things related to depression in pastors.

The church is both the source of the problem and the solution for depression in ministry. At its worst, the church does harm. It's made up of flawed people, sinners (the only kind of people available). It doesn't surprise me when a pastor shares a genuine concern with parishioners but then receives no response from them. Or when unsympathetic youth group members harm a child's fragile psyche. Where's the church of nonsinners that pastors could serve that would always get these things right?

But while some church environments may be harmful to pastors, others may be beneficial. Churches are full of people who pray for you, ask how you're doing, and offer to help and mean it. And corporate prayer itself is healing. I'm sympathetic with Rae Jean's suggestion that folks predisposed to depression find their way into ministry, which actually makes things better. The pastor isn't doing the work primarily for the sake of receiving benefit (or harm!), yet she can't help but be affected by the church she loves and tries so faithfully to serve. In this way, the church is also the solution. It's the place where we meet Jesus, the Great Physician, who heals all ills, including ours. Eventually.

Watching Over One Another in Love

Clearly the theology around depression is complex. However, returning to the beginning of this chapter, depressive symptoms can slow down pastors and sometimes overwhelm them, and that is not what we want for our friends or our leaders. So what can be done?

1. *Keep criticism in perspective.* Work closely with your lay leaders to keep criticism in perspective and handle it in a healthy way that doesn't put the full burden on the pastor. Ask together what strange gift might be hidden in this morass. Theologian Lauren Winner speaks of an art

critic, Peter Schjeldahl, who has a strategy for responding to a work he hates. Winner writes, "He asks himself, *What would I like about this if I liked it?*"[40] We can ask this even of mean-hearted criticism. There is always an opportunity to learn and grow. Your allies will be heartened by your willingness to accept a strange gift—and your enemies will be discouraged that they accidentally made you a better pastor.

2. *Set guidelines for yourself.* Pastoral work is by nature unpredictable. You can make it slightly less so by setting some guidelines for yourself based on your and your church's priorities. What kinds of calls will you always respond to personally and right away? What might you be able to hand off for a few hours and to whom? Not all twenty-one tasks in the pastor's job description (see chap. 1) can be top priority, but you can use common sense and your values to make bendable rules of thumb and avoid agonizing decision-making for every situation. If something unpleasant comes through on the phone or email or social media, I challenge myself, even though ministry isn't ordinarily a nine-to-five job, to take an approach that pretends it is: If I'm in the office, in the meat of a workday, I can open a difficult email. If it's the evening or weekend, or if I just don't want my day ruined, I won't. Somehow, this helps. For example, friends have told me about a critical review of a book of mine that's out there. I keep planning to read it on a day when I feel entirely too good about myself—but that day has never actually arrived!

3. *Discern your call.* Discern where your efforts are most needed—where God is calling you to be—and do that thing with all you have. Don't feel guilty about not doing enough. You can discern often and fervently, but then just recognize that God has only given you, in the words of poet Mary Oliver, one "wild and precious life."[41] If you are working in alignment with God, then it will have to be enough. You don't need to save the church by dying yourself. Christ's sacrifice is unrepeatable.

4. *Foster your relationships.* Foster friendships and relationships, and call on people when you are feeling down, but also before you are feeling down. You are more than the robe you wear. You may have to make a greater effort than some to keep your friendships strong. You might consider holding on to friendships in seminary with people who knew you before you wore a robe. Or you might consider having an annual weekend with two or three people you hold dear so that the tradition

---

40. Winner, *Still*, 41.
41. Oliver, *New and Selected Poems*, 94.

recurs on its own and you don't accidentally let a whole year go by without rekindling those friendships. You can find a way—just don't underestimate the importance of emotional support. I find that the longer I'm in ministry, the more friendships with fellow seminarians matter. Some of those friendships matter far more now than they did twenty years ago. We *get* one another. Make time for that.

5. *Don't forget the big three: sleep, exercise, and nutrition.* Everything comes more easily with adequate sleep. It will help you better respond to challenges. Experiment for a week and try it. Eight or nine hours of glorious sleep is a fantastic gift from our creator. Accept it. I try to be gentle with folks I notice sleeping during my sermons rather than beat myself up for being boring. "They must really need it to sleep through a sermon this good!" I joke internally. So do you.

The research supporting exercise is unequivocal—exercise is one of the best things you can do to lift your mood.[42] But you have to push through. Most people don't actually feel better while exercising—the lift comes twenty minutes or so *after* exercising. Exercise will also help you sleep better.

Your brain and body need healthy foods and vitamins to function well and to recover from stressors.

6. *Be open to trying treatment.* Depression often goes away on its own, but treatment can help it go away sooner, and sometimes it doesn't go away without help.

Seeking treatment for depression is common among pastors. As noted earlier, Rae Jean found that 44 percent of pastors had seen a therapist in their lives, and 18 percent had seen a therapist in the past year. Is that surprising? Sometimes stigma and cultural norms can lead to misperceptions. For example, did you know that 40 percent of people in the United States don't drink alcohol at all?[43] It can seem to me like everyone is drinking, when in fact those nondrinkers are just pretty quiet while the beer ads are pretty loud. A lot of pastors seek counseling, but they don't all proclaim it from the rooftops. You would be in good company to seek a therapist.

42. Exercise can both prevent depression and help current depression go away. In one experimental study, participants with major depressive disorder were assigned either supervised exercise, home-based exercise, antidepressants, or a placebo pill. After four months, participants in the exercise and antidepressant groups were far more likely to have had their depressive symptoms remit than those taking the placebo. In fact, the beneficial effect of exercise was comparable to the antidepressant! Blumenthal et al., "Exercise and Pharmacotherapy"; Hoffman et al., "Exercise and Pharmacotherapy."

43. "Alcohol Facts and Statistics," National Institute of Alcohol Abuse and Alcoholism.

7. *Focus on the greater meaning.* Hold on to the greater meaning of what you do, and try not to let the rest get you down. Or, as in the title of a famous book by Richard Carlson, "Don't sweat the small stuff . . . and it's all small stuff." In Christ, the victory that matters has already been won. Our work is then surprisingly free to succeed or fail or tread along just below standard. God will bring about the world God wants, either with our help or despite us or through us. Hang on tightly to meaning.

8. *Prepare for stress.* Understand the stress process and garner needed resources or skills—in advance. In the next chapter, Rae Jean walks us through the process of stress. Have you ever wondered why you find long-term planning or doing a devotional for a seniors group stressful but your best friend from seminary doesn't? The answer has to do with the resources you think are available to you, your personal strengths and coping skills, and whether you can see grace at work in challenges. Although depression involves biology and isn't always rooted in life situations, being maximally prepared to handle stressful situations may prevent depressive symptoms—and it sure can't hurt since we're all going to encounter stress at some point! We devote the next chapter to stress and proactive coping.

4

A Practical Guide
to Combating Stress Symptoms

In chapter 1 we described the pastor's experience as including varied work that requires multiple skill sets, long workdays, high and sometimes opposing expectations from parishioners, and conflicts that arise in church settings. In chapters 2 and 3, we looked at pastors' sacred call and at some pastors' experiences with depression. Stressful circumstances are inevitable and can potentially interfere with being fully alive, although they don't always have to. Handling stressful circumstances well can help pastors prevent anxiety and depression symptoms and avoid habits that are bad for their physical health.

Stress: Defying Definition

Let's start by unpacking stress. What *is* stress? Despite the ubiquity of the word "stress," some people question whether it even exists. A friend once told me about conversing with a poor, older man who said, "Only rich people have stress. What I've got are *problems*—financial problems, marriage problems, and job problems!"

But for those who believe that stress is real, how would they define it? A couple years after I started doing research with clergy, I read an article in a psychology magazine that defined stress as arising when (1) you feel out of control or (2) you feel out of sync with your values.[1] This definition of

1. Clay, "Is Stress Getting to You?"

stress spoke to me because it had such clear intervention implications: you "just" had to get more in control or get your activities in line with your values. When I shared this definition with our Clergy Health Initiative research team, one colleague came up to me later and said she didn't buy it. She argued that being out of control or feeling out of sync could be stressors for some people but that they didn't define stress itself and might not even be stressful for everyone.

Having read only one article, and a magazine article at that, we decided we should go in search of a definition of stress. Our search was fruitless—even the research journal called *Stress* didn't offer a definition of stress![2] The most helpful source we found was the American Institute of Stress, which says, "Stress is not a useful term for scientists because it is such a highly subjective phenomenon that it defies definition." They also wrote, "Everyone knows what stress is, but nobody really knows."[3]

So researchers can't precisely define stress, even if stress is the kind of thing you recognize when you feel it. Yet being precise can lead to knowing how to address a problem, and with so many studies connecting stress to poor health, I sincerely wanted to reduce stress for clergy.[4]

Fortunately, there is a way out of this quandary, and it is to look at stress models developed by psychologists. These models have multiple steps relating to stress, and each step has a specific name, such that the word "stress" is nearly avoided. A simplified model of the transactional theory of stress (see fig. 4.1) shows the interaction between a person and her environment.[5]

Figure 4.1
Stress Appraisal Model

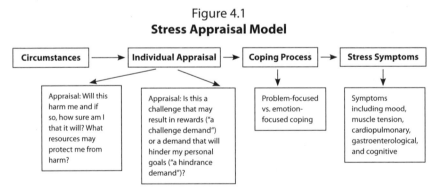

2. We searched *Stress: The International Journal on the Biology of Stress* (published by Taylor & Francis) to no avail.

3. "What Is Stress?"

4. Schneiderman, Ironson, and Siegle, "Stress and Health."

5. Folkman et al., "Dynamics of a Stressful Encounter," 992; Lazarus and Folkman, *Stress, Appraisal, and Coping.*

Once you understand the pieces of the trans-actional model of stress and coping, which I've simplified slightly and will call here the stress appraisal model, you can think about where to intervene to prevent stress symptoms, whether it's in your own life or in the lives of the clergy you care about.

Circumstances

The beginning of this model is circumstances. You'll see that the stress appraisal model uses the term "circumstances" rather than "stress" or even "stressors." Stress implies something negative, but viewed objectively, a situation just *is*. It's the reaction to those circumstances—which varies from person to person—that is either positive or negative.

It took stress researchers a long time to clue in to the fact that different people can have various reactions to similar circumstances. Indeed, several decades ago, researchers tried to measure stress by having people look at a list of presumably stressful circumstances and check off those that applied to them.[6] This list started with negative events like "death of a friend," "personal illness," and "job loss" and also included positive events like "planning your wedding" and "starting a new job." Researchers assumed that one's degree of stress corresponded to the number of items checked off. This approach didn't work; it didn't predict well who was anxious or depressed.[7]

Researchers then hypothesized that perhaps they were overemphasizing big events in life and underemphasizing small but regular events, so they created different stress measures, this time listing "daily hassles" such as owing money, not liking coworkers, and concerns about how others see you.[8] Although that

"**I try hard not to change [myself],** which has really upset some of the [lay leader] powers that be. . . . They saw me in the liquor store. I was getting some Irish cream to put in my coffee and I looked over and went, 'Well, hey! How are you all doing?' I put my bottle on the counter, paid, and walked out. And [one of the lay leaders] came up to me the next Sunday and he's like, 'I didn't know you drink.' I said, 'I didn't know you drink either.' And it was sort of like, 'Oh my gosh. She's a human being.' It shocked them to see me, but it wound up being a good thing that they realized that I was a human being and they've now come to my defense on certain things. It's like they said, 'Why are we holding her to standards we're not willing to keep?'"

6. Horowitz, "Life Events Questionnaires"; Holmes and Rahe, "Social Readjustment Rating Scale."
7. Kanner et al., "Comparison of Two Modes."
8. For one of the most commonly used daily hassles scales, see the end of this article: Kanner et al., "Comparison of Two Modes."

"When I got to my second appointment . . . my [personnel committee] chair came over to me one time and said we don't like it that you leave on Thursday afternoon and go down and visit your family and don't come back until Saturday morning. And I said, I'm sorry, you know, that's my weekend. I'll be here at worship, I'm available by phone, but [I am with my family] and if you cannot live with that, I am completely understanding, and all you need to do is . . . get another pastor. So I guess you can say I kind of laid the groundwork there, too, with the expectations, but after that, once we got that settled, we were fine."

approach was better, it didn't predict mental health problems as well as desired.[9]

Eventually, researchers got beyond the "circumstances" step of the model above and added the "individual appraisal" step, which we'll explore further in the next section.[10] It turns out that when some people are told that budget problems will squeeze out their favorite church programs, they worry about it for ten minutes, whereas others are despondent for weeks. The beauty of the stress appraisal model is that it takes into account individual differences in reactions to all kinds of events—positive and negative life events as well as daily hassles.

No pastor wants to get rid of all the circumstances that might be stressful. This is a world in which difficult and sometimes heartbreakingly sad things happen, and it's very much the pastor's role to be present at those times. I'm not suggesting that we change the life events of ministry. On the other hand, pastors may be able to do some things to change their daily hassles. In either case, pastors' reactions to circumstances—their individual appraisals of circumstances—can be changed. Let's see how it works.

Behind the Pulpit
Setting Up Your Best Circumstances

You can't always change your circumstances, but sometimes there are proactive things you can do that might prevent some harmful circumstances.

For pastors, these things may prove helpful:

1. *Set expectations.* Talk openly with your congregation about what you want your role to be and what they want your role to be and come to an agreement. This may prevent other people from putting you in a position you don't want to be in.

9. Cohen, "Contrasting the Hassles Scale."
10. Folkman et al., "Dynamics of a Stressful Encounter," 992.

2. *Choose your personnel committee members wisely.* Sometimes those who want to serve on such committees see it as their job to advocate for their congregation by giving the pastor a hard time. As a pastor, I first sought to make that committee "fair" by having not just friends but critics on that committee. But I quickly abandoned this approach! Instead I packed it with high-functioning leaders who loved me and appreciated what we were doing as a congregation. I made this a group of confidants. They weren't unwilling to confront me—in fact, their confrontations were more painful because I knew they loved me, so I couldn't dismiss them. But because they were close to me personally, they made me better. And so they made the church better.

3. *Teach your personnel committee members how to communicate on your behalf.* They can run interference for you. In order to do so, they need to know what you are up to and why, and sometimes they even need to know things they can't tell other people. They need to be trustworthy people to whom others can complain. Hopefully they will say, "Since personnel issues are confidential, I can't tell you all the details, but I can assure you we did the right thing."

> **"I told [my staff-parish relations committee]** that I will take time off, vacation time, and that I honor a day of Sabbath that is not a Sunday but a day of Sabbath. I expect that my staff will take time off too and honor their vacation time, and they've been very helpful with that. . . . They know what's on my mind and I know what's on theirs."

For bishops and other supervisors, the following describes how to support those under your care:

1. *Check in on the pastors under your care.* Send them cards and notes. Call them for no reason other than to check in and encourage them. Pray for them. Talk with them about ideas, theology, books, life—not just job mechanics. Your supervisees will be deeply grateful if you express genuine concern for them.

2. *Set expectations with congregations.* Listen to lay leaders and also listen to pastors. Don't allow congregants to expect pastors to do all the work without congregant contributions. Assist congregants in grounding their work in concepts like baptism; tools such as Pastor & Parish (described in the appendix) exist to aid personnel committee members in thinking of their work in spiritual terms.

For lay leaders and personnel committees, try the following to support your pastors:

1. *Listen to your pastors.* Understand them. Love them. Don't just give them gifts during pastor appreciation month (though that's nice!), but pass on praise year round. Deflect mindless criticism. Handle the parishioner complaints that are really just kvetching or hand-wringing. Most perfectionists want to leap into the fray when criticized, however irrationally. But you don't want your pastor wasting energy on this. And it won't cost you nearly as much energy to block those efforts on their behalf.

2. *Maintain a small expense account for your pastor.* Be sure there is enough money in an expense account for your pastor to do ministry functions like taking folks to coffee or meals, especially new folks whom you hope to cultivate into involved parishioners, or creatives in town from whom your pastor needs to learn for the sake of her preaching. Support her theologically by being sure she can buy books and go to conferences that will refresh and energize her to lead and serve.

3. *Support your pastor in creative ways.* Notice your pastor's strengths and play to them. Figure out ways to remove work that doesn't energize him and allow him to put more of his energy into work that does. This will make him—and you and your church's ministry—much more effective.

Individual Appraisal

After experiencing a circumstance, you move on to the next step in the stress appraisal model, "individual appraisal." This is where you decide whether a circumstance (1) is important to you and (2) could do you harm, followed by an assessment of what resources you have that might prevent the harm.[11]

Let's take a circumstance like being told your ministry in a certain place is done, which for UMC pastors is a possibility every July and is also something that runs through the minds of clergy from any denomination. Some pastors may hear this news and assess that moving is both important to them and potentially harmful. At the same time, they may decide they have the skills to navigate a move well, the money to move, and enough support from family and friends to move with little disruption to their important relationships. Thus, skills and resources affect one's individual appraisal. Alternatively, some pastors will hear this same news and assess that moving could do them a lot of harm, perhaps by tearing them and their children away from schools and friends.

11. Folkman et al., "Dynamics of a Stressful Encounter," 992.

Figure 4.2
Likelihood of Relocation

"How likely do you think it is that you will be asked
to change churches in the next 12 months?"

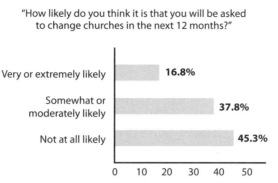

Responses are from 2016 surveys of full-time church-appointed pastors.

These individual appraisals happen in a fraction of a second—so fast that most of us don't even realize that our thoughts occurred. And yet through research, we know that often thoughts occur first and are quickly followed by emotions.[12] Usually these emotions are simultaneously paired with physiological arousal, such as increased blood pressure and heart rate, sweating, and getting butterflies in your stomach. So if you don't want to change churches, being told you will be appointed to a different church will result in a very quick thought of some kind ("My worst fear is coming true!"), followed by an emotion like anger or worry, combined simultaneously with your heart racing.

You can sometimes change your emotional reaction by changing your thought. Specifically, if you slow down and take time to think through the resources you might draw on to get through a potentially harmful circumstance, you may end up with a different thought and a less harmful appraisal. For example, a pastor might hear that there is an ugly rumor in the church ("If this spreads, my congregants are going to think I'm not trustworthy!") and react with anger or worry (an emotion) and feel her heart start racing (a physiological response). If she can slow down for a minute and reason things through, she might remember that there is a lay leader whom she can call on to rectify the rumor. And this might cause her emotional and physiological responses to dissipate.

12. Scherer, Shorr, and Johnstone, *Appraisal Processes in Emotion*. A number of theories speak about the order of thoughts, physiological arousal, and emotion. Most suggest thoughts (or interpretation) occur first. For a concrete example: hearing footsteps in a dark alley at night takes you through several of the theories. See Heffner, "Emotion."

Past experience also factors into your appraisal. If you have always been able to dispel rumors, your immediate thoughts will carry only a small degree of concern. However, let's say that a rumor once sent your church and your family into utter turmoil. In that case, you will have a rapid-fire response drawing on those memories associated with your previous experience. This is called "associative processing," and it happens much faster than reasoning does.[13] When new circumstances start to make you panic, it's a good idea to slow down and think about whether your previous experience still applies today. Sometimes enough has changed that you no longer need the emotion of worry or anger. Perhaps this time around you have new skills or a more supportive congregation.

So far we've only talked about circumstances that you appraise could harm you. But it is actually more nuanced than that, and perhaps the real assessment is not just whether a circumstance can harm you but whether it will be *difficult*. Circumstances that aren't difficult and aren't important to you don't create strong emotions, positive or negative. If you view a circumstance as beneficial and not difficult, that may lead to positive emotions like pleasure or relief. However, if you think a circumstance will be difficult, there are three categories you'll unconsciously put the circumstance in:[14]

1. Something that could do you future harm (called a "hindrance demand," e.g., a rumor)
2. Something that has already harmed you and that you now have to deal with (another example of a hindrance demand, e.g., a car accident)
3. Something that poses a challenge and might be difficult but also good for you in the long run (called a "challenge demand," e.g., leading a church after a tragedy, which carries with it the possible reward of feeling closer to doing God's work)

The third category—the challenge demand—is especially interesting because it's up to the individual to decide whether a difficult circumstance could lead to future benefit or just hinder her goals. Some pastors may be assigned to serve a difficult church—say, one undergoing conflict with members leaving— and decide that this is going to harm them, perhaps by being exhausting and preventing them from doing well. But other pastors may decide that being assigned to a church in conflict is a challenge in which they may learn to be a great leader.

13. Hogg and Cooper, *Sage Handbook of Social Psychology*, 166.
14. Podsakoff, LePine, and LePine, "Differential Challenge."

As a psychologist and researcher who has never been a pastor, I imagine that this appraisal process creates tension for pastors. Jesus embraced challenges during difficult circumstances. At the same time, not every challenge you encounter can be turned into a positive growth experience. However, if you can find a way to think about some challenging circumstances as making you and the body of Christ stronger, this will make all the difference in terms of circumventing stress symptoms instead of experiencing them.

Behind the Pulpit
Unwelcome Gifts

How do we pastors grow to see our challenges as, in some way, good gifts? We know to be careful with such dangerously pious advice in pastoral care. Christians often casually cite Romans 8:28, "All things work together for good for those who love God." We've all seen responses that were intended to comfort become more like a slap in the face for those mourning a loss. The problem is that because of repeated exposure to suffering, we may lose the ability to see pain and heartache as gifts, unwelcome though they may be. While our lives are part of the demonstration of God's glory, it is a dangerous spiritual teaching to think that whatever comes can be seen as a gift—one designed either to encourage us or to challenge us. This is dangerous in that we may end up equating suffering with having deeper spiritual experiences and that might lead to thinking that God causes suffering or evil. So what is the alternative?

I remember David Steinmetz, a church historian, commenting on the difference between the views of Calvin and Wesley on whether God causes pain. This has been taken as a difference between Calvinists who think God sends bad things and Wesleyans who think God does not. But Steinmetz jokes that if Calvin falls down the stairs, he dusts himself off and asks God what he should learn from it. If Wesley falls down the stairs, he dusts himself off and asks God what he should learn from it.[15] The lesson is this: The world is always hard. We are perpetual disciples. God is perennially good.

When challenges inevitably arise, pastors, parishioners, and denomination officials can be proactive in how they make their appraisals. When we pastors are doing the appraising, the following suggestions may prove useful:

15. Attributed to Steinmetz, church history lectures (Duke Divinity School, Durham, NC, spring 1997).

1. *After receiving difficult news, slow down and challenge your thoughts.*
   - How sure are you that this will be harmful? Perhaps after a good night's sleep, it will seem like less of a problem.
   - What resources do you have? Whom can you turn to and what can you draw on to minimize harm?
   - Not every cloud has a silver lining. Or maybe sometimes the silver linings are small. Take a calm, prayerful minute and think about whether something good can come out of you rising to this difficult occasion.
2. *At any time, build your social support.*
   - Try to have at least two people you can bare your soul to. Maintain those relationships even during good times. Don't hesitate to call them when you are struggling with something, and also call them with good news.
   - If you feel like your values are different from those of your church leaders and that it is a constant battle to lead them in the direction you think God would have them go, regularly talk to at least one clergy person who is in the same boat. You may never get praise from your congregants, but you might get support from another pastor.

The following are suggestions for denomination officials:

1. *Think of what resources you can offer clergy.* Perhaps you have ideas for resources that are currently lacking that you can try to get.
2. *Support your clergy.* Clergy will benefit just from knowing that you support them. If clergy believe that you have their best interests at heart, that alone will be more encouragement than you know.

For parishioners who wish to support their pastor through a time of difficulty, try the following:

1. *Encourage your pastor's friendships.* These will save her life. I'm not exaggerating. Her ability to be with folks who have known her since before she was a pastor—to retreat with them, to get away and have fun with them, to challenge and be challenged by them—will make your whole church healthier. When her friends and family visit, delight in them. Go out of your way to tell them how wonderful she is. This praise will get back to her and bless her.
2. *Be especially keen to divert criticisms of your pastor that he or she can do nothing about.* Sure, we all want a pastor with a young family and fifty years of experience, someone who's a brilliant preacher and master administrator who can cast vision and visit a hospital room like an angel and write award-winning poetry on the side. God only has human beings to work with, unfortunately—or fortunately. Pastors are human too. We get that everyone

has strengths and weaknesses. In a time of declining church power and influence, your church's struggles are part of God making you holy—they're not all your pastor's fault. Only go to your pastor with insight, not blame, and then only with insight that she or he can do something about. The pastor isn't going to grow a foot taller, his voice isn't going to drop an octave, and he's not going to miraculously acquire the gifts of some mythically remembered previous pastor. As a pastor friend said after visiting a former church, "They sure love you once you're gone." Why not start sharing love while the pastor is still there?

3. *The most important thing you can do for your pastor is to pray.* Our hearts follow our prayers. If you pray, your love will increase and your church will benefit.

Coping Process

After making an appraisal that a circumstance is difficult, you go about coping with it (step 3 in the model). Many coping strategies are possible, and it can be helpful to consider whether a circumstance calls for problem-focused coping, emotion-focused coping, or both.[16] Problem-focused coping strategies include:

1. *Anything that can help solve the problem* (in other words, exactly what "problem-focused coping" sounds like). If you can address the root source of the problem, doing so might put an end to it altogether. For example, if the problem is that an important member of the church has threatened to leave, then often letting that person go ends the difficulty.

2. *Getting instrumental help from others to reduce the problem.* For example, if the difficulty is that you are expected to add a Bible study to your week, then finding someone who can lead that Bible study instead will help.

3. *Improving your time-management skills.* If the problem is that you are stretched too thin, then being more efficient with your time can help. (Feel free to groan when you read this one. I know I did while reading the literature—but it is a common suggestion as a problem-solving approach.)

16. Carver and Vargas, "Coping and Health."

Each of these problem-focused coping strategies has a limit. Obviously, you can only become so efficient with your time. And sometimes the problem is unsolvable, such as when a loved one dies or you have to take an unavoidable exam. Fortunately, there is another set of coping strategies called emotion-focused coping.

> "I try to be in covenant with other clergy and other friends that are Christians outside of the church.... Support from other clergy and friends is huge for me, and I have a group of people that do support me and [that] I can call and talk to and say 'guess what happened today' and they're there for me. ... That's a huge difference."

In emotion-focused coping, the goal is to try to reduce the negative emotions you're experiencing.[17] You might talk with a friend or write in a journal. Just expressing your strong emotions might make them less strong. Truly this works, and it is part of what therapy is all about, but you don't have to go to therapy to find ways to express your strong emotions. Alternatively, you could distract yourself with recreation or work to get through an unpleasant situation. You could pray for guidance and strength. You could meditate. You could also do one of many things that carry harmful consequences like drink alcohol, eat too much, or suppress your emotions.

What do we know about clergy and their coping strategies? In terms of coping with ministry demands, a study of clergy from many denominations across the United States found that clergy have a tendency to turn inward to cope through spiritual devotion and hobbies and that when they do turn outward, they usually talk to their spouse and not others.[18] These are all examples of emotion-focused coping strategies; although the study did not ask about problem-focused strategies, it clearly showed that when engaging in emotion-focused coping, some clergy tend to shut out other people.[19]

It doesn't surprise me that clergy turn inward to cope. Turning inward makes a lot of sense when turning outward can be so complicated. Take the example of pastors complaining (also a form of emotional coping!) to one parishioner about another parishioner. Doing this can lead to gossip, concerns about confidentiality and trust, and divisions in a church when congregants feel forced to take sides. Turning inward is a safe way to avoid these kinds of scenarios.

17. Weiten, Dunn, and Hammer, *Psychology Applied to Modern Life.*
18. McMinn et al., "Care for Pastors."
19. In our survey data, pastors report drawing support from a wide variety of people, not just spouses, within the past six months. We discuss this later in the chapter. We don't know how often clergy do so, though, so the cautionary word about pastors turning inward too much still stands.

Figure 4.3
Social Isolation

"How socially isolated do you feel?"

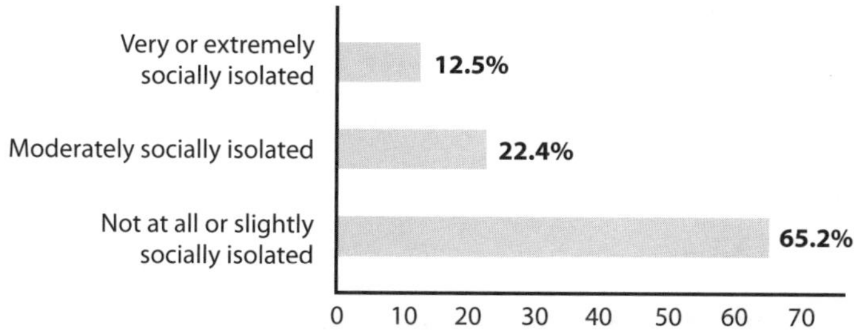

Responses are from 2016 surveys of full-time and part-time church-appointed pastors.

But while turning inward to cope with their own emotions, pastors must simultaneously provide emotional support for parishioners throughout the week, including offering pastoral counseling and spiritual guidance. Consequently, pastors may find themselves in the situation of "water, water everywhere, but not a drop to drink." They may be surrounded by people all day but not have anyone to turn to for their own emotional support. A large body of literature indicates that feeling socially isolated—even when surrounded by people—is powerfully harmful.[20] Our survey includes the question, "How socially isolated do you feel?" Approximately 12.5 percent responded "extremely" or "very" socially isolated. In other studies of clergy, social isolation is present for 10 to 17 percent of pastors.[21] Fortunately, most clergy do not feel socially isolated. However, in our studies those who do indicate feeling that way are far more likely to qualify for depression, with its symptoms of decreased interest in life, low energy, and feelings of worthlessness. (Socially isolated clergy are *not* more likely to qualify for anxiety, though, with its symptoms of worrying and feeling tense or restless.)

So how are pastors doing in their social and emotional support overall? We have a question on our survey that comes from the Centers for Disease Control and Prevention and was also asked of North Carolinians in 2010.[22] The question is, "How often do you get the social and emotional support you need?" Of our survey repondents (UMC clergy in North Carolina), 70.9 percent said "always" or "usually," compared to 80.9 percent of North

20. Hawkley and Cacioppo, "Loneliness Matters."
21. Two sources report studies suggesting that 17 percent of clergy are socially isolated: Carroll, *God's Potters* and Weaver et al., "Mental Health Issues."
22. "Behavioral Risk Factor Surveillance System," Centers for Disease Control and Prevention.

Figure 4.4
Social and Emotional Support

"How often do you get the social and
emotional support you need?"

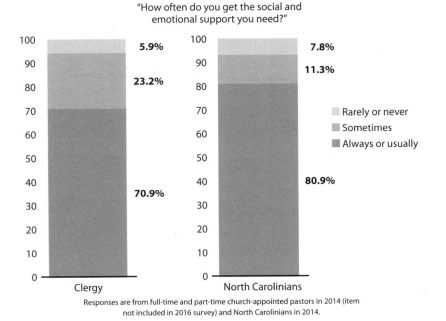

Responses are from full-time and part-time church-appointed pastors in 2014 (item
not included in 2016 survey) and North Carolinians in 2014.

Carolinians. Thus, North Carolinians fare better than clergy in terms of always or usually getting emotional support. However, they fare worse in terms of "rarely" or "never" getting emotional support: we found that 7.8 percent of North Carolinians reported this extreme lack of support, compared to only 5.9 percent of clergy.

Social support matters so much because clergy who use both problem-focused and emotion-focused coping strategies can benefit from drawing on other people for support. For example, when engaged in problem-focused coping, other people may be able to help you come up with ideas for solving the problem, or help you instrumentally by leading that Bible study or taking your sick child home from school, or even help you tangibly by loaning you money. When engaged in emotion-focused coping, telling your problems to others can help relieve the sense of burden and make you feel less alone, even if no new ideas or insights come from it. One interesting question is whether pastors in some situations might build friendships with parishioners and see them as a valuable source of personal support. This is not always recommended by clergy supervisors. They worry that leaning emotionally on parishioners will compromise healthy boundaries and potentially lead to pastors misusing their authority. Clergy supervisors worry that after a pastor has moved on, parishioners will maintain an enduring relationship. This raises the possibility that parishioners, if they don't like some of the new pastor's ideas or approaches, might communicate regularly with the pastor who has left, thus bolstering resistance and undermining the new pastor's authority and impact. No one wants that kind of situation, which is perhaps why clergy supervisors, as we heard from pastors, discourage long-term friendships with parishioners.

> **"I had a very wise person** recently tell me that wherever you are, you need three or four people that are going to see you through the fire. And in this particular setting I had three or four people who I met with on a weekly basis that would see me through the fire, whatever the fire was. And they were members of the church."

However, Jason tells me that, from a theological standpoint, pastors forging friendships with parishioners is worth considering. Jesus calls his disciples "friends." If there were ever a power imbalance, it is that between almighty God and sinners like the disciples (and us). Yet God risks that friendship with the people he's created and called. Looking specifically at Jesus's relationship with the disciples, we see that Jesus experienced deep anger and unsurpassable joy, moments of patience and moments of impatience with his disciples. Ultimately, he died for them and gave his life for them—and us. Jesus's relationships with his disciples are valuable examples for clergy and the parishioners they're called to lead.

If many pastors will not lean on the parishioners they are surrounded by every day for support, then where should they turn for emotional support? Here is what we know about other common sources of emotional support.

Spouses. An extremely high percentage (89.7 percent) of clergy are currently married, so talking to a spouse is a natural outlet. Across denominations more clergy men are married, though, which means that a lower percentage of clergy women have a spouse they can draw on for support (see fig. 4.5).[23]

Fellow clergy at the same church. Pastors of larger churches may have clergy staff, such as associate pastors, with whom they can talk. In our study, 33.2 percent of clergy reported working with an associate or head pastor. Associate pastors reported that their relationship with their head pastor is quite supportive (only 7.9 percent of associate pastors said their relationship with their head pastor is "slightly" or "not at all" supportive). When asked if they found their relationship with their head pastor to be

23. Associated Press, "Study Shows Average Divorce Rate among Clergy."

Figure 4.5
Marriage, by Gender

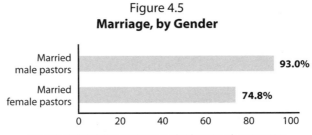

Married male pastors: 93.0%
Married female pastors: 74.8%

Responses are from full-time and part-time church-appointed pastors in 2016.

Figure 4.6
Satisfaction with Family Life

"At present, what is your level of satisfaction with family life? time spent with family?"

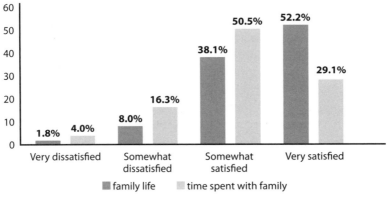

	family life	time spent with family
Very dissatisfied	1.8%	4.0%
Somewhat dissatisfied	8.0%	16.3%
Somewhat satisfied	38.1%	50.5%
Very satisfied	52.2%	29.1%

■ family life   ▨ time spent with family

Responses are from full-time church-appointed pastors in 2016.

Figure 4.7
Pastoral Roles

"In your current appointment, are you a . . ."

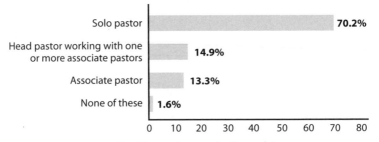

Solo pastor: 70.2%
Head pastor working with one or more associate pastors: 14.9%
Associate pastor: 13.3%
None of these: 1.6%

Responses are from full-time and part-time church-appointed pastors
in 2014 (2014 data preferred due to item language changes in 2016).

stressful, only 6.1 percent indicated that they found it to be very or extremely stressful.

We also reversed the situation and asked head pastors how supportive or stressful they found their relationships with associate pastors to be. The answers were even more positive, with only 3.7 percent of head pastors describing their relationships with associate pastors as slightly or not at all supportive and 2.6 percent reporting that they found these relationships to be very or extremely stressful. It makes sense that having frequent interaction with other clergy who understand both ministry work and the circumstances of your particular church can lead to good support—both emotional support and instrumental support in the form of concrete suggestions and help with tasks.

Clergy supervisors. Solo UMC pastors may not have a head pastor or an associate pastor to turn to, but they do work in a connectional ministry with other pastors and with supervisors, called district superintendents (DSs), who supervise 55–180 clergy in a geographic area. In other polities, clergy may interact with Presbytery heads or with deans in Episcopal dioceses. During focus groups, we heard mixed views from clergy on sharing their problems with their DSs. Some pastors were afraid of looking bad and then having their DS appoint them to a less desirable church in the future. Other pastors felt it was very important and useful to let their DS know what was going on with them and with their church or churches, with less concern for future consequences. Of the ten focus groups we held with church-serving pastors, pastors in only one focus group repeatedly mentioned DSs, and that was in a focus group of pastors serving large churches. These large-church pastors spontaneously discussed the benefits of talking with their DSs.

So from focus groups alone, we assumed that most pastors were not turning to their DSs for support. We were very much surprised, then, when our survey data painted a different picture. In our 2014 survey, we asked pastors very specifically whom they turn to for support. We asked them to identify people with whom they discuss important personal or professional matters and then asked for the roles of the first five people named, with an option to indicate for each person whether he or she was a DS. Of church-appointed clergy in 2014, 24 percent named a DS as one of the first five people they thought of with whom they had discussed important matters, and 3 percent of clergy named not just one but two or three DSs. We then asked how often the pastor talked to each person named, and 44 percent of pastors who indicated a DS said that they talked to the DS at least once a month. So now we know better that supportive relationships between pastors and DSs are active and ongoing.

We also asked clergy how close they are to this person and how guarded they are with this person. A very high 71 percent of pastors indicated that they were somewhat or moderately close to the DS they named, yet at the same time, 79 percent said they were somewhat or moderately guarded with the DS. In terms of the content of their conversations, 16 percent said they talked only about professional matters, 68 percent said they talked mostly about professional matters, and 15 percent said they talked equally about professional and personal matters (less than 1 percent talked mostly or only about personal matters with a DS). It seems about a quarter of pastors draw on DSs for professional support but are guarded with what they say even while feeling close to the DS. It also seems that a substantial minority (15 percent) of pastors discuss personal matters with a DS.

Friends. Back in elementary school, we all figured out that having a good friend can make your whole day go better. What does such friendship look like in a minister's day, and how does it hold stress at bay? Here's a personal example from Jason.

Behind the Pulpit
Friends Are the Antidote to the Fan(atic) Club

"The fan club," a friend called them. That collection of church people for whom you can do nothing right. It's a perfectly ironic description. Fan is short for "fanatic," which suggests just a hint of unreasonableness. There are little meetings where plots are hatched and strategies formed for how to undo you. If the fan club gets too large or loud, you're through. But it doesn't have to be large or loud to live in your head. And I was at a strange church—a large, vibrant, growing mainline church with resources in an era of decline in most mainline congregations. I can only imagine what the fan club is like without one or more of those traits in a parish.

I'd wake up in the middle of the night and the fan club would be on my mind. Then I'd be up; I couldn't sleep after that—best to go and get some work done. Or I'd preach my guts out one Sunday, and nearly everybody would take the time to say something more textured in response than "good job, preacher," except a fan club member, who would have a snotty comment about the bulletin (something over which I had minimal influence, but never mind). There was one fan club member I offended in some way that he took to be egregious. He took to sitting in the second row, right in my view, staring at me with an expression of sheer loathing. I rather enjoyed this actually. He looked comically small down there (is this why we originally made pulpits elevated?). Then he did something I appreciated even more. He quit showing up at all.

It is striking that I had so few fan club members in my time serving churches. I could count them on one hand honestly. One friend of the fan club told a friend of mine (it felt like junior high) that there were maybe one to two hundred people dissatisfied with my leadership. At a church with fifteen hundred people, that's not a bad number. And I think the source highly inflated it. In any case, there's a significant margin between having a few dissatisfied parishioners and facing an entire congregation on the warpath. My job was never in danger. The entire leadership apparatus of United Methodism is there to protect a pastor from an angry mob, as opposed to polities where a single vote in a congregational meeting can get rid of you. But I felt anxious *all the time*. Like the parishioners were one inch from being out to get me. Politicians only dream of the sort of approval ratings I had. No public figure has unanimous approval. So why the anxiety? And how did I cope?

Mostly by running. Not fast or well, but far. Really far. I wore out running shoes built by our best scientists and engineers. I ran a marathon and then a half marathon. I ran because, as Forrest Gump said, I felt like running. But I also ran because I could do it with other people. And I felt awesome for days afterward. And the fan club glances and comments bounced off me like arrows off steel.

Wade was my running partner for my first year in Boone. After church one day, he suggested we run. He's a real runner; he can go far and fast. But he slowed down for me. So I shuffled along, he ratcheted things down, and we "ran." And we laughed, and got to know one another, and talked politics and music and history. We had things in common—like a love for mission work, which Wade had fulfilled during a college internship at Mother Teresa's convent in India. He attended an excellent Christian college, and I've long been an admirer of places that love Jesus and promote the liberal arts well. He's also a riot. He'd have me in such hysterics that I'd have to stop running. A short example: For his birthday Wade invited all his friends to a rental place in Gatlinburg, Tennessee. And we, his friends from all parts of his life, all read aloud together the entire script for *The Princess Bride*. What a genius idea! How much ridiculousness can be had in one setting?

In short, Wade was my friend. He treated me like a human being—one he even liked being around.

We did talk about church sometimes: his kids went through preschool and children's ministry; he and his wife, Jenn, served on committees and had strong opinions and, more importantly, theological commitments. His story about a previous minister's kindness to them lured me in. This pastor went out of his way to

---

Preventing Stress Symptoms

Jason reviewed the stress appraisal model and developed these suggestions of actions you can take, proactively or in the moment, to prevent stress symptoms.

- *Try to engage in problem-solving coping, not just emotion-focused coping.* Two approaches are better than one. Problem solving can get rid of the problem altogether but may require you to involve others. There's a benefit to involving others, though—they may end up feeling closer to you and getting more involved in the church. These potential benefits will help to reduce the stress you are experiencing.
- *Cultivate at least two relationships in which you can bare your soul.* Sufficient emotional support can be hard to come by for pastors because we're always giving emotional support to others. For many pastors, one of these relationships will be with a spouse, but it would be good to have someone else to go to if letting off steam about the church upsets your spouse.
- *Avoid social isolation at all costs—it is highly detrimental.* It will take work and creativity to keep relationships strong when you move often and cannot always build enduring friendships with parishioners. It is essential to start cultivating friendships early, perhaps while you are in seminary or with people who knew you "before," and then continue to nurture those friendships. Consider having an annual getaway with one or two key friends.

---

draw the church's circle of care around the family when their twins were born and almost didn't make it. The pastor checked into a hotel room to be near them at a hospital hours away. He looked in on Wade's family daily. And when they were home again, he brought a case of beer to their house. What pastor does that? I gave thanks for a job well done by my predecessor. And I hoped that those who came after me would remember pastoral successes and overlook my failures. The words of Pope John XXIII seem appropriate once again, "Overlook much. Correct a little."[24]

Wade teased me, praised me when I needed it, disagreed with me, encouraged me. I did the same for him. I cried hard when I heard that he and his family were moving away. It was the hardest day I had in ministry there. I was tempted to think in apocalyptic terms—the devil had found my softest spot and punched me there. Hard. Wade was my most solid support. We're still friends, and I've since moved too, but of course it's different with distance.

I also stopped running regularly. There's something about someone getting up and being at your house at six in the morning that makes you get up too. If your buddy will be outside in the cold and the dark whether you're there or

24. Pope John XXIII, *Overlook Much.*

not, you drag your sorry self out there. It's the same reason we pray and raise kids and do much of anything that matters *in groups*. I can make an excuse not to drag myself out of bed, but if Wade is out there waiting for me, I'll go. Plus my whole day will be better for seeing him.

Stress Symptoms

If you have coped extremely well, you may not experience stress symptoms at all. Wouldn't that be golden? However, sometimes circumstances are just too difficult. For example, you cannot realistically hope to avoid all stress symptoms if you have just been diagnosed with cancer, not even if you believe that you might grow from that difficult circumstance and you are very skilled at problem-focused and emotion-focused coping. Regardless, you are going to experience some stress symptoms.

What are stress symptoms? You'll remember that researchers used to measure stress using a list of potentially stressful life events but that this didn't work because not everyone appraises the same event to be stressful. Some researchers now try to measure stress using stress symptoms, and this appears to be a reasonable approach, so long as a wide enough array of symptoms is measured.[25] We humans are different enough that we don't all exhibit the same kinds of symptoms, although they do cluster into certain areas:

1. Mood symptoms consistent with depression or anxiety
2. Anger and irritability
3. Muscle tension in various places including shoulders, jaw, and back
4. Cardiopulmonary arousal symptoms like a racing heart, irregular heartbeat, and rapid or difficult breathing
5. Sympathetic arousal symptoms like having trouble sleeping and sweating under pressure
6. Neurological symptoms like feeling dizzy and weak
7. Gastroenterological symptoms like nausea, stomach pain, and diarrhea
8. Cognitive disorientation symptoms like difficulty concentrating and making mistakes more often or thinking the same thought over and over
9. Upper respiratory symptoms like colds and having to clear your throat more often[26]

25. See, e.g., Carlson and Thomas, "Calgary Symptoms of Stress Inventory."
26. Carlson and Thomas, "Calgary Symptoms of Stress Inventory."

You already know these three important ways to reduce stress symptoms. Their power simply can't be overstated: (1) exercise, (2) eat healthy foods, and (3) sleep.

Exercise releases endorphins that improve your mood.* The repetitive motion of exercise can relax you. The physical release of energy can help you sleep better. Exercise is more powerful than any pill.

Eating healthy foods can help lessen the physical stress symptoms noted above.† For example, one stress reaction includes a buildup of carbon dioxide and lactates in the body, and healthy foods can help with this. If you drink soda, you'll only add carbon dioxide to the already too-high levels of it in your body. Vitamins and minerals can help heal many of the physiological stress symptoms. If you're eating junk food, you're substituting nutritionally deficient calories for otherwise healing food.

Sleep helps you think more clearly and so assists with your appraisals. Getting adequate sleep will provide you with the energy you need to exercise, and it will help you make more thoughtful decisions, especially regarding healthful food choices.

*"Stress Management," Mayo Clinic.
†"How Food Can Help Your Stress Levels," Stress Management Society.

There are lots of ways stress symptoms are experienced! But hopefully now you will understand that these symptoms aren't themselves "stress"; rather, they are symptoms. These symptoms are initiated by a circumstance that you may be able to prevent proactively. If not, you do have some control over your appraisal, or how you think about that circumstance. Even if you think the circumstance is difficult and potentially harmful, it's possible that you'll be able to see it as a challenge demand, which may be hard but will result in rewards, rather than a hindrance demand that will just get in your way. And regardless of how you think about a circumstance, you still have some control over how you cope with it. As clergy, experiencing some set of stressful circumstances is inevitable, but you have available to you the appraisal and coping steps that you can control and change.

A Final Note on De-stressing

It is not enough to remove stress-inducing circumstances. You don't immediately relax just because an exam or sermon is over. You have to do something to bring about positive emotions that will help you relax; otherwise you will stay tense and those stress symptoms will continue. You have to learn how to celebrate, how to let go. Consider putting in place a regular ritual that induces this relaxation response. You could keep Sabbath regularly (if you can't commit to a full day, try a few hours). You could have a family movie night every week. You could even do something simple like having a cup of tea on the back porch. Whatever it is, do something to kick-start the relaxation process, because it's not automatic.

Have you ever seen a dog shake? It is actually a remarkable gesture that starts with the dog's head, moves down the body, and ends with the tip of the tail. Shaking helps dogs remove water when they're wet, but if you've ever owned a dog, you'll know that they shake at lots of other times too. I read once that dogs shake to relieve stress ("shake it off"). I tried to find research on this and learned only that rats also do a "wet-dog shake" that sometimes is related to stressors.[27] Although I couldn't confirm the same findings in dogs, I like to think of this shaking as dogs' way of kick-starting the relaxation process.

Jason tells me that in *The Penultimate Curiosity*, a book on science and religion, the author discusses the waterfall dance that chimpanzees do.[28] Apparently, when chimpanzees see a waterfall, as a group they do a dance. Really! I suggest you need a way to kick-start the relaxation process for yourself after facing stressors. I also recommend allowing yourself to be moved in the presence of God and take the opportunity to engage in a chimpanzee dance at every waterfall.

27. Amano et al., "Effects of Physical and Psychological Stress."
28. Wagner and Briggs, *Penultimate Curiosity*, 39–42.

5

The Pastor's Paradox

Clergy Health and Disease

In chapter 3 we described our findings on depression rates in clergy. These rates are high compared to rates for Americans in general. Although we don't know whether the clergy profession is causing depression in pastors or whether something else could be going on, clearly it's important for pastors and those who care about them to be proactive in caring for pastors' mental health, which is inextricably intertwined with physical health. We ended chapter 4 recommending exercise, healthy eating, and sleep as ways to manage stress.

But now let's focus on pastors' physical health. Are pastors likely to have better or worse physical health than the average American? Think about this for a minute. Why did you give the answer you did?

Ten years ago, when I first started studying the health of clergy, I expected pastors to have *better* physical health than the average American. I made this judgment based on what gets in the way of the health of Americans. Poor health is driven primarily by poverty: not being able to afford doctor visits or medications, not having enough education about nutrition or health issues, not living in a safe enough environment to exercise, living too far away from grocery stores that sell fruits and vegetables, and not having transportation to get to those grocery stores.[1] When you read this list, do you think of clergy?

1. "Healthy People 2020," Secretary's Advisory Committee on Health Promotion and Disease Prevention Objectives for 2020.

I do not. While not rich, most clergy have a stable moderate income, health insurance, and transportation. Clergy are actually *more* educated than most Americans, with 45 percent of senior (or lead) US Christian pastors holding a master's or doctoral degree, and so they are as capable of wading through the plethora of health information on the internet and the labyrinths of health insurance as any of us.[2] Clergy who are currently employed generally have health insurance. Most clergy don't live in neighborhoods too unsafe to exercise in, or if they do, they probably have a car and can drive somewhere else to exercise. These things all relate to better health.

Furthermore, lots of studies describe how people who attend church have better physical health than those who don't (more on this later), which also points to the conclusion that clergy might be healthier than the average American.[3]

Clergy Health Historically

Clergy were once thought to be among the healthiest people in the world because some studies showed they lived extraordinarily long lives. This became common knowledge; I even recall hearing about a journalist who in the 1980s quipped that clergy are the last to get to heaven. In these studies, some excellent demographic researchers had rounded up mortality and occupation data encompassing four hundred years—but ending around 1960—from nine European countries and the United States.[4] They compared clergy to nonclergy: for example, Benedictine monks living in Paris between 1607 and 1746 to people living in the vicinity of Paris during those same years. They compared German clergy to Germans of other occupations from 1801 to 1833. They compared Baptist ministers in North Carolina to a group of North Carolinians with other occupations between 1944 and 1957. They made other comparisons between European populations and Protestant ministers, Catholic priests, Church of England clergy, and Roman Catholic missionaries. Rarely do you see a data set of such breadth and depth.

The researchers concluded that clergy lived longer than people of similar ages in the same geographic areas. They also found that clergy lived longer than other white-collar professionals—at least until 1910 when physicians

2. Chaves, Anderson, and Eagle, "National Congregations Study."
3. Ellison and Levin, "Religion-Health Connection"; Koenig and Cohen, *Link between Religion and Health.*
4. King and Bailar III, "Health of the Clergy"; King and Locke, "American White Protestant Clergy."

and lawyers began living nearly as long as clergy, and teachers began living longer than clergy. Compared to most people, clergy were less likely to die from tuberculosis, flu, sexually transmitted diseases, and many cancers. Clergy were especially less likely to die from lung cancer, which may have been baffling at the time because the link between smoking and cancer hadn't yet been made.

Studies such as these painted a picture of clergy being healthier than other people, but they couldn't explain why. And then, as humans do, we filled in for ourselves why clergy should be healthier. Many of us probably assumed that people who are healthy in spirit would also have lower blood pressure or that people with healthy spiritual practices would also have healthy eating and exercise habits.

It is quite a shock, then, to see today's physical health statistics on clergy.

Behind the Pulpit
Not Just One Buffet

If there's a theological adage that runs through this book, it's one from Irenaeus: "The glory of God is a human being fully alive."[5] We love it because it suggests that God's greatest delight is to see us, God's creatures, full of delight. This idea has its origin in John 10:10: Jesus has come that we might have life abundant. Add to this 1 Timothy 6:19, which wishes for hearers "the life that really is life." While Christian faith has often been mistakenly presented as world-denying, body-denying, grumpy, and misanthropic, the fact is, it's just not. A faith with a God-made-flesh at its center should be the most world- and body-affirming faith there is. There is brokenness, to be sure, but there is also "a crack in everything / That's how the light gets in," as the great Leonard Cohen put it in his song "Anthem."[6]

To look at me and my fellow ministers, maybe you'd say we're a little too life-affirming. We all look like we've put ourselves on a strict diet of carbs and no exercise. Though we know that our likelihood for longer life goes down as our waistlines expand, many of us just can't or won't do anything about it.

For some of us, partial blame falls on the region we live in. Especially in the South, where I'm from, church life doesn't work without food. Lots of food. Not healthy food. But we make up for that with abundance. Fried chicken, barbeque, breakfast meats, biscuits (big fluffy delicious buttery biscuits you could eat with

5. *Against Heresies* 4.20.7, in *Irenaeus of Lyons*, 153.
6. "Anthem," track 5 on Leonard Cohen, *The Future*, Columbia, 1992.

no teeth), and dessert. Tables full of dessert. Pecan pie made with Karo syrup and gobs of brown sugar. Chocolate pie, like a gooey candy bar melted into the flaky perfection of a pie crust. We even douse perfectly good fruits with sugar and encase them in carbs—and then we bake 'em and eat 'em and go back for seconds. Even now, when I'm well aware that clergy are unhealthy, if I go to a clergy event with only healthy snacks set out for us to eat (a promising development, I realize), something in my stomach turns over. Really? They want us to eat nuts and fruit? Where's the *actual* yummy food?

Good pastoral instincts can exacerbate this set of problems. There are really two buffets at church functions in small southern churches. One is main and side dishes. The dessert buffet is a whole 'nother meal, sometimes loaded with as much stuff as the first one. Some of them are amazing and you know it. You'll try those without reflecting. Then you consider seconds. And you notice desserts neglected by others. Someone baked those, poured their heart into them, consulted Grandma's recipes, risked life and limb carrying them all the way here, and there they sit uneaten. Well, how could you not take some? And when it's all over someone will look around, spy you, and say, "Pastor! You need to take some of this home!" It's a way of loving you. And you can't say no without hurting someone—or so you tell yourself. That's dessert, round three, for those keeping track at home.

Church gatherings are an excuse to eat badly, and we clergy attend these multiple times a day, every week of the year, slowly wearing ourselves down until we're less human, less who God calls us to be. And church work is hard enough when we're at our physical best. When I lived in Spain I followed bullfighting, a sort of national religion, and was stunned to learn that before any sane bullfighter enters a ring, the bull has already been substantially weakened by various kinds of gory instruments. The point isn't to anger the bull (though it works). It's to weaken him. By the time the bullfighter is waving a cape in front of the bull, the animal is already dying.

How many of us are in the ring weakened? Bleeding to death? Angry enough to see red and to charge but not to hit anything?

Given our dietary track record, it's surprising clergy live as long as we do. Maybe the benefits of our work outweigh the impressive demerits: we are surrounded by other people; we are doing meaningful work; and we have health insurance. We *expect* to like our jobs. Lots of people are stuck in jobs they don't enjoy just so they can pay the bills. We like to think we're helping God make the universe better.

Churches in the southern United States are the spiritual and economic engine for much of the church throughout the rest of the country. Even churches that aren't like those in the South have to react to those that are, just to stake out how they're different.[7]

One key emphasis in Christian faith in North America is evangelicalism—it may be *the* key emphasis in Protestantism, and in the South where I'm from, it is simply king. The primary *form* of that faith has been revivalist: all have sinned and fallen short of the glory of God (Rom. 3:23), but God has provided remedy in the form of Jesus. If you believe in Jesus, you'll have full life with him now and unendingly. This, oversimplified, is the gospel that most shapes us, whether we personally preach or believe it or not (lots of Christians spend their lives adamantly rejecting this version of the gospel, with recourse to liturgy or social justice). It assumes that after conversion, folks will live holy lives. And holiness often gets narrowed down to a few behaviors. A representative slogan describing this says, "We don't drink, or chew, or go with girls who do." There are other things we don't usually do, like smoke, even in states whose economies were built on tobacco. We don't swear. We don't gamble. We don't watch R-rated movies. As the list grows, notice something: the number of activities left for folks to blow off steam is becoming short indeed. Now when I say "we don't," I don't mean we *actually* don't. In general, my clergy friends drink and watch the same movies as anyone else. But our church people expect that we ought not, and therefore we end up shielding these activities from public view even when we do them. The point is, you can feel like you're living a veiled life.

So what's the only entirely acceptable indulgent activity left to us ministers, especially in the South, but also far beyond? Overeating. So we do that. Thank you very much.

Clergy Health Today

In 2008 we collected data that allowed us to compare the health of United Methodist clergy to that of a similar group of North Carolinians who weren't clergy (see fig. 5.1).[8] Most strikingly, we found that the obesity rate for clergy was 39.7 percent, compared to 29.4 percent of similar North Carolinians.[9]

7. This is true beyond the United States as well. Phyllis Airhart's remarkable history of the United Church of Canada, *A Church with the Soul of a Nation*, can be read as a history of the United Church's engagement with Southern pastor Billy Graham: from enthusiastic to tepid to hostile.

8. In 2008, our survey was taken by 1,726 clergy; over 15,000 North Carolinians answered the same survey questions on the Behavioral Risk Factor and Surveillance System survey that year, allowing us to compare them.

9. First, to clarify: Obesity means having too much body fat. Like many researchers, we calculated body mass index (BMI), which is a combination of one's height and weight.

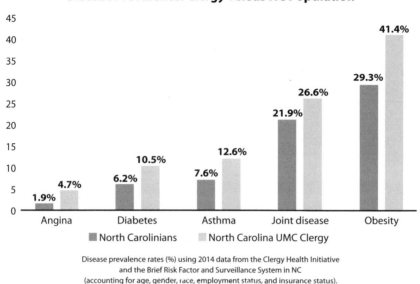

Figure 5.1
Disease Prevalence: Clergy versus NC Population

Disease prevalence rates (%) using 2014 data from the Clergy Health Initiative
and the Brief Risk Factor and Surveillance System in NC
(accounting for age, gender, race, employment status, and insurance status).

That's a difference of more than 10 percentage points! More recently, using 2014 data for both clergy and North Carolinians, we found that this obesity disparity still exists: 41.4 percent of clergy were obese versus 29.3 percent of comparable North Carolinians. When we combined the percentage of both obese and overweight clergy, this left only 25 percent who were of normal weight.

The high rate of obesity among clergy is taking a toll on—and truly fracturing—their physical health. Obesity is a significant problem not just in and of itself. We should also note that it both causes and complicates a variety of chronic diseases, including diabetes, arthritis, asthma, joint disease,

We then used a cut-off number (30) to indicate being obese rather than normal weight or overweight. While not perfect, this measurement is generally a good estimate of having too much body fat.

With regard to the 2008 comparison data: To be able to make a direct comparison between clergy and North Carolinians, we standardized to the age and gender distribution of the North Carolina population that were white, employed in the past year, possessing health insurance, and age thirty-five to sixty-four (preretirement). Because age and race are tied to health, we conducted separate analyses for various age groups and races. Only about one hundred clergy (6 percent) in the UMC annual conferences in North Carolina are black, and that sample size is too small to be certain of disease prevalence rates. Therefore, we report numbers in this chapter just for white clergy, but in our analyses comparing black clergy to black North Carolinians, all the trends for black clergy were the same as for white clergy.

angina (chest pain), heart disease, and hypertension.[10] And North Carolina UMC clergy experience high rates of multiple chronic diseases such as these.[11]

Across the board, clergy experience worse chronic disease than North Carolinians from similar demographic groups. The difference in rates is especially pronounced for people between the ages of 55 and 64.[12] Female clergy in this age bracket have particularly high rates of diabetes (10.9 percent vs. 5.2 percent), joint disease (47.6 percent vs. 39.0 percent), and obesity (43.5 percent vs. 24.6 percent). Male clergy these ages have much higher rates of angina (9.5 percent vs. 4.8 percent) and obesity (43.7 percent vs. 29.5 percent). By age 55, many pastors have been serving in ministry for decades. However, we can't say for sure that there's something about being a pastor that, over time, causes pastors to become obese. For example, it could be that new people entering the ministry are healthier today than their counterparts were years ago.

Comparing rural-serving clergy to all other clergy, we found that pastors serving in rural areas had higher body mass indexes (a mean of 30.1 compared to 29.3) and higher rates of joint disease (42.0 percent compared to 30.9 percent), even after accounting for many other possible explanatory variables.[13] It seems, then, that high rates for clergy in general can go higher still for rural pastors.

So United Methodist clergy in North Carolina have serious health problems. What about clergy of other denominations and in other areas of the country? There are few studies of clergy physical health, but they all point in the same direction. The Center for Health within the UMC's General Board of Pensions and Health Benefits administered a survey to a large random sample of United Methodist clergy across the country in 2012 and then repeated this survey with new United Methodist clergy samples in 2013 and 2015.[14] Each year they found above-average rates of obesity, asthma, and high cholesterol for clergy, compared to general US rates. They reported rates of obesity between 40 and 43 percent. A survey of the Kansas East and Kansas West Conferences of the United Methodist Church revealed a 40.4 percent obesity rate, compared to 29.6 percent of Kansas residents.[15] These figures are remarkably similar to the rates we found in North Carolina. So, unfortunately for United Methodist pastors, clergy obesity is not isolated to North Carolina.

10. "Clinical Guidelines," National Institutes of Health; Reynolds and McIlvane, "Impact of Obesity and Arthritis."
11. Proeschold-Bell and LeGrand, "High Rates of Chronic Disease."
12. Proeschold-Bell and LeGrand, "High Rates of Chronic Disease."
13. Miles, Proeschold-Bell, and Puffer, "Explaining Rural/Non-Rural Disparities."
14. "Clergy Health Survey," General Board of Pensions and Health Benefits, Center for Health.
15. Lindholm et al., "Clergy Wellness."

Other denominations have seen similar trends. A 2002 survey of Evangelical Lutheran Church in America clergy across the United States found above-average rates of obesity for clergy.[16] Higher obesity rates have also been found for African American clergy in the African Methodist Episcopal (AME) Church[17] and a combined sample of Methodist, Lutheran, Baptist, Church of Christ, and Catholic clergy in the United States.[18] One mortality study found that white and black male clergy ages sixteen to sixty, during the years 1982–92, were more likely than other male Americans in white-collar professions to die of ischemic heart disease (i.e., reduced blood supply to the heart, usually felt as angina).[19]

Unfortunately, this kind of data is limited. It would be helpful to have more health studies of clergy. While the analyses are not quite as systematic, we do know that the staff of multiple denominations review health claims and expenditures for clergy. In conversations with numerous officials in the Episcopal Church (USA), the Unitarian Universalist Association, the Presbyterian Church (USA), and the Evangelical Lutheran Church in America, all indicated that the health claims of their clergy are high and that they believe the diagnosis rates among clergy are high too. The expense of health insurance for clergy is one reason why the UMC annual conferences in North Carolina and our funder, The Duke Endowment, have been so supportive of our clergy health studies.

I do not know of any studies investigating the physical health of Jewish rabbis or Muslim imams, but I would love to see these done.[20] Likewise, I have not seen any physical health studies specifically conducted with Seventh-Day Adventist Church pastors; I suspect, however, that they may be an exception to the bad news about clergy health. The Seventh-Day Adventist practices of eating plant-based diets, not drinking alcohol, and regularly keeping Sabbath may benefit them. It would be great to have examples of pastors from any denomination who are in good health so that we could learn from them.

In one bright spot, we found that only 3.2 percent of clergy currently smoke, compared to 15.4 percent of similar North Carolinians.[21] This is important

16. Halaas, "Ministerial Health and Wellness."
17. Baruth, Wilcox, and Evans, "Health and Health Behaviors."
18. Webb, Bopp, and Fallon, "Factors Associated with Obesity."
19. Calvert, Merling, and Burnett, "Ischemic Heart Disease."
20. Farrah Abbasi organizes Muslim mental health conferences. She told me that using convenience samples of conference attendants, she has found that imams face mental health difficulties. There are articles on rabbis helping congregants with their mental health and a nod toward rabbis sometimes needing their own mental health care and being reluctant to go. See, e.g., Flannelly et al., "Rabbis and Health."
21. Proeschold-Bell and LeGrand, "High Rates of Chronic Disease."

because smoking exacerbates health problems such as angina and diabetes. However, data from multiple sources, denominations, and geographic areas all point to a serious physical health problem for clergy: obesity.

The causes of obesity are more complicated than just eating and exercise. Looking at the reasons why someone eats too many calories, we often find that stress is involved. If you've ever been stressed and reached for carbs and dessert, there's a biological reason. Under stress, your body secretes more glucocorticoid hormone, which leads you to want to eat more carbs and energy-dense food.[22] Eating these so-called comfort foods actually *does* work—temporarily, at least—by stimulating the pleasure centers in your brain and making you feel better. (You *knew* this worked, right?) So when searching for ways to address the obesity problems faced by clergy, we have to also consider what we learned about the stressors clergy experience in the previous chapters.

Some pastors and denomination officials I've talked with think it may be possible to categorize multiple stressors under one big stressor: lack of agency.

Behind the Pulpit
Agency

"Or do you not know that your body is a temple of the Holy Spirit within you, which you have from God, and that you are not your own? For you were bought with a price; therefore glorify God in your body" (1 Cor. 6:19–20). You went to seminary. You know you have to read a passage in its context. And in context Paul is teaching the Corinthians not to have sex with prostitutes. You do not likely have this particular problem—if Rae Jean's interpretation of the data is to be trusted, one reason we pastors historically live longer is that we have fewer venereal diseases. So you skip right over this passage. Until it's time to teach the youth group participants not to have sex—then you pull this one out.

But what about the temple of the Holy Spirit that is between the crown of your own head and the bottom of your own feet?

I heard a pastor confess to his congregation once that he ate compulsively. He especially liked to do it alone. It was his way of getting out of the glare of his people and doing something only slightly forbidden. He never wanted others—especially his spouse—to see. Another friend, a Catholic priest, told me of leaving the parish hall, buying a box of cookies, and eating the whole thing in the grocery store parking lot. That dark car was a space where he was in control and

22. Dallman, Pecoraro, and la Fleur, "Chronic Stress and Comfort Foods"; Laitinen, Ek, and Sovio, "Stress-Related Eating and Drinking."

no one could stop or even question him. I've never done this . . . except that I have. I used to refer to these as my "blowouts." They also involved entire packages of cookies.

But here's the thing: our bodies are temples of the Holy Spirit. Temples are places where the Shekinah, the very presence of the Lord, the fiery, cloudy, physical, smoky presence of God, fills the house and everyone bows in worship. God dwelled in the tabernacle (Exod. 25:8; 40:34) and then in the Jerusalem temple (2 Chron. 5:13–14). In the days of the temple, priests tended to God's house. They helped people sacrifice and pray. They performed sacrifices in accordance with Old Testament law. The temple had such a presence in Jewish life that it is still revered nearly two thousand years after its most recent destruction. Jews gather to pray daily at its one remaining wall. It's a holy place. You can feel it. One of the most powerful religious moments of the twentieth century was when a very unsteady Pope John Paul II wrote a prayer on a piece of paper and tucked it into the crevice between two of the temple's stones.

And Paul says your body is like that (1 Cor. 6:19). It is holy. Beautiful. The Holy Spirit lives there. We have to tend to our body as priests tended to the temple. Our bodies are temples. We should care for them as God deserves.

Pastors would never knowingly let the church be left dirty when folks are coming for worship. Imagine—trash strewn about, the place unswept, unvacuumed, smelling like a cheap hotel. We wouldn't allow it. So why do we allow ourselves to treat the temple of our own body that way? Filling it with trash. Letting it sit idle, without the exercise it needs. Neglecting it. Actively killing it. Israel's priests treated God's temple well. We as pastors treat the house that is our church well. Our own bodies? Bring on the cookies!

"Blowouts" or binges have something to do with ownership. We live in somebody else's house. Preach in a church somebody else built. Go where we go on someone else's authority. Not much is ours. Except our bodies. Or so we think when we hit the cookie aisle. The thing is, we're wrong. Paul says as much in these verses: "You are not your own. . . . You were bought with a price" (1 Cor. 6:19–20). Our creator says to treat ourselves not harshly, as we're prone to do, but gently, like he does.

I do think the whole-box-of-cookies phenomenon has something to do with agency. There are very few areas of our lives where we can do what we want, full stop. No permission is needed, no committee has to weigh in, no one can even gossip about us (to our knowledge). Just us and the cookie box and the dark.

We pastors often feel we have very little agency. Committees tell us what to do in every part of our lives. If we're Methodist or Catholic, we go where sent; if we're something else, we go to the best placement we can secure, which is often depressingly below our own view of our abilities. And there's not a lot we can do about it. If we think tweaking the worship style may help more people come and stay, we have to get it approved by multiple people. If we change the staff—whoa, don't do that, it'll get you fired. We are responsible to have this part of the body of Christ thrive, and yet we can hardly move around money or personnel or change the color scheme without begging. Bishops say we preachers whine that we have no power. They're right; we do whine.

But we're wrong to say we have no power.

One of the best books on agency I know is Michael Lindsey's *Faith in the Halls of Power*. The evangelical sociologist interviewed dozens of leading figures in sports, business, politics, entertainment, and other sectors to see how their faith interacted with their work and vice versa. One common theme he found is how little power these enormously powerful people felt they had. *Presidents* whined they couldn't do anything—Congress stymied them or unforeseen events handcuffed them. Business moguls complained they couldn't work with their boards. Athletes felt they had terrible coaches. Every one of us has some reason to pretend we can't do anything. And we're wrong. God has stamped God's own image onto each of us. There's something of the One who cast stars into space, and who chose our eye color, present in every single human being. We have agency. We just don't recognize it.

We *can* bring about change in the church—not all at once, not as fast as we'd like, and not without pain and struggle, but we can. It won't be the way we want and it won't happen overnight. In the meantime, we can build up what's sometimes called a "church within a church." The description—*ecclesiola in ecclesia*—comes from pietist branches of the Reformation. Luther and Calvin reformed the churches' beliefs; these folks wanted to reform ordinary Christians' behavior. These Christians weren't sure whether their fellows among the baptized were really Christian or not, so they set up demonstration plots: little groups trying to live out the Christian life in an obvious way to be a model for others. Methodists started life this way—as a disciplined little band of Anglicans trying to show the rest of the Church of England how it's done. Things don't always end well for such groups. They can be superior, pious, annoying. And they're right. Christian faith requires our every ounce of effort, body and soul. We can't make anybody else change (we can hardly make ourselves change). But we can provide a model for others, should they want something more rigorous and beautiful to emulate.

Some of my friends in the United Church of Canada have modeled this. They have quit trying to change their denomination. Instead they've tried to build something more compelling. They've taken parishes and worked at turning them into congregations that bless their neighborhoods, preach the Word powerfully, and administer the sacraments faithfully. They are a church within the church. Whether the rest of the church notices or cares is beyond their power or concern. They're a demonstration plot, showing that another way of life is possible.

We can build this in even the dreariest parish. Some folks will be drawn to our preaching and leadership. Some were already present but hardly engaged. New people will come. And those we inspire can become a demonstration plot for the others. They'll want to engage and know how they can do more. Take them up on it. Form them into a body of disciples doing it right. And even if this doesn't catch on in the rest of the parish, who cares? You'll have built authentic Christian community—and you'll be surprised who all will find this attractive, even powerful.

Robert Jenson describes God as whoever raised Israel from Egypt and Jesus from the dead.[23] This resurrection power is the power by which we do our ministry. We are not then without options, power, or agency. We just don't realize the power of the live volcano on which we sit.

And I can't prove this to you, but I bet as you start to notice the agency you *do* have, as you see God do new things in your church's midst, you'll celebrate with a salmon and kale salad and just a tiny bite of dessert. And you won't have to hide the empty box of cookies in the back of the car.

Clergy Health Then and Now

How is it that four hundred years of data indicating better physical health for clergy across multiple European countries and the United States could be overturned? When we made this discovery, it felt rather like whiplash.

If you take a very close look at the historical data, you will find that although clergy lived longer overall, some clergy died sooner from specific diseases that were either chronic (e.g., heart disease and diabetes) or possibly stress-related (examples using the language of the time include "malfunctioning of the digestive system" and "psychoneurotic disorders").[24] The historical health advantages for clergy include fewer infectious diseases like tuberculosis, fewer accidents, and fewer suicides.[25]

The demographers' data ends mostly before 1920, and society as a whole has gained certain health benefits since then. By the late 1940s, antibiotics were widely available and clergy were no less likely to die from infections

23. Jenson, *Systematic Theology*, 1:63.
24. King and Bailar III, "Health of the Clergy," 34.
25. This is my interpretation of King and Bailar III, "Health of the Clergy."

(including sexually transmitted diseases) than was the general population.[26] The advantage clergy had in having fewer accidents was probably also gone. It's likely that the clergy occupation one or two hundred years ago was safer than other occupations, which often involved manual labor, but as fewer people toil physically today, the source of accidents has changed to car accidents, and clergy do their fair share of driving. On the flip side, clergy were historically disadvantaged in terms of heart disease, and that is not a condition we've been able to solve yet. Heart disease was the number one cause of death in 1960 and still was in 2015.[27]

Perhaps clergy on the whole were never that good at managing their stress, and as we noted above, eating can be comforting. Since 1960, food industrialization has made calories cheap and plentiful. Among adults ages twenty and older, the prevalence of obesity in the United States doubled between 1980 and 2002.[28] Although obesity rates have stayed steady since 2003, they are still shockingly high.[29] Clergy are not immune to the things that drive weight gain and may in fact, as suggested by their obesity rates, have more reasons to eat. We are affected by the inventions of our time. Furthermore, behaviors are catching. If clergy are around potluck lines where everyone piles their plate high, that is catching. The good news, though, is that behaviors like taking the stairs rather than the elevator are also catching. We are social beings, and that fact certainly extends to the church as well.

Behind the Pulpit
You Become Like Those around You

The South wouldn't be the South without air conditioning. Mr. Carrier's invention means that Yankees can move south for lower property taxes and not sweat all day six months a year. The South's economy has also changed dramatically from agriculture, textiles, furniture, and the like (industries largely outsourced now) to high-tech, health care, education, and more white-collar jobs. I had older parishioners across North Carolina who all remembered growing up working in the fields. They could still clean a squirrel if they really had to. But their daddies came back from World War II and went to college. People moved en

26. "History of Antibiotics," Microbiology Society.
27. "Vital Statistics of the United States," National Center for Health Statistics; "Health 2015: With Special Feature on Racial and Ethnic Health Disparities," National Center for Health Statistics.
28. Hedley et al., "Prevalence of Overweight and Obesity."
29. Flegal et al., "Prevalence of Obesity."

masse from the Rust Belt to the Sunbelt and property values went up. They became middle class.

But one of the slowest things to change culturally is how we eat. So meals
still looked like what Granny would cook for a holiday. Fried chicken and col-
lard greens and barbequed ribs and Jell-O with marshmallows in it (really). Never
mind that that food didn't hit the table every day back then: it came for feasts.
Now we have the money to do it often. And food manufacturers have figured out
that adding sugar to their products makes us eat more and buy more of them. We
used to labor in fields and work off some of that food. Now we work in offices.
The only people conscious of their waistline are people who eat things like Swiss
chard and have that hungry, distance-runner look. People cook less now. Products
used to be peddled as "homemade," but now they're marketed as "restaurant-
style." Cracker Barrel serves up massive portions for a few dollars. The walls are
decorated with antiques, fake china teapots, and trinkets, and people line up for
the experience, remembering their granny's table, even if they never ate at one.

Now that I live in the lower mainland of British Columbia, where evangelical
revivalism was never so dominant, I'm struck that there is hardly a road without
a bike lane, sushi is cheaper than fast food, and people are maniacally healthy—
the healthiest of any province in Canada, at least physically speaking. Culture
sets strictures for what's acceptable and what's not. Ministers here in British
Columbia have just as sedentary a professional life as the ones in North Carolina, but they look skinnier. They live in one of the healthiest places in North
America. You become like those around you.

I noticed this phenomenon during the Spirited Life intervention for clergy
(more on Spirited Life in the appendix). We'd go to pastor gatherings, and after
the initial disappointment over being served tangerines and cashews (as described above), we'd discuss H$_2$Orange—that is, the water with a little bit of
orange juice added in. We'd talk about how much weight we'd lost. We'd notice
how others would eat only half a plate and bag up the other half right away. And
sometimes people showed up to a meeting looking like half of their old self. That
was inspiring (if not infuriating). Peer pressure is a subtle thing. We can look
around at others, conclude we're skinnier, and feel better about ourselves—and
eat another biscuit. Or we can notice others losing weight, gaining energy and
happiness, and realize, wait, I could do that too.

In the recent past, the form of the gospel in the South has changed from the
straight revivalist version I mentioned above. Christians have realized that our gospel was too focused on otherworldly matters and neglected sources of instruction
and models for virtuous living in this world. Our approach to teaching theology
has changed as we've tried to take stock of the incarnation. God came in flesh—
how did the church writ large end up neglecting flesh then? Some clergy are trying

hard to reevaluate this. As a pastor friend of mine summarized in response to a question about the afterlife, "Actually, I'm more interested in life *before* death." Our theology emphasizes life here in this good world in our bodies. Does this theology of our bodies match how we live our lives? It doesn't always look like it.

And yet . . . do you have to be healthy to be a good minister? Of course not. Western culture has grown more superficial regarding appearance. It's hard to imagine FDR or Winston Churchill getting elected in the television age, but try to imagine the United States and the United Kingdom without them.

Proper care for our bodies requires as much attention as care for our souls. Perhaps you've seen people who care entirely too much about exercise. They wear workout clothes all the time and just sort of stay sweaty all day. Or you're hanging out with them and their kids at the park and they suddenly start doing chin-ups or suggest playing tag and then actually run during the game. The thing is, we have to *become* those people. I noticed as a pastor that I buried very few ninety-year-olds who weren't skinny.

And this isn't all our responsibility alone. We changed the conversation around smoking in this country by working on several levels to make it socially frowned upon. Of course, smoking is not eradicated, but it's dramatically curtailed.[30] In the church, we can move as a public on a social problem. We can encourage one another to be healthier the way we have long implicitly encouraged one another not to be. At my church in Boone, we ran a marathon together to raise money for a local antipoverty program. Suddenly church people were calling one another, giving one another rides to the track, reminding each other to run their seven miles that day. It was a positive contagion. We weren't frowning at what others were doing. We were smiling and encouraging one another to do something fun together. Fun is the only motivation I've found that really works for getting healthier. If we love something, we'll find a way to do it. So too with exercise. We have to do what we love. The more we do it, the more we'll love it, and the more we'll change. Not we alone, but we in community with others. We pastors apply that concept to some parts of our lives. Now we just have to understand and apply it as we tend God's temple.

I believe Jesus offers the fullest form of life both now and unendingly. Other pastors and theologians believe that too. If we're indeed as physically unhealthy as the Duke Clergy Health Initiative has shown, then there's a hole in our gospel. It's one of many holes. We've been blind concerning race. We've been silent about economic injustice. We've neglected our own Scriptures and their demand to care for the poor and love God's creation. So add personal health to the

---

30. From 42 percent of US adults in 1965 to 17 percent in 2014. "Trends in Current Cigarette Smoking," Centers for Disease Control and Prevention.

list. And now you can see why we reach for another slice of pie. We can't reach for much else to find instant relief, and when the list of things we have to do is so endless, it's near on hopeless.

But this is interesting. Somehow we've not managed to ruin the church yet. God still seems to turn up, birthing resurrection in our midst, sometimes even despite us. Churchgoers have faced the temptation to go and start a "better" church, one in which the people don't engage in whatever compromising activity that was so upsetting as to make them want to leave. That approach rarely works because we take ourselves with us when starting something new. God only has sinners to work with, us included. If we tried to start a Church for Fit Ministers, with Richard Simmons as its patron saint, we'd all flab out. That's just how it works. And despite all that—look at how God has deigned to use even us. This is the God who chooses Israel, out of which emerged the Scriptures we still use, which chronicle failed episode after fumbled opportunity. Most people groups write their histories as chronicles of glorious successes. Not the Jews. Here's why: each failure is a chance to show how good and patient God is. So too God is with us. If God can work with us this well despite our physical state, what could God do if we were as healthy as God desires all people to be?

Thomas Aquinas taught that virtue is a matter of practicing certain excellences until they become a sort of second nature.[31] We *are* the habits we keep. We don't need to despair about our bad habits. Instead, we can determine to change them. We've built them up over a lifetime. The church, it's fair to say, has enabled these bad habits over generations. So they will take time to curtail and even more time to develop better ones. But it can be done. We can build new habits, which are the key to building new selves. We can't do it alone, and we can't do it overnight. But we can do it. Tending God's temple deserves no less.

The Mystery

In spite of what we know, a mystery remains. We can only speculate as to why clergy have historically had higher rates of some chronic physical health conditions. Earlier I suggested that these may be due to stress, but are clergy really more stressed than other American workers? Researchers have found that employees working in hostile work environments have higher obesity rates (31.0 percent) than those who don't (27.4 percent).[32]

31. This material comes in the first half of the second part of the *Summa*. For an excerpt with commentary, see Bauerschmidt, *Holy Teaching*, 109–32; Dobson, *Health as a Virtue*.
32. Luckhaupt et al., "Prevalence of Obesity."

There is no doubt that occupation can play a large role in one's health. Take obesity, for example. Counselors, social workers, and probation officers have very high rates of obesity (35.6 percent) as do home health aides and nursing assistants (34.8 percent) and transportation and material movers, such as taxi drivers and freight movers (32.8 percent). Police, private detectives, and security guards have obesity rates (40.7 percent) similar to the rate we found in our clergy study (39.7 percent).[33] We even found one population—long-haul truck drivers—with an obesity rate of 69 percent.[34] But salespeople (24.4 percent) and building and grounds cleaning and maintenance workers (23.5 percent) have lower obesity rates.[35] Clergy are not unique in that their occupation may affect their health. The key is to figure out specifically how it affects their health and where there is room for change.

Believing in God by itself is not enough to protect clergy. It's true that being religious is linked to better health.[36] One fascinating study even quantified this relationship. If you're twenty years old and attend church more than once a week throughout your life, you are likely to live seven years longer than if you never attend church. But why is this so? Is it because church attenders are stronger believers? If so, that would be particularly relevant for clergy, whom we assume are strong believers. This study's authors argue that three things are going on: (1) Healthier people tend to go to church; (2) churches often promote healthy behaviors like not smoking and not sleeping around; and (3) churches provide social support.[37] So the results were not about beliefs alone. In different research, Lynda Powell reviewed existing research to test nine possible pathways connecting church attendance and better health.[38] She did not find that believing in God or using religion to cope with difficulties resulted in better health. What did seem to lead to better health was church attenders engaging in healthy behaviors such as exercising, going to the doctor, not smoking, and having more social interaction.

So church attenders start off healthier than those who don't attend church. Can we extend that finding to clergy? While we know that clergy spend a lot

33. Luckhaupt et al., "Prevalence of Obesity"; Proeschold-Bell and LeGrand, "High Rates of Chronic Disease."

34. "National Survey of Long-Haul Truck Driver Health and Injury," US Department of Transportation.

35. Luckhaupt et al., "Prevalence of Obesity."

36. George, Ellison, and Larson, "Relationships between Religious Involvement and Health"; Koenig and Cohen, *Link between Religion and Health.*

37. Hummer et al., "Religious Involvement."

38. Powell, Shahabi, and Thoresen, "Religion and Spirituality." See also VanderWeele, "Religious Communities and Human Flourishing."

of time *in* church, we don't know whether that leads them, like other church attendees, to exercise or go to the doctor more.

What about social support? Although clergy do have a lot of social interaction, it's possible that the kind of social interaction they have isn't as healthy for them as it is for parishioners. Clergy give a lot of support to parishioners, but, as we wondered earlier in the book, do parishioners give support to their pastors? And even if some do, might they also dole out criticism to their pastors more often than is common between friends?

And then there's this: despite their heavy chronic-disease burden, clergy do not perceive that their physical health gets in the way of their work.[39] In a survey, we gave clergy a common measure of physical health functioning, which asks things like, "During the past four weeks, as a result of your physical health, have you . . . 'accomplished less than you would like' [or] 'been limited in the kind of work or other activities' you do?"[40] The great thing about this measure is that its developers have given it to thousands of people across the United States. A score of fifty means someone's physical health functioning is right at the US average. The pastors who took our survey scored two to four points higher than Americans of the same age and gender,[41] indicating that they perceive themselves to function very well—in fact, their perception is that they are functioning *better* than most Americans. This is puzzling because given their higher rates of angina, diabetes, asthma, and joint disease, clergy should find it difficult to attend all their meetings, do a great deal of outreach, and work long hours. And yet they tell us they are doing just fine.

We're not sure what is going on here. I wonder, though—could it be that pastors pay more attention to their spirit than their bodies and are just unaware of how much their physical health affects them? Could it be that their job is so sedentary that they are less often reminded of physical health limitations? Or could it be that clergy *are* aware of their physical limitations but just push through them, which allows them to accomplish their goals, only with more sacrifice because they are tired or in pain while working?

We designed and tested an intervention to improve pastors' holistic health, including physical health.[42] Over 1,100 clergy participated in Spirited Life, and

39. Proeschold-Bell and LeGrand, "Physical Health Functioning."

40. The measure is called the Medical Outcomes Study, Short Form. See Ware et al., *SF-12v2*.

41. Although 2- to 4-point differences may sound small, they are clinically meaningful. Hundreds of studies have been done using this measure with people with different health diagnoses. People with musculoskeletal complaints score 2 points lower, and people with asthma and irritable bowel syndrome both average 2.7 points lower (see Ware et al., *SF-12v2*).

42. Proeschold-Bell et al., "Two-Year Holistic Health and Stress Intervention."

we learned a lot from them. For anyone inclined to design or fund a health intervention for clergy, we've included in this book's appendix many of the program lessons we learned. If you're a pastor, here is what the Spirited Life participants, speaking straight from the heart, would tell you:

- Proactively set aside time for healthy behaviors. No one will do this for you.
- Be clear on your health goals and then be creative. You may need to use a different strategy every day. Can't go to the gym today? Go for a walk, do jumping jacks, set up a basketball hoop in your office.
- Develop a strategy for making choices in the potluck line, for food at meetings, and for food delivered to the parsonage. When you begin a new appointment, make your food preferences known—if you say you love salad, you just might get some and then you just might eat it, even if you really prefer pie.
- Develop a strategy for eating on the road to hospital visits and for days with unpredictable schedules. Could you stock healthy frozen meals in the freezer at your office? Store healthy snacks in your car? Keep a supply of a drink you like that isn't sugary?
- As much as you can, prevent weight gain in the first place. Every pastor needs to know they are at risk for obesity.
- Remember that eating carbs and sweets is something we do because it is adaptive in the very short term. We temporarily feel better because those sugars help us regulate stress-induced arousal in the brain. The problem is that this results in weight gain in the long term; you need other ways, as suggested in chapter 4, to regulate stress symptoms.
- Don't pursue good health alone. Take a companion or two with you on this health journey. They will make it more fun, and they might help you step into the full life God intends for all of us.
- Remember that, as Paul says, each of us is a temple of the Holy Spirit. Pray over your health—long before you're sick. Pray over your colleagues' health. God longs for full flourishing for each of us. Join in that divine longing through prayer.

As this chapter indicates, physical health and stress are connected. Indeed, physical health and mental health are inextricably linked. Strengthening one improves the other. In the next chapter, we suggest that positive mental health can, to some extent, prevent depression and play an important role in improving physical health.

6

Feeling Alive

The Role of Positive Emotions

Preventing Health Problems

I wonder if any of you who picked up this book will turn first to this chapter on positivity. I certainly don't mind if you do. I mean, who wants to start with all that bad news about high rates of obesity and depression in pastors? But if you *did* read through the bad news first, it should make you appreciate the good news even more. I could bury the good news in the middle of this chapter, but I've been practically bursting to share it with you, so I'm going to go ahead and share it first; I hope that you will read this chapter in full to understand how this works.

There is a way to prevent depression, and this same way also seems to prevent some physical health problems. It's not painful, and it doesn't have bad side effects. It's called positive mental health. People who have positive mood,[1] which is a short-term kind of happiness, plus deeper feelings of meaning and belonging, which is a longer-term kind of happiness, have good outcomes—actually, really good outcomes. They do better at work and miss less work.[2] They have fewer chronic diseases, medical visits, and prescription

---

1. Keyes, "Mental Illness and/or Mental Health?"
2. Keyes and Grzywacz, "Health as a Complete State"; Keyes, "Mental Health Continuum."

medications.[3] And in studies that follow up with them in the future, they are less likely to become depressed.[4]

This doesn't mean that positive mental health fixes everything. We still lose loved ones, have difficult work quandaries, and can be diagnosed with serious health problems. But positive mental health does make the hard things better and can prevent depression, and maybe even some physical health problems. Here is a possible solution to offer clergy (and all of us)! Here's how it works, and how we know it works.

Positive Emotions: What They Do and Undo

Why do positive emotions exist? What role do emotions like contentment and joy play in keeping us alive and well? Think about this for a moment, first in terms of negative emotions. We know why we feel fear—it's a signal to run away from, say, a lion so we aren't eaten and can live another day. We also know why we feel anger. Anger is a signal that someone has wronged us, for example, or taken something from us, and it might motivate us to take back our possession (or our right).

But why do we feel positive emotions? There are many of them: hope, gratitude, interest, awe, and love, just to name a few. Just as fear triggers the action of running from the lion, positive emotions also trigger actions.[5] Joy triggers the urge to play or become involved, awe triggers the urge to absorb and accommodate, and amusement triggers the urge to share and laugh.[6] Evolutionarily speaking, the benefits of negative emotions like fear are clear—negative emotions can literally keep you alive. But what about positive emotions? Do they help us survive?

Exciting research has been done on this by Barbara Fredrickson. I get enthusiastic about her work because she does what I can't. She brings people into her lab and manipulates their experiences, whereas I do research in the very messy, uncontrolled world. Specifically, Fredrickson conducted a series of experiments that built on each other and led her to create a theory. When

3. Keyes, "Chronic Physical Conditions"; Keyes, "Nexus of Cardiovascular Disease and Depression"; Keyes and Grzywacz, "Health as a Complete State."

4. Keyes, Dhingra, and Simoes, "Change in Level of Positive Mental Health"; Keyes, "Mental Health Continuum."

5. Negative emotions trigger specific actions, whereas positive emotions trigger urges to act but are less prescriptive about the specific action to take, and in fact, they might trigger thinking and cognitive activity rather than physical acts per se. See Fredrickson, "Cultivating Positive Emotions."

6. Fredrickson, "Positive Emotions Broaden and Build," 5.

she did more experiments to test that theory, it panned out. What's more, it's a really useful theory! Not many psychological researchers make such a contribution, and I'm eager to introduce you to her work.

When Fredrickson started her research, it was not at all clear that positive emotions offer us a survival edge, but she had a hunch that they must. She persisted, and her work gives us insight into what positive emotions do for us.

In a number of Fredrickson's studies, she shows participants videos and then measures various cardiovascular and behavioral reactions.[7] Imagine, for example, that she shows you a video of puppies playing or of ocean waves. You enjoy it, but your pulse and heart rate don't change. She shows you a video of a boy crying about his father who has died, and this makes you sad, but it doesn't change your pulse or heart rate very much. She shows you a screensaver, and you don't feel much, and your pulse and heart rate don't change at all. Seemingly, these videos, while effective in eliciting emotion from you (or no emotion, in the case of the screensaver), don't play an important role in your cardiovascular system. There's no evidence yet that positive emotions are physically adaptive for you.

But now imagine that she shows you a video called "The Ledge," taken from the film *Cat's Eye*. You watch a man out on the ledge of a skyscraper, with traffic moving like ants below. He creeps along the edge of the building, hugging it, trying not to fall off. He loses his footing, scrambles, and just barely avoids falling to his death. This video takes only eighty-three seconds, and yet it creates fear in its viewers, including elevating their pulse and heart rate. In just eighty-three seconds, you can go from calm to terrified, and your body shows it.[8]

Fredrickson wondered if we can undo an emotion like this and its effect on the body, and if so, whether positive emotions might play a role. She experimented with showing people different videos after the ledge video. If you're shown the screensaver afterward, it takes your heart forty seconds to recover from its fear-induced elevated rate. If you're shown the sad video, it takes even longer—sixty seconds—to recover. But if you're shown puppies or ocean waves, it takes only twenty seconds to recover.[9]

The lesson is this: taken out of context, positive emotions don't seem to do much for you, but put into the context of a scary event, positive emotions can cut your recovery time in half.

7. Fredrickson narrates her research journey and consolidates these studies in "Positive Emotions Broaden and Build."
8. Fredrickson and Levenson, "Positive Emotions Speed Recovery."
9. Fredrickson and Levenson, "Positive Emotions Speed Recovery," fig. 3.

When I learned this, I thought immediately of my colleague Kate Whetten, who studies the plight of orphans around the world. She studies their coping strategies and many positive things, but she also studies the physical and psychological trauma they experience. Many people might need to numb themselves just to read through the list of possible horrors that make it onto her questionnaires (burns, deaths, beatings, sexual abuse). And yet her team laughs *all the time*. No kidding, they laugh so loudly that I can hear them ten doors down. This laughing is not an intentional strategy for them, but by unconsciously turning to laughter, they work better—take in the bad, but also work in something good or funny, and you can recover in half the time and get back to the important work you're doing. Laugh to keep from crying, laugh to keep on going, and laugh to pay attention again sooner. What other trick do you know of that saves you half your time *and* makes you feel better?

This is called "the undoing effect of positive emotions."[10] A plethora of studies have manipulated positive emotions through showing people videos of waddling penguins, giving people compliments and gifts of candy, and telling people they did well at a task. They then compare the thoughts and actions of those who received the positive emotions to those who received a neutral condition (like a video of colorful sticks) or a negative-emotion condition (like telling someone they did not do well at a task). Universally, these very brief introductions of positive emotions resulted in good outcomes, including

- thinking more flexibly;[11]
- socializing with people you don't know;[12]
- cooperating, helping, and enhancing relationships;[13]
- feeling playful;
- having greater interest in engaging in physical activities;
- generating more solutions, and more creative solutions, to a stated problem;
- literally seeing more on a computer screen, and seeing the forest and not just the trees, so to speak, when looking at shapes clustered on the screen;[14]

10. Fredrickson et al., "Undoing Effect of Positive Emotions."
11. Fredrickson, "What Good Are Positive Emotions?"
12. Fredrickson and Branigan, "Positive Emotions Broaden the Scope of Attention"; Isen, "Success, Failure, Attention."
13. Fredrickson, "What Good Are Positive Emotions?"; Isen, "Success, Failure, Attention."
14. Fredrickson and Branigan, "Positive Emotions Broaden the Scope of Attention."

- persisting longer at a task;[15]
- setting higher goals for oneself;[16]
- experiencing increases in willpower over temptations;[17]
- negotiating an optimal agreement;[18] and
- being more creative.[19]

Take a second look at this list of actions that resulted from positive emotions and think about clergy this time. These are exactly the kinds of behaviors that would serve pastors well. Actually, they would serve anyone in a leadership position well.

The Broaden and Build Theory

These studies hint at the evolutionary value of positive emotions like amusement. But Fredrickson goes further and proposes a theory, the broaden and build theory, which plays out the long-term benefit of having frequent positive emotions.[20]

It goes like this: Positive emotions broaden your thinking, making you open to new ideas.[21] When you are open to new ideas, you might solve a problem at work or come up with a new strategy. This broadening because of positive emotions also makes you more sociable, which might lead you to make a new friend or deepen an existing relationship. A broadened mindset also makes you more open to trying new behaviors, such that you might sign up for a class that stretches your skill set (computer programming, say, or trombone lessons or hang gliding).

Having a little extra broadening on a daily basis relative to those who don't—and thus are less open to new ideas, experiences, and relationships—gives you

15. Erez and Isen, "Influence of Positive Affect"; Kavanagh, "Mood, Persistence, and Success"; Sarason, Potter, and Sarason, "Recording and Recall."

16. Baron, "Environmentally Induced Positive Affect"; Hom and Arbuckle, "Mood Induction Effects."

17. Tice and Wallace, "Mood and Emotion Control."

18. Carnevale and Isen, "Influence of Positive Affect."

19. Isen, Daubman, and Nowicki, "Positive Affect Facilitates Creative Problem Solving."

20. Fredrickson, "Role of Positive Emotions."

21. Note that Gable and Harmon-Jones (see "Approach-Motivated Positive Affect" and "Blues Broaden") conducted studies that found some complexity to this finding about positive and negative emotion. It may be that whether you broaden or narrow your thinking hinges on whether there's an opportunity to take action after an emotion. In some laboratory studies, inducing sadness when there was no way to act on that sadness caused broadened thinking, despite sadness being a negative emotion (negative emotions usually narrow thinking). More real-world studies on this are needed.

Figure 6.1
Broaden and Build

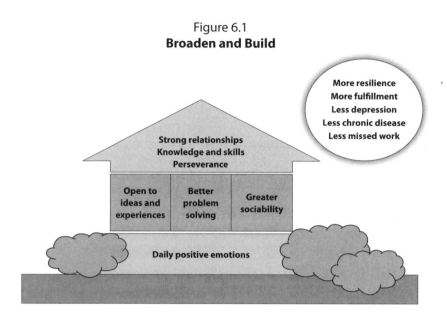

an advantage. The behaviors that come from a broadened mind build up your resources. You end up with more skills, more friends, and yes, even a better job and higher pay.[22] Enhanced doses of positive emotions improve your life. Then, when faced with a difficulty, you have resources to draw on in the form of friends, money, and skills and are in a much better situation to cope.

You might think of the presence of positive emotions as allowing you to build something akin to an extra-strong foundation of a house (see fig. 6.1). While it's true that Christ is always our strongest foundation (as Jason reminded me), in this analogy positive emotions also serve as a sort of foundation. They hold up the house's walls: openness to ideas and experiences, better problem solving, and greater sociability. These walls, in turn, support the roof—which is made up of things like strong relationships, knowledge, skills, and perseverance. With the particular shelter of this kind of roof, you

22. This finding is suggested by an incredible review of hundreds of positive-emotion studies by Sonja Lyubomirsky and colleagues. They analyzed the findings of three kinds of studies: (1) cross-sectional, in which happy people are more likely to be successful, with better mental and physical health; (2) longitudinal, in which long-term happiness (being "chronically happy") is associated with more social activity, better coping, active pursuit of goals, and more productive and fulfilling work; and (3) experimental (meaning researchers manipulated variables), in which positive emotions promote more sociability, more effective conflict resolution skills, more altruism, and better immune systems. Based on their review of these studies, they conclude that positive emotions may actually be the cause of success. See Lyubomirsky, King, and Diener, "Benefits of Frequent Positive Affect."

are in better shape to survive a storm; for example, friends will be there to help you, and you'll have more skills to navigate challenges. And the results of this shelter, at least in correlational studies, are shown in the sun: more resilience and personal fulfillment and less depression, chronic disease, and missed work.

This broaden and build theory also helps explain the evolutionary benefit of positive emotions. Although none of these broadening behaviors will save your life immediately like running from the lion will, positive emotions help you *in the long run* by building up your resources, which also gives you a survival edge. The whole puzzle of whether positive emotions benefit us evolutionarily was hard to solve because researchers were thinking of it in the wrong time frame—taking a short-term rather than a more long-term view.[23]

Spiraling

As we've seen, positive emotions can lead us to take a variety of actions. On the flip side, studies have shown that when we're faced with emotions that make us feel threatened, we not only fail to broaden our thinking, we also turn inward. In those same video studies, participants who experienced fear through the ledge video were less likely, compared to those who watched falling sticks or swimming penguins, to report urges to contemplate problems, to work, or to relish life.[24] Study participants who saw an anger-inducing video were less likely to report wanting to work, to relish life and reminisce, or to be contemplative. They also reported wanting to be antisocial, even to the point of wanting to hit someone. In other words, fear and anger make us attend to what's right in front of us—and that may be adaptive at the time. But it's amusement and other positive emotions that make us see larger patterns and spawn creative ideas, which benefit us in the long term.[25]

It's easy to see how fear and anger can lead to downward spirals. However, Fredrickson wondered if there might be such a thing as upward spirals—and found that it is indeed possible to spiral upward! One good feeling can lead to a positive interaction with someone, which leads to more good feelings, which then makes it more likely that something like our work will go well. As work goes well, we then have more creative and quality ideas to contribute. With positive emotions, we also continue to interact in positive ways with friends and a wide variety of people, and we are more open to what other people tell

23. Fredrickson, "What Good Are Positive Emotions?"
24. Fredrickson and Branigan, "Positive Emotions Broaden the Scope of Attention."
25. Wadlinger and Isaacowitz, "Positive Mood Broadens Visual Attention."

us—and this positive spiral goes on and on. Then, if something bad happens during our otherwise enjoyable day, positive emotions set us up to problem-solve better or to shake it off, which helps prevent a downward spiral.

As you might imagine, very small and reciprocal interactions, like a compliment leading to a smile, make a difference in your emotions. Barbara Fredrickson terms these spiraling moments "positivity resonance." Although it can be tricky to study such a diverse and quickly unfolding array of events, she found a way to do so by turning to our bodies. Some of her studies measure oxytocin, which is the calm-and-connect hormone. In other studies, she measures vagal tone, which is how efficiently the vagus nerve, a nerve that goes from your brain and weaves around many of your organs, oxygenates blood. Oxytocin and vagal tone predictably increase and improve when a positive spiral is at play, providing evidence that positive emotions don't just make us feel good, but that they are also good for us.[26]

Emotions on Both Sides of the Aisle

By now it should be clear that both positive and negative emotions give us information and that being in a good mood and experiencing more positive emotions gives us an edge on broader thinking, which serves us well in the long term. What about pastors though? What kinds of emotions do pastors feel during a typical week?

One available measure of emotions, the Positive Affect Negative Affect Scale (PANAS), consists of twenty items, ten each of negative emotions (e.g., distressed, guilty, irritable) and positive emotions (e.g., excited, interested, determined). Episcopal priests completed these surveys, reporting which positive and negative emotions they had experienced during the past few months. The researcher, Joseph Stewart-Sicking, then compared their answers to the answers of healthy Americans. He found that Episcopal priests had much higher levels of negative emotions.[27] However, he also found that Episcopal priests comparatively had even higher levels of positive emotions.

This finding is interesting to me. It seems that clergy can hold it all—the good and the bad, the joy and the grief—and they can feel it all. Clergy may be different from people in other professions in this way, and we should keep it in mind when we turn to thinking about promoting the positive mental health of clergy. Jason suggested to me that clergy should linger on this insight as well—yes, you do feel more pain than other people, but you also feel more joy. And isn't that a trade worth making?

26. Fredrickson, *Love 2.0*.
27. Stewart-Sicking, "Subjective Well-Being."

At minimum, we should always be sure to measure the positive emotions of clergy alongside the negative, because if we only measure the negative emotions, clergy are likely to score high and we may falsely assume that they are doing poorly. But what about the balance of positive to negative emotions that clergy experience? Some studies suggest that people with a high ratio of positive to negative emotions experience higher levels of positive mental health and other advantages like increased creativity.[28] It would be exciting to study clergy, with their high levels of *both* positive and negative emotions, to learn whether they experience the advantages of high positive mental health even with high levels of negative emotions. Jason reminds us in what follows that the intermingling of highs and lows has been a characteristic of the human condition since its biblical beginnings.

Behind the Pulpit
Joy in Riffing Off the Blue Notes

Biblical Christianity has a deep interest in human flourishing. God creates all people, stamps God's own image on each of us, gives us laws to bless one another, and designs the entire cosmos to be a place of abundance for all. God's original word over all creatures is one of blessing. Eden was a place of the most positive emotions imaginable.

But the story doesn't end there. In fact, it doesn't stay there very long at all. Martin Luther imagines that Adam and Eve fall just a few minutes into their life together—as soon as there are rules, we frail human beings look for ways around them.[29] And then they (that is to say, *we*) blame one another, and the serpent, and even God, and God banishes us from the essential goodness for which we're created. Human beings are creatures who long for Eden and yet defy how God invites us to re-create it, not just with Adam and Eve's disobedience, but also with Cain's and so many others'. And of course our own.

God doesn't give up on us. God would have been fully justified in destroying us all and starting with a blank slate. God sees the carnage yet promises not to lay us all low again. God chooses a favorite people from among all the earth—Israel—to be his conduit through which to bless all peoples. God pours everything he is into this people—guiding them with the law, correcting them with

28. Fredrickson, "Updated Thinking on Positivity Ratios."

29. Steinmetz, lectures on biblical interpretation in the Reformation (Duke Divinity School, Durham, NC, spring 1997). For Luther's exegesis of the opening chapter of Genesis, see *Luther's Works: Lectures on Genesis*, ed. Jaroslav Pelikan (St. Louis: Concordia, 1958), chaps. 1–5.

the prophets, keeping them hopeful with promises of a messiah. And they (we) ignore and deny God's blessings. So God pours himself out entirely into one person: Jesus, God's own self and Son. Jesus is God's fully alive humanity among us. He invites us into the sort of flourishing that God eternally is. And Jesus's people, in our faltering and fragile way, have tried and mostly failed to live into God's dream for the world. We call this church.

Given this history, we're never surprised when human beings misbehave or even when creation itself revolts against what God wants. It's a dangerous world out there that we have wrought. And yet God has not left us to our own devices. God is determined to get the world God wants and yet is unbearably patient in bringing it about.

We need a gospel that tells the truth about the brutal world we live in, not one that veils our eyes from it or downplays our experiences of negative emotion. We also need a return to cosmic joy, and in Christ we get precisely that: the world newly made—not yet entirely, but in places, starting with his empty tomb and breaking out in places like the civil rights movement, the fall of the Berlin Wall and the end of apartheid, and above all in *the* social revolution called the Christian church. We need what Otis Moss Jr. calls "blue note preaching":[30] It can sing the blues over the hash we make of the world. Its music allows us to feel deeply the sorrow of the ones singing and playing and being described in the music. And then we can find joy along with the blue notes, positive emotion alongside the negative. As one blues musician said, "I took the energy I usually use to mope, and I wrote a song instead."[31] The gospel is not that there is no cross; it is that there is a resurrection after that cross.

Positive Mental Health: Feeling Good and Functioning Well

Imagine how we might view the world and behave in different ways if we experienced emotions deeper than what a penguin video can induce—emotions like finding personal meaning in our work, as clergy do.

Until now, we've been talking about emotions. Emotions are relatively short-lived feelings that result from a specific event. Something happens and you feel an emotion in response. This emotion can quickly change if something else happens and elicits a different emotion. Emotions give us important information about how we're doing and whether or not we need to act, but they are plentiful and short-lived.

30. As his son Otis Moss III discusses in *Blue Note Preaching*.
31. Attributed to Duke Ellington in Bell, *Till Victory Is Won*, 17.

Contrast emotions to mood. Mood is the background noise (or symphony!) of your day. You wake up in a certain mood, which might just continue throughout the day unless it is utterly shifted by an event that elicits other, more powerful emotions. Otherwise, as you handle various events and their concordant emotions throughout the day, you likely revert back to the same mood. You may have the same general mood for months at a time. Some researchers have shown that there are patterns to people's moods across the day,[32] and it repeats a pattern you may have for months at a time. Figure 6.2 shows the pattern for a typical US worker.

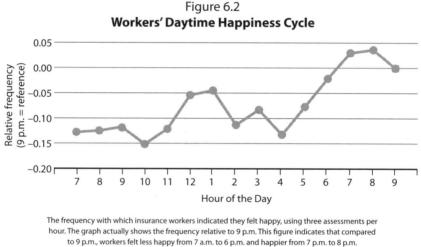

Figure 6.2
Workers' Daytime Happiness Cycle

The frequency with which insurance workers indicated they felt happy, using three assessments per hour. The graph actually shows the frequency relative to 9 p.m. This figure indicates that compared to 9 p.m., workers felt less happy from 7 a.m. to 6 p.m. and happier from 7 p.m. to 8 p.m.
Source: Stone et al., "Daily Mood Variability," 1294.

Fredrickson's studies cited above are among many showing that a person's emotions can be altered through videos. But even though watching a cat video right before a meeting might broaden your thinking, its emotional benefits won't last for very long. Changing your mood would last much longer and possibly sustain broadened thinking. So an important question is, can you change your mood?

As it turns out, the answer to this question is yes, you *can* make changes that will likely boost the degree of positivity you wake up with every day, within limits. These limits are due to personality and how your brain is hardwired. Based on identical twin studies and brain scans of babies, we know that our brains are "preconfigured to see good in the world"—or not to.[33] A key area

32. Figure 6.2 is taken from Stone et al., "Daily Mood Variability"; Golder and Macy, "Diurnal and Seasonal Mood."
33. Haidt, *Happiness Hypothesis*.

of our brains is the frontal cortex, which is where we process information and make decisions. It turns out that some people show more brainwave activity on the left side of the frontal cortex and other people have more activity on the right side. People with more activity on the left side won the "cortical lottery," so to speak.[34] They are hardwired to experience more feelings of happiness on a daily basis and also to feel less anxiety, fear, and shame than those who have more activity on the right. There's evidence that your experience of these feelings remains relatively the same from infancy through adulthood.[35] You can think of this hardwiring as a "set point." Maybe you won the cortical lottery and will naturally experience the world more positively. Or maybe you didn't. Regardless of which side of the cortical divide you fall on, this set point is only a default place. It has a range that can go quite a bit higher or lower. Someone born with high right-cortex brain activity may never experience the high positive mood of someone born with high left-cortex activity, but he or she can still do things to get to the highest point of his range.[36]

This possibility of shifting your baseline mood is good news! Who wouldn't want to wake up at the height of their mood range? So how do you get there? A sociologist and a psychologist—Corey Keyes and Carol Ryff—scoured old and new texts and conducted a number of studies.[37] We can take their research and condense it to this: the things that affect your underlying mood are wrapped up in your functioning, and two key kinds of functioning are essential components of positive mental health. These are psychological functioning and social functioning.[38]

Psychological Functioning

Good *psychological functioning*, or psychological well-being, is made up of qualities and skills individuals have that allow them to function well in the

34. Haidt, *Happiness Hypothesis*.
35. Headley, "Set-Point Theory"; Diener, Lucas, and Scollon, "Beyond the Hedonic Treadmill."
36. The studies in this area are based on the set-point theory of well-being and are very helpfully explained by Haidt in *Happiness Hypothesis*. I love this term "cortical lottery," coined by Haidt—I apply it all the time when I see someone quickly shake off a bad emotional event ("Well, *they* won the cortical lottery!"). Researchers drawing on longitudinal data are still determining how much we can change from our set point. It seems major life experiences like the death of a child can permanently impact us negatively, and that extroverts may increase their feelings of well-being more over time, possibly due to taking risks more often and some of them paying off. The point is that we shouldn't underestimate our biological makeup, but we can still make changes that should result in improved mood.
37. Keyes, "Social Well-Being"; Ryff, "Happiness Is Everything, or Is It?"
38. Keyes, "Mental Health Continuum."

world.[39] Some examples of these are meaning in life and having good interpersonal skills (see table 6.1 for more examples). It's not so much the psychological functioning itself that matters as what it brings you. Good psychological
functioning gives you the skills to grow as a person or at work, which leads
to lasting satisfaction. Good psychological functioning can also give you the
skills to do things like show kindness, which leads to more positive attitudes
toward yourself. With the skills provided by good psychological functioning, you
interact with the world in ways that result in a deep kind of life satisfaction—a
deeper sort of happiness than those offered by positive emotions and mood.
For example, if you watch a comedy, you'll experience positive emotions, but
those will likely go away shortly after the movie ends. By contrast, if you volunteer at a homeless shelter, you may or may not laugh as much, but the sense
of purpose and meaning that comes from it should stay with you much longer
than the humor from the movie. Thus, good psychological functioning leads to
deep life satisfaction, which persists longer than positive emotions and mood.

Social Functioning

At one time, researchers believed that positive emotions plus good psychological functioning pretty much covered positive mental health.[40] However,
is that enough? Emotions and psychological functioning are individual-level
perceptions, which may fit best for cultures like the United States that are
more individualistic in nature but may leave out something important for
cultures that are more community oriented. However, even for those of us
in an individual-oriented society, focusing on how you feel about your mood
isn't enough to describe functioning well because if we don't interact well
with others, our life satisfaction cannot run as deep. For example, someone
like Ted Kaczynski, the Unabomber, could have good psychological functioning in the sense that he might feel like he has purpose in life and high self-
acceptance and (before prison) satisfaction with life. Yet if we stopped there,
we'd leave out a key part of the picture—everything about his lack of feelings
of belonging, of comfort with others, and of making a positive contribution
to society. It's therefore essential to consider social functioning too. Social
functioning is made up of the ways people evaluate their functioning in public
life, such as feeling like you belong or like you contribute to the world (see
table 6.1 for more examples). As with good psychological functioning, good
social functioning leads to deeper life satisfaction, in this case derived from
belonging and contributing to others.

39. Keyes, "Mental Health Continuum."
40. Keyes, "Social Well-Being."

Table 6.1 Components of Good Psychological and Social Functioning

Psychological Functioning	Description
Self-acceptance	Holding positive attitudes about yourself
Positive relations with others	Feeling empathy and affection for others, having deep friendships
Purpose in life	Having goals and a sense of meaning and direction in life
Knowing yourself and making good choices	Being able to discern which settings are best for you and then choosing them or improving them (e.g., figuring out what kind of classes work best for you and, if you learn better in smaller classrooms, choosing small classes when possible)
Independent living skills	Being able to regulate your own emotions and behavior and generally function as an adult, including working
Personal growth	Engaging in a lifelong process of continually changing and developing as a person
Social Functioning	
Social integration	Feeling that you are part of society, you have things in common with others, and your fate is linked with that of other people
Social acceptance	Experiencing some groups of people that you are comfortable with, can trust, and believe are capable of good
Social contribution	Believing you have something valuable to offer the world
Social actualization	Believing that the world can progress and that you or people like you can benefit from the world's improvements
Social coherence	Feeling like you can understand what is happening in the world around you

Source: Keyes, "Mental Health Continuum."

Now, finally, you have the background to fully understand positive mental health. Figure 6.3 puts this all together. It depicts the two components of positive mental health: (1) positive emotions and mood and (2) functioning well. Overall life satisfaction and positive functioning come from good psychological and social functioning, which each lead to positive feelings. Although the term "happy" is too vague to be of much use, as a shorthand you can think of positive mental health as emanating from the short-term happiness that comes from positive emotions and the longer-term happiness that comes from deep life satisfaction.

These components of positive mental health—positive emotions and mood versus functioning well—differ in their time frames. As noted earlier, emotions vary throughout the day in response to small events. The background noise of mood is a little more stable and yet still susceptible to larger events. To maintain positive mental health in the long term, we would do well to tend to our psychological and social functioning. Unlike emotions and mood,

Figure 6.3
The Components of Positive Mental Health

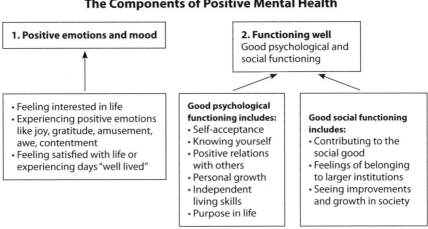

psychological and social functioning take months to shift, and they are very important in how we cope when something shakes up our mood.

Let me give a personal example. In 2014, I was shocked to be diagnosed with breast cancer. As you might imagine, it was a highly emotional time during which I became very worried, and it was hard to find pleasure in things at first, even though life became suddenly all the more precious. My emotions and even my mood took a nosedive as soon as the doctor issued the word "cancer." On the other hand, my psychological well-being stayed quite stable, because I still had meaning and purpose in life and was still growing as a person. As for my social well-being, at the time I would have said it was stable because I continued to be connected to people and felt like I was making a contribution to the world through raising my kids and through my work (especially my work with pastors!). But in retrospect, I think my social well-being actually *grew*, because I was blessed with so many people telling me how much they cared about me and giving me repeated signs that they were thinking of me during my treatment. I now also have a new connection to people who have experienced cancer. As my own example shows, mood can quickly change, whereas deeper life satisfaction takes much longer to shift.

Measuring Positive Mental Health

Do you want to try to measure your own degree of positive mental health? The Mental Health Continuum, Short Form, is designed to help you do just that (table 6.2).

Table 6.2 Mental Health Continuum, Short Form:
A Measure of Positive Mental Health

	During the *past month*, how often did you feel the following?	Never	Once or twice	About once a week	Two or three times a week	Almost every day	Every day
Emotions	a. Happy	0	1	2	3	4	5
	b. Interested in life	0	1	2	3	4	5
	c. Satisfied with life	0	1	2	3	4	5
Social functioning	d. That you have something important to contribute to society	0	1	2	3	4	5
	e. That you belong to a community (a social group, faith community, church, school, neighborhood, etc.)	0	1	2	3	4	5
	f. That our society is a good place, or is becoming a better place, for all people	0	1	2	3	4	5
	g. That people are basically good	0	1	2	3	4	5
	h. That the way our society works makes sense to you	0	1	2	3	4	5
Psychological functioning	i. That you like most parts of your personality	0	1	2	3	4	5
	j. That you are good at managing the responsibilities of your daily life	0	1	2	3	4	5
	k. That you have warm and trusting relationships with others	0	1	2	3	4	5
	l. That you have experiences that challenge you to grow and become a better person	0	1	2	3	4	5
	m. That you are confident to think or express your own ideas or opinions	0	1	2	3	4	5
	n. That your life has a sense of direction or meaning	0	1	2	3	4	5

Source: Developed by C. L. M. Keyes (see "Overview of the Mental Health Continuum").

The first set of items (a through c) map onto emotions. To be diagnosed as having very high levels of positive mental health, also called "flourishing," you need to indicate "every day" or "almost every day" to at least one of these three items.

The second set of items (d through h) map onto social functioning, and the third set of items (i through n) map onto psychological functioning. To be diagnosed as flourishing, you need to indicate "every day" or "almost every day" to at least six of these eleven social and psychological functioning items.

This survey can also be used to diagnose "languishing," which is a lack of positive mental health but not necessarily to the point of mental illness, such as depression. Languishers need to indicate "never" or "once or twice" to at least one of the first set of items and also six or more of the eleven social and psychological functioning items.

Positive Mental Health among Clergy

In our own study of United Methodist clergy, we gave the Mental Health Continuum, Short Form items to pastors in 2014, and we were able to compare our data to data from a sample of people across the United States who took a survey through the Centers for Disease Control and Prevention.[41] The comparison results can be seen in figure 6.4.

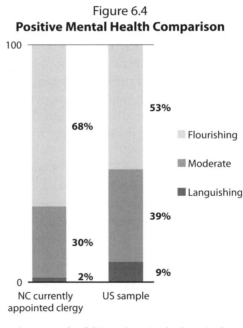

Figure 6.4
Positive Mental Health Comparison

Responses are from full-time and part-time church-appointed
pastors in 2014; US comparison data is from 2012.

Looking at the left bar stack, we see that 68 percent of North Carolina clergy qualify as flourishing, compared to only 53 percent of people in the United States. Looking at the left bar stack, we see that only 2 percent of clergy qualify as languishing, compared to 9 percent of people in the United

41. Centers for Disease Control and Prevention. The data is from a representative sample of 3,935 US residents in 2012, provided by C. L. M. Keyes.

States. This is great news! Clergy seem to be doing better than the average American and to have very low rates of languishing.

These findings are also somewhat surprising given that about 10 percent of clergy qualify for depression. Here's what I think is going on: (1) the measure may work slightly differently for clergy[42] and (2) compared to other Americans, clergy—even depressed clergy—may have deeper life satisfaction that comes from better psychological and social functioning; they have meaning in their lives (from good psychological functioning), and they contribute to society (part of good social functioning). This is good because, as noted above, the deeper kinds of life satisfaction will sustain you during tough times.

The Connection between Positive Mental Health, Mental Illness, and Physical Health

You'll recall that watching penguins led to changes in people's behavior, including making them more social and better problem solvers. Yet those positive emotion boosts are temporary, and they are lighthearted when compared to actual positive human interactions, such as being generous. A natural next question, in light of the long-term, deeper life satisfaction that we've been exploring, is whether deeper life satisfaction also comes with positive behavior changes. The answer, in short, is yes!

This is truly the good news I've been dying to share with you. It's taken a long time to get to this point in the book, but I think it is essential in moving forward to improve the health of clergy and keep them healthy.

To put it simply, having high positive mental health seems to prevent future mental illness and also future physical health problems. This is important, so let me say it again: the evidence seems to indicate that having high positive

---

42. I am confident that the Mental Health Continuum, Short Form, works as intended with clergy. In a diary study that we did with clergy, which included this measure, those who scored as flourishing also rated their daily activities the highest on meaning and enjoyment. Giving me further confidence, clergy who had lower mental health scores rated their daily activities lowest on meaning and enjoyment, as expected. However, there may be a limitation for this measure for clergy. I think that conceptually the "emotions" category is fairly easy for clergy to positively endorse; respondents simply need to say they've been "interested in life" nearly every day for the past month, which a full 96 percent of the pastors indicated, allowing them to clear the bar set for positive emotions. Because it is easy for clergy to qualify as having positive emotions, I think depressed clergy show up in the "moderate mental health category" more often than nonclergy US respondents did—the latter may show up in the "languishing" category instead. In general, I think this measure may overestimate the percentage of clergy with flourishing and moderate mental health, especially among clergy with depression. But because of our diary study, I still think it does a good job. I believe the results showing clergy having higher positive mental health than US adults still stand, but they may be somewhat attenuated.

mental health achieves a double punch of preventing future mental illness and preventing future physical health problems. We know this largely through a series of studies using the Midlife in the US (MIDUS) data, which come from a random sample of adults in the United States in 1995 and ten years later, in 2005. These studies use the Mental Health Continuum, Short Form, items that you saw earlier in this chapter.

Our understanding of the benefits of positive mental health unfolded first with the data from just 1995. From this data we know that flourishers (who also did not have a mental illness) had

- the least missed work in terms of full days or half days missed;[43]
- the fewest limitations in tasks of daily living like getting around and getting dressed;[44]
- the fewest chronic physical health diagnoses;[45] and
- the lowest use of health care.[46]

In addition to the prior list, flourishers who also reported having no or only one chronic disease, experienced the following work and medical advantages. They

- placed greater thought and effort into work;
- had fewer work injuries;
- had fewer medical visits, including hospitalizations; and
- had fewer prescription medications.[47]

Using the 1995 MIDUS data, researchers looked at how many chronic diseases Americans of various mental health and depression statuses had.[48] Flourishers without depression had on average 1.5 chronic diseases. People with moderate mental health but without depression had an average of 2.1 chronic diseases. The number of chronic diseases increased to 3.1 by adding in depression (to either flourishing or moderate mental health). And languishers with depression had the highest number of chronic diseases: 4.5. We don't know which came first (for example, a chronic disease may lead to being depressed), but these studies clearly show a correlation between physical health

43. Keyes and Grzywacz, "Health as a Complete State."
44. Keyes, "Mental Health Continuum."
45. Keyes, "Chronic Physical Conditions."
46. Keyes and Grzywacz, "Health as a Complete State."
47. Keyes and Grzywacz, "Health as a Complete State."
48. Keyes, "Chronic Physical Conditions."

and whether or not a person has depression. While these particular findings may not be surprising, other findings in these studies show something that is perhaps less expected: a difference in physical health relative to how strong one's positive mental health is—including when we look at just one chronic disease at a time (see sidebar).

Percentage of Americans reporting cardiovascular disease relative to positive mental health status:

- Flourishing mental health, 8.2%
- Moderate mental health, 11.8%
- Languishing mental health, 12.0%

Note: Keyes, "Nexus of Cardiovascular Disease and Depression Revisited."

These findings are impressively positive. It would be fantastic to avoid physical health problems and do better work through better positive mental health. But the findings described so far were all from data at a single time point and are susceptible to the chicken-and-egg problem; we can't tell whether positive mental health leads to fewer medical visits or whether fewer medical visits (i.e., being physically healthier) leads to better positive mental health. In truth, it's hard to get around this problem. Fredrickson's lab studies get around it by randomly assigning participants to watching videos that induce positive versus negative emotions, but those studies are necessarily contrived. You can't randomly assign someone to a series of real-world events. While still imperfect, some research by Keyes comes closest by its longitudinal nature (that is, by using the MIDUS data from 1995 and 2005).[49]

The first question he explored is whether people's positive mental health changes across time, and he found that it does. A lot of people changed mental health categories during those ten years.[50] People were unlikely to change by two mental health categories, such as going from languishing to flourishing (4 percent) or from flourishing to languishing (3 percent), but high percentages of people moved by one category. Specifically, in terms of improving mental health, 51 percent of people who were languishing in 1995 were moderately mentally healthy in 2005, and 19 percent of people with moderate mental health in 1995 were flourishing in 2005. In terms of declines, 46 percent of those flourishing in 1995 had declined to moderate mental health in 2005, and 14 percent of those with moderate mental health had declined to languishing. So positive mental health is a resource to protect and cultivate.

Perhaps more importantly, the study findings suggest that staying stable at the highest possible level of positive mental health can prevent mental illness. Compared to people with moderate mental health in both 1995 and 2005, people who were flourishing in both 1995 and 2005 were three times less likely

49. Keyes, Dhingra, and Simoes, "Change in Level of Positive Mental Health."
50. Keyes, Dhingra, and Simoes, "Change in Level of Positive Mental Health."

to have a mental illness in 2005. This is a reason to try to boost the 30 percent of clergy who have moderate mental health up to flourishing mental health.

As one might suspect, languishing isn't good for mental illness, and the data bears this out. Compared to people who stayed flourishing, people who stayed languishing or who newly moved from moderate or flourishing mental health to languishing were seven times more likely to have a mental illness in 2005.[51] Boosting the mental health of languishing pastors is really important.

How can this be? You may recall that even this longitudinal data is imperfect. It's possible that a third variable, such as having more money, is the true explanation—it could explain having both higher positive mental health and better health. But it is also possible that the broaden and build theory explains how these good outcomes are achieved.[52] Consider the following: Positive emotions make you open to new ideas, people, and experiences. You act on that openness and build up your skills and social support. With more skills, you are likely to enjoy your job more, earn more money, and have health insurance. With more social support, people are likely to take care of you if you get sick, and with your broadened thinking in which things feel doable, you're more likely to get health care when you need it and less likely to let ailments linger until there is permanent damage. High positive mental health essentially makes you more resilient because you have more creative thinking, are more likely to reach out to others, and have not only more people but also more diverse people (think of all their knowledge and resources!) to call on.

As we saw in chapter 4, stress is not just a state but rather a series of thoughts that happen in reaction to an event. Building on this idea, if you experience positive emotions and broadened thinking, and if you also have social support to draw on, then you are likely to appraise events as more manageable and less stressful than if you are lacking in positive mental health. Appraising events as manageable prevents the symptoms of stress, which include things like respiratory ailments, GI problems, nausea, muscle tension, and pain. The mind-body connection can really come through for you if you have high positive mental health.

Sign Me Up for Positive Mental Health! But What If I Am Already Depressed?

Even though positive mental health can sometimes prevent future cases of mental illness, this isn't always the case. As we saw above, our surveys found

51. Keyes, Dhingra, and Simoes, "Change in Level of Positive Mental Health."
52. Fredrickson, "Role of Positive Emotions."

that few pastors are languishing. But we also saw in chapter 3 that roughly 9 to 11 percent of pastors qualify for depression on those same surveys.[53] How can these findings coexist?

Let me first say a word about the term "mental illness." It can be off-putting, but in this particular chapter I think it's important to distinguish positive *mental health* (in the form of positive emotions and psychological and social functioning) from *mental illness*, which in most of my clergy studies is measured as depression or anxiety. Please try to let go of any stereotypes you might hold that all kinds of mental illness are severe and stigmatizing, and think for a minute like a psychologist who seeks to understand the experience of people nonjudgmentally and who uses terminology that clearly distinguishes between different experiences. Here, I use "mental health" to mean positive mental health and "mental illness" to describe states of negative emotions that likely need clinical attention, as well as diagnoses of mental illness (e.g., panic attacks).

With that definition of mental illness in mind, let's return to how it is that someone can have moderate mental health and be simultaneously depressed. To understand this, you have to understand a concept that initially shocked me, which is that mental illness and mental health are not on the same continuum; rather, they are on *two separate continua*. Remember, we are not talking about emotions that are in response to an immediate event but about moods and one's mental state across a longer period of time. If we were talking about emotions, it might be hard to be sad and joyful at the same time. But across the course of a week, you might have both sad moments and happy moments. Or you might be sad consistently for a couple of weeks or more but still feel like you have purpose in life and a sense of belonging to one or more communities. In that case, you might qualify for depression but still have robust psychological functioning and social functioning.

Figure 6.5 may help you visualize this. First look at the lightest columns, which represent languishing pastors. Some clergy (5.6 percent) with languishing mental health do not have any depressive symptoms, and 16.7 percent have only mild depressive symptoms. Lacking positive mental health is not the same as having a mental illness; it is just the absence of positive emotion, personal meaning in life, and social connectedness. It wouldn't be a great life to lack all these, and lacking them may be the precursor to becoming depressed, but it also wouldn't necessarily mean having depression or anxiety. As seen in the figure, over 61 percent of clergy with languishing mental health experience depressive symptoms to the extent that they qualify for moderately severe or severe depression.

53. Proeschold-Bell et al., "Using Effort-Reward Imbalance Theory."

The figure also makes clear that pastors with flourishing mental health (the darkest columns) experience very few depressive symptoms, whereas pastors with moderate mental health exhibit varying degrees of depressive symptoms. Positive mental health is correlated with depressive symptoms, but it is not perfectly correlated, and an individual's experience of positive mental health may differ in surprising ways from their ratings of depressive symptoms.

The key point is this: mental health is different from mental illness. Of note, there is a (nonclergy) literature that supports this. Mental health and mental illness have been shown in several studies to overlap but not completely—in fact, far from it (they correlate at about 0.5, which is only a moderate relationship; 0.7 would be a strong relationship, and 1.0 would be the strongest relationship possible).[54] It is true that people experiencing mental illness indicate less positive mental health, but there is still substantial diversity in that experience.

Ministry is complex work. Is it any wonder, really, that pastors might experience multiple symptoms of depression or anxiety while also experiencing interest in life and finding meaning in their work? Jason gives some examples of living into this complexity.

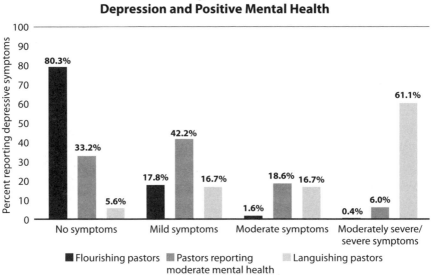

Figure 6.5
Depression and Positive Mental Health

Data is from 2016 survey responses of full-time and part-time church-appointed pastors.

54. Keyes, "Mental Health as a Complete State," esp. 182; Golder and Macy, "Diurnal and Seasonal Mood."

Behind the Pulpit
Happy Angry People

A pastor friend of mine told me recently that she'd had a hard week. "I've been in the hospital with a dying man who's been a creep to me," she said. "I'm not the only one he's mistreated. He's alienated from everyone he's loved. I'm trying to nudge them all toward reconciliation here at the end. And it's hard. I'd rather punch him in the face. But I'm holding his hand while he dies, because of Jesus," she said. She is, in this book's parlance, a human being fully alive. But that doesn't mean she's having fun or is happy about it. Grace is beautiful, but it's also hard.

Looked at one way, she's just doing the drudge work, dutifully doing the job (however joylessly). Looked at another way, she's growing in the image of Christ. Paul taught us this—his pain in ministry is a re-presentation of Christ's own suffering. Paul's sufferings (which he goes out of his way to catalog) are filling up what is lacking in the sufferings of Christ (Col. 1:24). This is strange to hear—in every branch of the church through time, Christ's sacrifice has been considered a once-and-for-all act, requiring no supplementation (Heb. 10:10–14). Yet Paul speaks of what is "lacking" in Christ's sufferings. We might parse this problem by saying that Christ's self-offering completes salvation for the human race writ large, but for us to become part of Christ's body, our life becomes like his. To be joined to the suffering one, we must also suffer with him—though of course infinitely less than he. Paul elsewhere describes his life with Christ as a matter of having been "crucified" with him, so that he will rise like him (Gal. 2:19–20). In this account, suffering isn't meaningless, and it isn't mere duty. It's taking part in God's redemption of the world. Christ, on his cross, forgives his tormenters (Luke 23:34). So Christians, acting in grace where others act in spite, become more like Jesus. It's not fun. But it is beautiful. And it's the narrow way to life to which all human beings are called—the most beautiful way to live (Matt. 7:14).

One of the best movies about parish ministry in recent years is *Calvary*. It portrays the ministry of one Father James, the Catholic priest of a small clapboard church in an Irish seaside village. He's an excellent priest. He's wise without being patronizing; he can see the evil in folks' lives and the good that will eventually overwhelm it. And precisely because he's such a good priest, someone who is a survivor of sexual abuse at another priest's hand plans to kill him. The film walks through Father James's daily, ordinary ministry—only it's anything but ordinary knowing your life will end after church on Sunday.

The film is brutal. He knows one parishioner is beating his wife, but the man denies it and insults the priest. A wealthy congregant wants to give a gift to the church in order to do penance, but Father won't accept it, and the man shows his nihilism and self-importance. A philandering parishioner admits his serial affairs but not their immorality. His associate priest is a fawning nincompoop. His bishop is spineless.

These are all relatively normal pastoral events. But the movie piles on. First, Father James visits a murderer behind bars who seems to feel no remorse for his actions. Father James, a widower, is then visited by his daughter, who arrives for a visit after a failed suicide attempt. An older man asks for a gun to commit suicide and escape dementia. A visiting French couple is hit head-on by drunk teenagers, and the husband dies. "Where are the teenagers?" Father James asks the ER tech. "Where they belong: in the morgue." Father James slides back into his long-abandoned alcoholism. His church burns to the ground. He picks a bar fight, pulls the gun he got for the parishioner, and gets beaten up, after which he tells the idiotic associate priest precisely what he thinks, sending him packing. And worst of all, his dog dies—murdered, by whom we're never told. All this before the date on Sunday with the would-be murderer.

Life in the parish is not normally this apocalyptically catastrophic. The film is trying to show that human beings can be horrible to one another in a compressed timeline. And yet, for all this, the movie hints that grace is more powerful than the misery we inflict on one another. The film ends with Father James's daughter visiting his murderer in prison. Her face suggests she's about to offer the murderer the sort of unmerited forgiveness that marked her father's life. Why else would she be there? But the camera breaks away before she forgives him—as if to suggest that depicting her offer of forgiveness would necessarily render it cheaply won. Grace, at the movie's crescendo, is only alluded to, not made explicit. The daughter's tears are the last thing we see.

Now, here's the question: Would anyone expect Father James to have a positive outlook on life? He's certainly high energy! No sluggishness is obvious. He's fully alive, as one often is at the precipice overlooking death. But he's not happy about where his life is headed. He loves life, he loves God, he wants to see people be healthy and considerate of one another. And when we are not, God suffers. The priest lives the way of Calvary—that is, the place where Jesus dies. When God lives the perfect human life among us, he is strung up on a torture device and dies naked before the world. For God incarnate, all is not right with the world.

And yet the data that Rae Jean presents here is clear and impressive. People with positive mental health live happier, healthier lives. And positive mental health exists on a different continuum from depression, anxiety, and other mental illnesses. One can languish in positive mental health and not be depressed. And one can be depressed but have the kind of thick network of friends and meaningful work that make life worth living. This is a wise set of observations for how we contribute to the fully alive life that Christ desires for all his people, pastors included.

And yet I struggle with the material in this chapter for reasons illustrated by the film above. Would we even think to use registries of depression or positive mental health to describe Father James? They seem limp somehow. Would we think to use them when discussing Jesus and his first disciples? Jesus's most famous sermon brims over with promises of blessing now, in this life, for all kinds of folks normally called anything but blessed: the poor, the meek, the persecuted. One would worry if Father James had positive mental health or anything but depression filling his ghastly final week.

And yet, as ever, there is something to Rae Jean and her colleagues' findings. I'm thinking of time spent with Chamber of Commerce–type professionals when I've been in parish ministry. I can assume these folks will be high-energy, pleasant, engaging. They'll often ask about my work, really listen, and more often than I would have thought, they turn up for church. Some even stay. By contrast, I think of gatherings of ministers who can be surly, mean, unpleasant. Give me Chamber of Commerce–style peppiness over the pastor gathering any day.

Further, I'm sure Rae Jean is right about the beneficent spiral—that over time, positive mental health accrues more benefits and even provides an evolutionary advantage (I'm hoping my great-great-great-grandchildren times one thousand thank me one day). It can make you open to new ideas from surprising places. It connects you with other people, perhaps unlikely people on face value, people who in turn make for more job opportunities and greater happiness. I see this spiral at work in flourishing pastors. They're well-connected, integrated into their communities, and engaged with others. People want to do things for people like that. You'd turn up to hear them preach from the phone book in Pig Latin. You'd join their committees and invite your friends to come to their church. I believe that churches are meant to grow and flourish and that life in Christ is the fullest life for all. And you rarely see a depressed pastor leading a vibrant church. According to Rae Jean's data, it *could* happen—one could be depressed and also have positive mental health after all. I've just not seen it.

And yet, and yet, and yet. Think with me for a moment of the American civil rights movement. How would its leaders respond to the Mental Health Continuum, Short Form? I'd love to know how the social well-being questions would be answered by Martin Luther King Jr., Rosa Parks, Bob Moses, and friends. How do you respond to a question about whether "society is a good place, or becoming a better place, for all people"? When John Lewis endured a beating to within an inch of his life on the Edmund Pettus Bridge in Selma, how would he answer that question? What degree of social well-being would there be in answering the question of whether "our society is basically good" when you're Medgar Evers, gunned down in your Mississippi driveway in 1962 for agitating for voting rights?[55] Or think about later emulators of the civil rights movement who have engaged in people's revolutions for things like gay and lesbian rights or the anti-Apartheid movement, or think of the Velvet Revolution in Eastern Europe, the uprising in Tiananmen Square, or advocates of Black Lives Matter today. Think of the look you'd get if you asked such freedom fighters whether "people are basically good."

This is a harder set of questions than it seems. I don't think social justice warriors would simply answer no. Often the camaraderie between social justice warriors can make for some of the happiest times of their lives. The war veterans I've known say something similar when they look back over their time in combat. They feel full of meaning and purpose as they face dogs or hoses or tanks or worse. And these people's movements share a sense of togetherness that bystanders who aren't involved in or even sympathetic with the struggle, watching on TV at home or otherwise from the sidelines, will see their demonstration and have their sympathy tilted against the billy club wielders and for the peaceful protestors. Civil rights protests in the United States were quite carefully aimed at communities where law enforcement would overreact—especially toward children—as in Bull Connor's Birmingham, so that the basic human sympathy in other Americans' hearts would be outraged and the tide turned.[56] Even in the darkest days of segregation, freedom fighters could manage to appeal to the basic goodness in otherwise not-obviously-nonracist Americans' hearts. Even a hard-right reactionary doesn't want to see dogs turned loose on children. And these uprisings resulted in good for oppressed peoples and for society as a whole—eventually (James 1:2–3).

John Hope Franklin was an eminent scholar of African American history at Duke. At his memorial, President Bill Clinton called him "a genius in being a passionate rationalist, an angry happy man, a happy angry man."[57] He was, in the language we've been using in this book, a human being fully alive. I'm not sure how he'd respond if asked, or even whether I'd want to ask him, whether he "liked all parts of his personality."

55. As ever, Lewis's own words are more apt than mine. In a recent podcast with Krista Tippett, Congressman Lewis said this: "The movement created what I like to call a nonviolent revolution. It was love at its best. It's the highest form of love. That you beat me, you arrest me, you take me to jail, you almost kill me, but in spite of that, I'm gonna still love you." J. Lewis, interview by K. Tippett, "Love in Action."
56. "Freedom Has Come to Birmingham."
57. Jarmul, "Franklin Celebration."

Perhaps there is a joy in sacrificing for justice that is deeper than mere happiness. This kind of sacrifice includes happiness—those suffering would be glad to enjoy the world for which they labor—but until it comes, they're happy (!) to bear their cross.

Intervention Implications

We devoted an entire chapter to depression in clergy. Depression and anxiety are important to address, often through treatment. One interesting thing that the current chapter highlights is that pastors can be depressed or anxious and simultaneously have some degree of positive mental health. Maintaining strong social relationships and meaning in life is especially important when experiencing difficulties. People who have positive mental health—even when experiencing some kind of mental illness—do better than those who don't. Having positive mental health helps them do better at work, prevents future physical illness, and keeps their closest relationships strong, even while they struggle with depression, anxiety, or other mental illness. For this reason, it's important to attend to positive mental health even when someone has a mental illness.

So how can we promote positive mental health in pastors and others who desire to flourish and thrive, no matter their context? Understanding the broaden and build theory, positive emotions, and deeper life satisfaction will help. In the next chapter, we'll look at what we know about the behaviors, attitudes, and ministry conditions of flourishing pastors.

7

Clergy Flourishing

In Their Own Words

If I had to just summarize in a nutshell what I've said, I think that expectations, yours and theirs, are crucial to overall clergy health. . . . They're crucial to maintain a close relationship with God because after everybody else is mad at you and abandons you—even your own family—God is not going to, so you've always got . . . to keep that relationship nourished. That's really important. And take care of yourself because, as a caretaker, you cannot take care of others if you're not taking care of yourself.

From an interview with a flourishing pastor

If our findings have struck a chord with you, you might be thinking, "Sure, this all sounds lovely. Who wouldn't like to have high positive mental health, which can prevent depression and physical illness? But it is all so much easier said than done."

And you are right! So our team conducted an in-depth, qualitative study comparing pastors with flourishing positive mental health to pastors with low mental health and burnout.[1] We got as specific as possible in order to

---

1. We conducted qualitative interviews with fifty-two church-appointed pastors who, on an initial survey, scored as having either (1) high positive mental health (flourishers, of whom there were thirty-four) or (2) low mental health, experienced as both work-related burnout and lower levels of positive emotions, social connection, and meaning (there were eighteen in the low mental health group). We sought to create two groups of pastors who had very different levels of mental health. Each pastor in both groups participated in one or two in-depth

determine how the flourishing pastors maintained positive mental health. Some of the strategies we report here are going to seem like "no-brainers." It's true that there's a lot of common sense in here. But because our findings are from a systematic study of what differentiated pastors with flourishing mental health from those with low mental health, these strategies hold more weight than any you hear recommended, say, on talk TV or in self-help magazines. They are strategies by clergy and for clergy, and they come not just from pastors who *seem* like they might be doing well but from pastors whose surveys, diaries, and interview data all align to indicate that they do, in fact, have flourishing mental health.

It is time now to get to recommendations. Ready? Go watch a penguin video to open your mind, and then we'll dig in!

Relationships

A great strategy to maintain positive mental health is to foster strong friendships and relationships with partners, spouses, and family members. We found that pastors with flourishing mental health were more likely to have strong relationships than pastors with low mental health.

Clergy are surrounded by people. However, we shouldn't confuse social interaction with supportive relationships. Clergy may interact with people all day, and they may frequently provide support to others, but that doesn't mean they're receiving support from others. Our survey data suggests that 23 percent of pastors "sometimes get the social and emotional support [they] need," while 6 percent "rarely" or "never" get it.

What are sources of emotional support for pastors? The most frequently mentioned sources were spouses, friends, and clergy colleagues. Several clergy indicated that drawing on close relationships was one of the key ways they coped with the demands of ministry. Friendships helped them air

"**My biggest thing** is having someone to be accountable to. . . . I have a best friend. Literally, they are my best friend because they don't take no stuff. . . . 'Did you do your exercises today?' We're both pastors, so we know the day-to-day stresses, and strains, and everything. We're able to relate [and] hold each other accountable."

interviews, completed a survey, and kept a diary for seven days. We looked across these data sources—especially in the diaries—to make sure the participants belonged in their flourishing or low mental health group. Although fifty-two participants may sound like a small number, it is a large number for a qualitative study. Andrew Case, a community psychologist, expertly led the extensive qualitative data analysis of this study. Case et al., "Attitudes and Behaviors" (forthcoming)."

their troubles, provided social connection, and even gave them someone to help make sure they adhered to their personal, nonministry goals, including health goals.

One particularly amazing study—not one that involves clergy but still worth mentioning here because there just isn't any other study like it—is the Grant Study, which began in 1938 and followed more than 260 Harvard graduates as well as a sample of low-income Boston teenagers until they died.[2] (You can't get more long-term than that.) In his prominent book on the study, *Aging Well*, George Vaillant describes how the people who had the most fulfilling lives when they were in their seventies had the most friendships then, as well as earlier in life.[3] Relationships are so powerful that this finding was true for both wealthy and poor people. Also, the people with the least fulfilling lives in their seventies were those who drank too much alcohol across their lives, but not because their alcohol use was harmful to their health. Rather, their alcohol use led to behaviors that pushed away those who provided support. (As a case in point, this study was able to tease apart which comes first—drinking or divorce—and determined that too much alcohol use causes people to get divorced and not that being divorced leads people to drink more.) This study and many others indicate that deep emotional relationships are crucial to physical health and joyful living later in life.

Participating in God's Work

Flourishing pastors were also distinguished from low mental health pastors in their orientation to ministry. Flourishing pastors spontaneously narrated their orientation to ministry as one in which they saw themselves as participants in "God's work." Clergy with this orientation understood God to be working through them. They focused on the *process* of working in alignment with God. They were less concerned about seeing the immediate results of ministry (e.g., the number of people in the pews) and more concerned about whether they were doing their best to work with God.

I had heard this way of thinking before—way back in 2008 during the very first clergy focus groups we held. Here is what one pastor said:

> We've been talking about things that we can do in establishing these boundaries and stuff. And this is something I've been struggling with this year. My wife

2. Stossel, "What Makes Us Happy."
3. Vaillant, *Aging Well*.

and I pulled back; our lives just got chaotic. And for us, we said every demand that comes our way—the children, the church, our finances—are legitimate, powerful needs in our life. And some of them still need to be dropped. And we're like, "Well, how do you decide that?" . . . What I'm trying to do this year is I need to know who I am. I can't establish boundaries unless I know who I am and what my purpose is in life. . . . Half the congregation says that means you work forty hours in the office. Other half says that means you work forty hours outside in the community. And they all have legitimate and valid hardships, but it really comes down to, What does God want me to do? I have a thousand different people telling me, "This is what/who you are as a pastor." . . . I've heard all these voices but I've never sat down and said, "God, who am I? What is my place? What am I supposed to do?" And I think it would be easier to establish boundaries and say no before yes.

And here's what another pastor said:

But it's taken me three years to come to that point. . . . I'm like, "Yeah! The heck with some of these folks." I'm going to have these people in any church I go in. Some are going to be more vocal than others or nastier than others, but they're everywhere. And the turning point for me was one of those [times at] three o'clock, four o'clock one morning, [when I'm] wide awake going, "Oh!" And couldn't switch my mind off and it was a really good prayer time with God. I finally sat down and got quiet and listened. "God, . . . let me know that I am on the right track." [Yet] God isn't going to say, "You're doing a really good job. Just keep at it." And the other ones . . . there's nothing I can do that will ever please them. . . . And that was a big turning point for me.

When asked how they structure their lives to try to keep God and the process of ministry at the center, flourishing pastors told us that they were always discerning; listening for God's voice is what it means to be a disciple.

So in a practical day-to-day way what does that look like? I think it begins in prayer and ends in prayer, following the promptings of the Holy Spirit. I can't express how many times in my life in ministry, both as just a person in Christ, but also as a pastor in Christ, that I felt like the Holy Spirit was saying you need to go speak to this person or you need to go visit this person or you need to just take some time to read the Bible or whatever. And then without fail, if I'm obedient to that voice, even if it's not like an audible voice, but if I'm obedient to that prompting, then it becomes clear why I need to do that.

They also said that they tried to remember who they serve.

I think in the end it's about remembering who we serve and who's the King of kings and the Lord of lords.

Finally, flourishing pastors reported reminding themselves that they are part of a process of working with God and are not privy to the full picture—they are missing information. One of the flourishers quoted the words of theologian Reinhold Niebuhr.

> Nothing that is worth doing can be achieved in our lifetime; therefore we must be saved by hope.
> Nothing which is true or beautiful or good makes complete sense in any immediate context of history; therefore we must be saved by faith.
> Nothing we do, however virtuous, can be accomplished alone; therefore we must be saved by love.
> No virtuous act is quite as virtuous from the standpoint of our friend or foe as it is from our standpoint. Therefore we must be saved by the final form of love which is forgiveness.[4]

Each of these approaches requires a nonsecular orientation to success and praise, so we asked the flourishers directly about those. One pastor stated, "I think that if your sense of partnership with God is authentic, if it is really not just a position that you take for survival but if it's authentic, . . . then the normal indicators of success are not significant. It just changes the entire paradigm." Another said that he tries not to work for praise, but rather to remain faithful to his ordination vows and work within a covenant with God.

Not relying on worldly sources of praise can indeed be hard. If possible, bringing your church into that same vision could make it easier to work in alignment with God. To that end, one flourisher said, "I always tell them we need to do what God is blessing and not ask God to bless what we're doing, and there it is in a nutshell. I think I should ask them to put that on my tombstone. The important thing is if this is something that God wants us to do, things will work and fall into place."

However, it may be uncommon to convince your parishioners to share your vision. I once had a long conversation with a pastor who felt strongly that church was more than a building, and yet his congregation was bent on trying to revitalize itself through an expensive building restoration project. He and his parishioners were at loggerheads for years, but he was sticking to working alongside God and not endorsing the more materialistic, human approach. I asked him how he managed to stay strong while enduring threats and anger

4. Niebuhr, *Irony of American History*, 63.

from parishioners. He said he met regularly with a small group of pastors who were also discerning God's will and often defying what parishioners most wanted. His mental health seemed strong.

As someone who isn't a pastor, it seems like "working in alignment with God" could get a little dicey as a strategy to protect your positive mental health. Where does working in alignment with God end and turning the work over to God begin? I can imagine a slippery slope in which I would give the work over to God too often. Yet from a secular perspective, working in alignment with God is similar to focusing on the mission of any organization, which is generally a good way to take heart in a job well done and not to become overextended. There's no better time in this book for Jason to walk into these deep theological waters.

Behind the Pulpit
"God, Here I Am"

"Here I am." In the orginal Hebrew, this is a way of saying, well, here I am. When God calls someone, they respond in this way—*here I am, Lord.* It's saying more than just "hey" or "what's up?" when we answer the phone. It's a way of saying, "I'm altogether present to you, God. Like the prophets of old, I am ready for your word. Even if it kills me, it'll make me more fully alive. And even if your people are as stubborn as you say, God, I'll serve and love them."

To respond with "here I am," we pastors can't hold anything back. The church is in a cosmic battle between Christ and his saints and the devil and his legions. And none of us can afford to participate with only half measures. That may sound overly dramatic, but hear me out.

One source of burnout I notice is the gap in expectations between what we thought we would be doing (taking part in God's saving of the world) and what we actually end up doing (filing reports worthy of the shredder). One defense mechanism we might employ against disappointment is that we don't throw our whole heart and soul into the thing. The church is so often disappointing! It can feel like we're ripping open our ribcage and offering our whole selves, only to have that whole self rejected—and for silly reasons (I don't like you, your hair, your jokes, etc.).

Let's be clear here: these things are not fair. I once asked a successful pastor what he noticed about other successful pastors, expecting an answer about leadership skills, tenacity, preaching, or something along those lines. He said, "They're tall." What? "Really—look who does well. They tower in the pulpit."

OK, but that excludes most human beings, let alone most ministers. And more importantly . . . who cares?! I fear he's right. Not necessarily about height (I recently heard Eugene Cho absolutely burn a pulpit down at a mere five feet and change), but about the sine qua non. Folks judge us on stupid stuff we can't control. Some little Podunk church has heard tales of congregations growing by leaps and bounds. All they need, they think, is a charismatic young (and, let's be honest, also white, male, and heterosexual) preacher. Instead they get a second-career female caring for an aging parent with seminary debt and stress. They're disappointed. She can tell and she's nervous. She's newly transplanted, away from friends and familiarity, and she doesn't thrive. The parishioners blame her, the denomination—anybody but themselves and their town—for not growing. A world still sexist and structured to benefit white males receives no blame; the pastor blames herself, and everybody suffers. Many of these factors are out of the control of the pastor and the parishioners. There is no clear fault to assign; a path forward seems challenging at best.

In one of Jesus's wildest parables, he compares the kingdom to laborers picked up to work at all hours of the day (Matt. 20:1–16). The ones who work an hour are given a day's wage. The ones who work all day expect ten times as much, but they also get the same amount. The employer is fair to them. He's just exceedingly generous to the ones who worked less. In other words, God is fair at the end of all things. And God is generous far beyond fairness. When God takes stock of all things, God will be generous far beyond what we were able to muster workwise. God doesn't count those as more blessed who were given a great deal to work with (on the contrary, God seems to hold them especially responsible). The gospel is replete with stories of God tending to tiny acts of faithfulness: a mustard seed, a little coin, an overlooked widow, the hairs on our heads. God regards every ounce of energy we expend and blesses it abundantly. We're not only blessed if we're growing a church by being tall. On the contrary, God has a soft spot for those who are failing, losing, trying, and considered by the world to be of no account. It's why God choses Israel, Jesus, the church, and you and me.

So we can't hold anything back. Our leadership may indeed fail. Parishioners may not like us. We may lead the congregation in the wrong direction. Stuff outside of our control will happen—a key employer in town closes its doors, a crucial leader dies or moves, or a better, cooler church opens up within hailing distance and steals all the young people. The world is in constant, chaotic motion, and if we try stand still or stay the same, things will continue to change all around us and we'll be left behind. So, yes, we may fail. But we must not fail because we did not try our best. If we threw everything at it—every ounce of energy into sermon prep, every inch of imagination into creative leadership, every iota of love into every difficult relationship—if we did all that and it still comes unraveled, we can look at ourselves in the mirror. More importantly, we can face God at the judgment. We didn't hold anything back. We gave it everything we had. And if that wasn't good enough, well, there was nothing more we could do. And here's the amazing thing: we'll find that energy is like manna. If we try to preserve it, it'll rot. If we spend it, it'll renew itself. I can't explain that or prove it; it just seems to be so.

And I don't mean we need to burn ourselves up. We don't have to destroy ourselves to save the church. Only God can do that. So keep a Sabbath, grow your friendships, throw yourself into a hobby with joy, count as God counts (not people in the seats but more interesting things—say, little girls whose eyes light up, old men who dream dreams). God is no taskmaster who demands a pound of flesh. God delights in saving the world and asks for your deepest delight too. We minister best when we're as God intends all human beings to be—fully alive.

And surprising opportunities may open up. The single, female pastor imagined above is leading mostly single women who are themselves caring for difficult family members. These women are at once similar and dissimilar, and beneath the dissimilarity is possible empathy, friendship, and love. The reason she went into ministry in the first place is because of her best friend, Jesus, who is close to the poor and brokenhearted. He's given us Scripture to feast on and to feed our people. He is indiscriminate about who he calls and sends. And he has a soft spot for nowhere places and dead-end endeavors. Churches there don't have to thrive by leaps and bounds. They can thrive by tiny steps of faithfulness and kindness. And she can do that. Churches can get past their initial misgivings and grow despite themselves.

And nobody has to be tall for it to work.

Boundaries

In expounding on what it means to work in alignment with God, Jason references the tension between giving the church your all and yet trusting that God will save the world without you having to run yourself into the ground. This tension was very much on the minds of the pastors we interviewed. From the church-appointed pastors with flourishing mental health, we overwhelmingly heard about the importance of creating boundaries between their work and other parts of their lives. About two-thirds of the clergy we interviewed with flourishing mental health, compared to only one-third of the clergy with burnout and low mental health, practiced this bounded orientation to ministry. These boundaries included setting expectations with the church—for example, agreeing that the pastor will keep a weekly Sabbath, take annual vacation time, or go on a sabbatical. Other ways of creating boundaries that pastors described included setting specific office hours, letting others know he or she will not take calls during a specific time of day (e.g., the dinner hour), and promoting privacy in the parsonage (see table 7.1, for Jason's thoughts and some quotations from flourishing pastors). Some pastors set boundaries by delineating their roles and responsibilities from those of lay leaders and staff or by opting not to attend certain committee meetings, especially when lay leaders could be responsible (see table 7.2).

"I think that it's important for a new pastor to go into their [personnel committee] first of all and ask . . . what are the three most important [things to them that a pastor does], and then to ask [them] how they keep the Sabbath and say, this is how I keep the Sabbath. . . . I think from the very beginning that lays down the boundaries and says 'this is what I do to keep close to God,' and I think they'll honor that."

Table 7.1 Planning Daily Life in Ministry

Suggestions from Flourishing Pastors	Action Steps
1. *Arrange your schedule in a way that works for you.* Being overwhelmed by your calendar is a choice. So is choosing to do what matters first.	• Schedule things in lumps so that you have back-to-back meetings, thus protecting a block of time for either family or non–meeting work. • Schedule evening meetings all on the same night so that only one night is taken up by church-related issues.
2. *Manage your phone and email; don't let them manage you.* We didn't go into ministry to check email all day, did we? The best ministers are out in the community, reaching new people, advocating for justice, praying, tending the flock. This is no desk job.	• Don't look at email on your day off (although you may have to look at the subject line of emails to determine whether there is an emergency). • Ask others to text you if there is an emergency so there is no real need to look at email. • Do not talk on or look at your phone while exercising. • Turn your phone off at night. • Don't read email right before bed. • Don't read anonymous emails or letters or respond to gossip.
3. *Give yourself permission to take care of yourself.* No one else is going to give it to you! Schedule time for yourself during the day (checking Facebook doesn't count).	• "So just try to look at the day as a whole and say, OK, I've only got a limited amount of personal energy, where is that energy going to be best applied? And if I feel like I need to spend time talking with my wife and eating lunch with her, then I arrange my day so that I can do that. If I feel like I just need to spend time with a book or walk or go to the gym and work out, then I don't beat myself up over blocking out those hours to do that, because it would be so easy just to go all day [and] be completely exhausted at the end of the day."

Suggestions from Flourishing Pastors	Action Steps
4. *Create routines, especially morning spiritual devotion routines.* Most flourishers set aside time for spiritual activities, and many carved out this time first thing in the morning, perhaps out of practicality, but also to start the day reaffirming their identities as beloved children of God. It may not always be possible to keep to a morning routine. Some flourishers talked about proactively looking at the week ahead and making a plan so some of these priorities don't get lost in work.	• "That's a focal point of my life, in terms of having a God view of things. . . . Instead of me waking up in the morning with my own agenda, just allowing the Word of God to wash over me and refocus my heart on the things of God and the way God looks at the world." • "I am an introvert . . . but I have to balance all the putting myself out with a lot of quiet time, and I think this is when it has worked best for me in the morning. . . . It's just me and God, and you do your Scripture reading, you do your prayers, you do your sacred reading, not always studying for a sermon." • "Every week plan: where's my downtime, where's my exercise time, where's my . . . personal spiritual growth time apart from sermon preparation?"

Table 7.2 Mutual Submission: Answering to Your Personnel Committee

Suggestions from Flourishing Pastors	Pastor Quotations and Action Steps
1. *Get clear on expectations.* Discuss the expectations of the pastor's commitments with lay leaders and personnel committee members. This can include personal needs like commuting and caring for family.	• "I can't be at everything and do everything. And if that is the expectation, then you're going to limit the growth and the ability of this church to do what God's called them to do based on that pastor's individual personal energy. So I try to do what I think are the important things."
2. *Talk with lay leaders about the need for clear and direct communication.* How we communicate is crucial. You want feedback. But you want to be affirmed too. Say as much. They want you to be better and the church to be better and they don't want to be mean. When this communication channel is clogged, the sewage will come out in some less healthy way.	• "I really like for us to operate under the auspices of Matthew chapter 18. If you have a concern with me or with anybody else, go one-on-one to that person and try to work it out and don't run around and tell everybody else what your gripe or grumble is. Try to create an environment of direct communication and good communication. We're in this together as a part of a team. And I'm not perfect and you're not perfect; we're moving on to perfection, and one of the ways we do that is by respecting each other and caring enough about each other to speak the truth in love."
3. *Communicate your schedule to others.* Don't be shy about Sabbath and sermon prep and vacation—announce it. They'll be proud of it and pray for you.	• Schedule your vacation days in advance. • Use a calendar that all can see and put on it time for prayer and sermon prep and Sabbath. • If you are serving a larger church, ask your assistant and staff to put the pastor's scheduled time off on their calendars.

In contrast, two-thirds of the pastors with low mental health gave a narrative consistent with having ill-defined boundaries. Pastors experiencing ill-defined boundaries said things like,

> My life is more likely out of balance. . . . It looks like working a lot, taking work home with me. Even when I'm at home, I'm sitting on the couch doing some paperwork on the computer. . . . I think one of the huge difficulties is turning it off, setting boundaries so that the other things in my life are addressed appropriately, like family relationships.

Pastors with low mental health were often experiencing difficult and time-consuming circumstances, such as caring for sick loved ones. Trying to balance work and family is especially hard at those times, as is discerning which boundaries to keep when one's attention might be shifting to family during work hours. Even in the absence of extra caregiving responsibilities, pastors with low mental health were more likely to report working a lot at home and having a hard time "disconnecting" from work when spending time with their families.

Of course, when considering boundaries, it's important to acknowledge that individual churches are different, and the demands a pastor experiences at any one church differ. It may be that having a very demanding appointment leads to burnout and that burnout can't be avoided even while having excellent boundaries and preserving time for family and nonwork pursuits. But for churches that aren't downright toxic, flourishing pastors deemed personal time to be a regular antidote to burnout. It may be that flourishing pastors have lives so rich in people and activities that preserving personal time isn't a struggle. They may be so eager to go on that family reunion and hike that mountain and see that play that their attitude is less one of "protecting their time" and more one of "living into the joys of their life." As seen in table 7.3, to help us live fully, God asks us for—nay, *gives* us—one day per week.

Realizing that protecting your time off may come with uncomfortable consequences, we asked the flourishers: What do you tell yourself when your boundary upsets someone? Flourishers said they reminded themselves that they had been proactive and had prayed on it, that people were typically more frustrated than upset, that they were engaging in direct communication about it, and that, when looking at the big picture, it would be OK. Here are their own words:

> My feeling is that church folk are probably more reasonable than I have given them credit for through the years, and that if I had just been wise enough to engage them in that conversation, I would have found more support early on and perhaps been more comfortable.

Table 7.3 God Asks Us for One Day Per Week

Suggestions from Flourishing Pastors	Pastor Quotations and Action Steps
1. *Set aside a day and keep it holy.* God asks us for one day per week. Keeping a weekly Sabbath was far and away the most frequent suggestion made by flourishers. Some flourishers only mentioned a "day off," but more indicated keeping a Sabbath with both spiritual and relaxing activities.	"I preached on Sabbath-keeping and I let them know that my Sabbath starts after church on Sunday and goes until after lunch on Monday, so they're pretty good about not—well, they're just good about not bugging me anyway."
2. *Model for others taking your own Sabbath or day off and respect theirs.* This is important to demonstrate for the benefit of fellow clergy and for lay people who are watching.	"Consistency. It was like discipline with children being consistent, and truly . . . about trying to model [my day off] for others as well. [Otherwise] . . . it's kind of like saying, well it must be OK to break her [Sabbath]."
3. *Get outside.* The outdoors is more than "nature." It is creation. God loves it. You will too.	Several flourishers spontaneously mentioned that going outside helps. There is ample research showing that time in nature is good for your mental health. Pastors talked about gardening, bird watching, and walking. But you don't need an outdoor hobby to go outside and breathe.

I have to keep reminding myself that I had given care . . . that it felt right in my spirit, that God was saying it was OK. . . . And I do remember having a conversation with them saying, I'm really sorry that you were upset, but this is important for me to have been caring like I did, and to continue to care and all to do what's here, I really need this time. And I flat-out asked them, what would you have needed me to do that I didn't do in the phone call with you? And they really couldn't say. . . . But I always offer an apology for expectations that they have and try to balance it out.

I basically say that I'm looking at the big picture and I have set my standards and I'm living by those standards because they are the right standards. And I confirmed those kinds of standards with the other pastors and with other lay people whom I trust.

It's kind of like I'm not there for the praise of people, I'm there to be true to the calling that God has in my life and the life of that congregation that God has called me to serve and lead.

Why is this personal time so important? I suspect that having more personal time explains two other differences that we found between pastors with flourishing versus low mental health. These differences are (1) having close relationships (described above) and (2) proactively making time for exercise and personal care, which we'll explore more in the next section.

Healthy Behaviors

The vast majority of pastors with flourishing mental health, compared to only about half of those with burnout, expressed intentionality in personal care. The personal care that flourishing pastors described included things like physical activities (exercise), spiritual practices (like prayer or Bible reading), relational activities (such as spending time with friends and family), and recreational activities (hobbies like fishing or hiking).

These activities could all be classified as "lifestyle activities." Roger Walsh is a psychiatrist who sought to identify evidence-based lifestyle changes that therapists could recommend to patients to treat mental health problems or promote positive mental health. He found extensive studies supporting eight kinds of activities that he dubbed "therapeutic lifestyle changes":

> "I learned pretty early on that personal care was essential and I just built it into my daily routine, and I'm pretty habitual and methodical about it."

1. Exercise
2. Nutrition and diet
3. Spending time in nature
4. Relationships
5. Recreation and enjoyable activities
6. Relaxation and stress management
7. Contribution and service
8. Religious and spiritual involvement[5]

In our Spirited Life holistic health intervention for clergy, we offered small grants of $500 for clergy to spend on any of these eight lifestyle activities.[6] These activities are powerful approaches to mental health with solid evidence bases and are so well proven that they can be considered active ingredients in promoting positive mental health. However, seeing this list of eight activities prompts the multitasker in me to ask, what would happen if you tapped into more than one lifestyle activity at the same time? Perhaps there would be some amazing and efficient benefit to exercising, in nature, with a friend.

Given the extensive research on beneficial lifestyle activities in nonclergy, it really isn't surprising that clergy with flourishing mental health spontaneously mentioned spending time on four of these activities: relationships (which came

5. Walsh, "Lifestyle and Mental Health."
6. Proeschold-Bell et al., "Randomized Multiple Baseline Design."

up very strongly, as noted above), exercise, spiritual activities, and recreation. Perhaps if we had specifically asked pastors about the other four areas, like spending time in nature, they would have endorsed those as well.

Part of what is so interesting about pastors is that the very nature of their work already has them tap into three lifestyle activities: religious involvement, contribution and service, and relationships. However, compared to laity, pastors may miss out on some of the mental health benefits these activities tend to bestow. First, take religious involvement. Much of the research on the health benefits of religious involvement point to the calming and meditative effects of prayer or the support that parishioners give to each other.[7] Yet, if you're the pastor, leading a congregation in prayer may require an active kind of energy (How am I performing? What are my parishioners thinking?). Because of this, prayer may lack an experience of contemplation or meditation for those who are leading it. Hopefully leading a service is still energizing for pastors—or else they may be in the wrong line of work! But for pastors serving in churches with conflict and harsh criticism going on, leading services may be far from calming. In another example, Bible reading may be done in preparation for a sermon but take on a different feeling than turning to the Bible for personal reasons only. As for relationships, as noted earlier, my guess is that the experience of support looks different for pastors than it does for parishioners.

So religious involvement for clergy may or may not bestow the same degree of mental health benefit that it does for laity. What about contribution and service? Roger Walsh talks about the "helper's high" that people engaged in altruistic acts can feel.[8] Others have written about meaning making and how it can promote positive mental health. I believe that clergy can experience a mental health benefit from contribution and service, but maybe not all clergy do, depending on their perspective. I imagine that some clergy enter the pastorate hoping that 80 percent or more of their time will be filled with serving others and meaning making, but if their work falls shy of this 80 percent, some may suffer from disappointment. This is not a new phenomenon for clergy. In a 1956 study of 690 Protestant parish clergy, the clergy ranked administrative tasks as least important and least enjoyable out of several pastor roles, and yet in logging their time, those administrative tasks consumed more minutes per day than any other role.[9] For other workers, though, perceptions of contribution and service may be different. Construction workers who volunteer once a month at Habitat for Humanity may have lower expectations of how

7. Koenig, McCullough, and Larson, *Handbook of Religion and Health*; Powell, Shahabi, and Thoresen, "Religion and Spirituality."

8. Walsh, "Lifestyle and Mental Health," 588.

9. Blizzard, "Minister's Dilemma."

much of their time needs to be spent in contribution and service in order to be valuable and may experience a mental health boost from the meaning that comes with relatively few volunteer hours. Although I don't know that this is true, I wonder whether pastors with flourishing mental health are more accepting of the low-meaning paperwork and activities that can come with being a pastor, while pastors with burnout are more frustrated by such work. Pastors are very willing to work; the problem may be linked to their expectations of what their work will look like.

Alternatively, it may not always be the content of the work itself but rather the expectations of the process for how the pastors and the parishioners will do it. If the parishioners expect that the pastor will do the work alone, that may be draining indeed. Flourishers indicated that ideally, church work is the work of the whole church body. As one flourisher put it,

> doing church as a team is really important. A lot of smaller churches, when you're first starting out, look to the young, energetic pastor to be the savior. . . . A leader makes a big difference, but that impact is multiplied if other leaders come alongside and it becomes a team effort.

Sometimes ministry work can be great and even rejuvenating for pastors, when the whole church is working as a team. However, everyone needs a break sometimes, even when their work is amazing. Pastors need to protect some time for themselves to engage in the kinds of therapeutic lifestyle activities outlined here. From research involving eight kinds of activities, we know that there are lots of helpful (and even inexpensive) options to choose from. Individual pastors can choose for themselves the activities that interest them the most, and across the board with these activities, pastors are likely to experience a positive mental health benefit.

So what strategies do flourishing pastors use to help them enact healthy behaviors? Flourishers pointed to an interesting mix of routine and flexibility—but the flexibility required planning. They also reported incorporating their own interests in church and finding a kind of exercise they could get used to. (For details, see table 7.4.)

Table 7.4 A Fully Alive You

Suggestions from Flourishing Pastors	Pastor Quotations and Action Steps
1. *Pay attention to your body.* Your body talks to you. Listen. God loves bodies enough to become one—take care of your only and precious one.	• Notice when you are experiencing muscle tension, aches, and fatigue, and then take time out or go to the doctor. • Ask friends to help you exercise, eat right, and sleep enough.

continued on next page

Suggestions from Flourishing Pastors	Pastor Quotations and Action Steps
2. *You don't have to eat it.* You don't have to sample every food item in the potluck line, even if it was made out of love. Try one parishioner's dessert this time, another next time—don't worry, you'll get around to everyone, one at a time!	• "There is something to accepting people's hospitality with them in their homes and sharing their meals, but that doesn't mean you've got to eat and eat and eat. . . . A lot of pastors are overweight or even obese, and so if you're . . . not yet there, then it's a whole lot easier to adopt practices now that will lead you to health than it is to get it out of hand and then try to rein it back in."
3. *Find a form of exercise that suits you.* Half of the flourishers spontaneously brought up exercise: find an exercise buddy, walk places, or take the stairs. Many mentioned pedometers and walking programs, which allow for flexibility during the day and encourage membership in a social group—like "walking to Jerusalem together" or competing to outpace each other. Don't feel guilty about exercise. It makes you a better pastor. And person.	• "So this is the very best thing happening to me lately. . . . I sync this thing [pedometer] every night—every night. And it enables me to engage other people and it pushes me out of my house on cold evenings to walk four or five miles. It's incredible. And I'm probably healthier from a mental health perspective now than I have been in a long, long time because of that exercise program." • "I even tell people the reason I do this is for my mental and physical and spiritual sanity. I want to be a great pastor for you."
4. *Combine interests with church mission.* We noticed a theme of combining a personal interest with church work. Flourishers discussed starting church walking programs or turning a love of gardening into content for sermons and church projects.	• "Everywhere I've ever been, I've gardened. And . . . then talk about it on Sunday—to talk about cultivating and pulling weeds as a therapeutic activity, and [about how] sometimes in our congregations we cannot weed out difficult challenges, but at least I can in my garden. And so all of that just works together for me."

Behind the Pulpit
Work Hard, Play Hard

It doesn't surprise me at all that Rae Jean's flourishers are people with strong boundaries. They know how to work hard and how to play hard. They have relational support that goes beyond small talk. They pray and rest and play. In other words, they're fully human. Others want to follow and be with someone like that. And when they point somewhere else, as preachers point to Jesus, others look in the direction they're pointing. And walk. Of course, as a pastor, it can be discouraging to be shown a portrait of another pastor and be told, "Here, be more like that person." But these are practices one can engage in, one at a time, however haltingly, that will make for greater health and wholeness, more of a self to offer God and others.

The primary agent in the coming kingdom and the renewal of the world is God. This divine agency explains why we should take a Sabbath. If God could take a rest after the six days of creation, then surely even as fragile as our churches seem, they won't fall apart if we take a day off, take a nap, look our spouse in the eye, ask our kids how their day was and really listen, or do something simply for sheer delight. Pharaoh's economy in Egypt included no rest for his Israelite slaves. So God's economy in Israel includes a Sabbath, not only for the Israelites, but for their animals and slaves, the resident aliens in their midst. The command to keep Sabbath (Exod. 20:8–11) was meant to be unmistakable: no one is indispensable, no one's work maintains the world's existence, not one of us can save the world by destroying ourselves. And as many have found, to rest one day is to make the other six more productive. Sabbath keepers don't do it for that reason necessarily, but it is a nice benefit.

Even so, I worry a little about setting forth our expectations of rest right out of the gate when beginning with a church. How do churches hear it if their pastors' first words are about *themselves*, their sabbatical, their family, their need for time off? A friend of mine was unemployed and fretting, but eager to hear from his new pastor, and more eager still to hear a word from the Lord on Sunday. And all he heard was about how the man was going to take time to get centered, to vacation, to pray . . . My friend was pleased for him, but thought, "Gosh, resting and praying are *all* I'm doing. I'd sure like to be working too." The enthusiasm for Sabbath can become a prophylactic against fear of failure. ("Sure, the church blew up, but I was doing centering prayer.") Rae Jean's findings suggest that boundaries are important. But when setting out these expectations with a church, it would be wise to lay out the passionate expectations too: "I will give your church my all; I will partner with you completely to do God's work and to do incredible things. And I have faith that we will work together, that I won't have to do this all alone. I have faith that we will both give the work our all and still be able to rest, so we can do God's work for the long haul."

Maybe it's just me, but I notice a temptation not to risk too much, especially if an institution's future doesn't look promising. That way if it fails, if *I* fail, there's a protected psychological space to fall back on. "Well, at least I didn't stick *my* neck all the way out because then I would have lost it, too." We may look for this protected space, especially if we're at cross-purposes with our congregation relationally or theologically. But think about it—who, on their deathbed, thanks God that they didn't try too hard? Who gives thanks at the end of life that they didn't risk too much? I noticed my own preaching took off when I started treating each sermon like it would be my last. If I knew I was going to drop dead on Monday, what would I say to my congregation on Sunday?

Ultimately, we pastors have to figure out how to work as though the result depends entirely on us. At the same time, we should work as if none of it depends on us. Because none of it does. This is God's world. God will finally save it all—down to every last particle of creation. God made the world in the first place and is currently redeeming it in Christ. And we, God's chosen coworkers, can't do a thing to stop God getting the world God wants. God will bring the kingdom whether we lift a finger to help or not. We can't stop it, slow it, hurry it, inaugurate it. All we can do is bear witness that God is bringing God's kingdom in God's own time.

Certainly we can make a total hash of our church. Many pastors have: we can drink on the job, make up sermons on the way from our pew to the pulpit, and neglect pastoral care and the care of our own and others' souls. And God will still bring the kingdom in God's own time. The tragedy would be then that God will work through someone else other than us. We won't get to take our full part in the world God is renewing. We won't be fully alive. But with God's kingdom, the victory is sure. Christ's resurrection shows that. Death is defeated. Now we get to take part in the full toppling of death that God will complete in God's own time.

Eugene Peterson wrote a marvelous essay on the psychology behind the pulpit titled "Teach Us to Care and Not to Care."[10] Everyone in the building, the preacher included, is a sinner. So our criticisms of the church and its preacher are wrapped up with our own sin. Folks have family issues. Folks are disappointed with God or their lives or who knows what. And they take it out on the church. Or, alternatively, folks are naturally spiritual. They're in touch with God. Their lives have turned out pretty well and they're thankful. They'll give you credit you don't deserve. We preachers would do well to get out of the way of both criticism and praise that comes our way. Much of it, maybe most of it, isn't about us. We don't have to fix people. We can't, in fact. Only God can, and God takes God's sweet time about it. Somehow we have to learn to care passionately about what matters—the beauty of the preached word, the sacraments elegantly administered, the neighborhood noticed and loved and entered into missionally. And we have to not care about what doesn't matter—the popularity contest, the gossip mill, folks' inaccurate expectations of us, our own inaccurate expectations of ourselves. As we seek to work in alignment with God, we might remember Peterson's caution that God only has sinners to work with. Our expectations and theirs will continually get out of alignment and hurt us and others.

Here's what Jesus does: he disentangles us from our sin, pries us loose, unraveling its hold on us. One day we will stand fully free of sin. For now, in certain moments freedom starts to emerge, and then it gets swallowed back up again. One day freedom will come in full. And again, we can't hurry or stop it.

10. In Peterson, *Subversive Spirituality*, 154–68.

God is so good and so powerful that God will do it, with or without our help, for us and for all creation.

Flourishing under Different Ministry Conditions

So far, I've talked about flourishing from the perspective of the attitudes and actions that pastors can take, and I've lumped together all pastors. I'm well aware, though, that the conditions of a pastor's appointment may make it easier or harder to experience positive mental health. For example, perhaps small or large churches make it easier for a pastor to flourish.

In this qualitative study, we tried to conduct enough interviews to check for differences among a few kinds of pastors and ministry conditions. Our work is ongoing, which is a way of saying it is incomplete. We haven't yet listened closely to all groups of clergy—not by a long shot—but we plan to continue the listening process. For now, table 7.5 shows the groups that were included in substantial numbers in our qualitative study on positive mental health.[11]

Number of Church Appointments

In the UMC system, a pastor can be appointed to one, two, three, or even four churches simultaneously. This is also increasingly true in Roman Catholic, Episcopal, and other settings that lack clergy sufficient for their ministries. Pastors serving just one church praised that system:

> It's nice not to have to get in the car and drive down the road on Sunday morning, fighting the traffic, [to get] to the next service . . . to be able to focus all of your energy on one community.

Pastors serving multiple churches were hard-pressed to find ways in which splitting their time between churches benefited their well-being. However, I

---

11. To understand differences in the ability to flourish in these groups, we used two approaches. First, we simply asked pastors about these conditions directly. For example, we asked short-tenure pastors questions like, "Are there conditions associated with having served in ministry fewer than seven years that promote your well-being?" This was a direct approach that relied on pastors having an insight they could articulate. We also used a comparative approach in which we looked for differences in the kinds of statements that pastors of different groups made throughout their entire interview. For example, we looked to see if flourishing pastors with shorter tenures in ministry *spontaneously* brought up different things that might support their well-being than did low mental health pastors with shorter tenures in ministry. Although this second approach is kind of sneaky, I like it because it's more likely to yield something unexpected. It's hard to articulate what you don't realize.

had to chuckle occasionally—by now you can predict that a flourisher will find *some* way to lend a positive spin! Here it is:

> It keeps me alert. . . . I have to write it on the calendar, what's going on at the different churches, but it just keeps you alert and you're dealing with a different group of people. None of them are the same.

Gender

While denominations can disagree over the validity of female ordination, we can't disagree over whether women were important leaders in the ancient church. "I have seen the Lord" is the first Christian sermon, preached by a woman—one Mary Magdalene. Some churches recognize the power in Mary's sermon by ordaining her female descendants. We haven't yet figured out all the challenges (we haven't even figured out the challenges inherent in ordaining *anybody* yet, as this book makes clear), but here is some of what we have found about the particular challenges of ordained female leadership.

Male and female pastors alike indicated that they thought female pastors face extra challenges in ministry. Although it is unfortunate that this was still the case in 2014, it was heartening that male pastors were unanimously attuned to discrepant treatment. Male pastors said things like,

> I don't have to deal with anyone sort of saying you're male so you're not perhaps called to this, which I know still happens quite frequently [for female clergy]. I probably don't reflect on that as much as I should.

The only specifically male barriers that some male pastors discussed were feeling like (1) some congregants assume that the male pastor knows everything and will lead in a "take charge" manner, and (2) female pastors may have an advantage in ministering to female congregants.

Female pastors reported gender-based challenges from every level, including colleagues (e.g., not being taken as seriously or respected), congregants (e.g., not being readily accepted and having to work harder to prove oneself), and families (e.g., balancing the roles of pastor, wife, and mother). Female pastors said things like these two participants:

> I think being a woman, I've always felt like I had to do more. I had to prove that I was better or as good [as male pastors]. . . . I have observed that there are still churches that will not accept a female pastor, or do not want a female pastor. Therefore, if you had any aspirations to have a larger church and be the pastor in charge, there would be roadblocks.

I'm also a wife and a mother and I'm still not used to having these multiple roles, and I don't think it's the same for a man. My husband is great. He does a lot, but I still feel like I can't just run off without having made arrangements for child care.

At the UMC conference level, female clergy indicated believing they received lower salaries and less favorable appointments. We checked into this using our survey data and controlled for factors such as number of years served in ministry and ordination status. We found that in 2014, female pastors were, in fact, disproportionately less likely to be serving mid-size churches. In terms of salary, it appeared initially that female clergy earned less than male clergy, but upon further analysis we found this discrepancy was driven entirely by associate pastors. While there was no salary difference by gender for solo and head pastors, female associate pastors earned on average 9 percent less than male associate pastors. However, many factors go into determining salaries, so we cannot be sure that we accounted for them all. Also, for men and women in the United States, the lower salaries for women are often explained by women having less access to the better paying jobs. We also see this happening in data on clergy, in which women are proportionally less likely to be head pastors of mid-size and larger churches.

In terms of advantages that female pastors may have, some female pastors indicated that pastoral care may come more naturally to them as a result of having been raised to be nurturing. Thus, they may be more able to minister to female congregants. One female pastor said, "I think that it's really easy for people to talk to a woman sometimes, and I think that because there tends to be a greater percentage of women in the church than men, they will sometimes relate to a woman better."

Some of the female pastors we interviewed had flourishing mental health and others had low mental health. Looking for differences between the groups, we found three areas that none of the flourishing female pastors mentioned, but that were commonly named by female pastors with low mental health. First, female pastors with low mental health did not feel supported by their congregants; some, but not all, believed this was due to their being female. Second, they lacked intimate, trusting friendships. Third, female pastors with low mental health experienced stressful personal circumstances, such as caring for ill relatives and balancing being a pastor, mother, and wife.

Female pastors may especially need safe opportunities to make and maintain friendships. Early in our work at the Clergy Health Initiative, we heard from female pastors that they feared "letting their slip show" (seriously, I couldn't make that up!), even to other female pastors, because they needed to maintain the image to *everyone* that female pastors are worthy of the job that many congregants still prefer for males. When there is stigma, it is harder to build and maintain emotional support, even among female pastors.

Denominational leaders need to take a strong stand to defend the abilities and desirability of female pastors. In an all-female pastor focus group we held in 2008, we heard things like,

> I think we, because we're women, we try so hard because, with the ordination of women being as young as it is still, you know, we go places where we're told. Every place I've been I've heard the comment, "Well, we were hoping it was going to be a man." Or, "We asked for a man.". . . And I think you try and compensate, you overcompensate for that. Because you are female, you think, "I've got to work four times harder."[12]

There's no easy answer for women—or men—when it comes to balancing all the roles they have and the important caregiving they do. The female pastors in our focus group were able to joke about it.

> I need a wife is what I need!

> Even in my secular job, [I always worried that] I wasn't doing enough. The guilt was there that I was not taking care of my family. I had to go out of town. And the pressure was constant. And I brought that over into ministry. And so I'm doing the same thing that I worry that . . . I'm not doing this, I'm not doing that. So, it's constant that I beat myself over the head. Is that more female than it is male? I've always been told it is. Do they hold it in? But I think, you know, when my husband comes home he just kind of shuts it off and he goes to bed at night and goes to sleep and I sit there and stare at the ceiling and worry about things. I "fret" about things. (I'm not supposed to worry so I changed it to another word!)

Despite this joking tenor, what these female pastors are saying is the same thing that has been found across occupations: women engage in substantial caregiving outside of work, and when the people they serve have extraordinarily high time expectations for them, their male counterparts are better able to bear up because they are doing less caregiving. This is a real struggle. Either female pastors need help for their family caregiving roles or congregants' time expectations need to be consistent with a forty-hour work week and not a fifty-five-hour work week.

In addition, it would be wonderful if male and female pastors alike could feel supported by their congregants and have the flexibility to fully participate

12. LeGrand et al., "Healthy Leaders."

in family life and not worry when spending time on family issues, such as picking up a sick child from school. For our ordained sisters, perhaps we can support them by encouraging their friendships and remembering the amount of caregiving they are likely doing outside of their work. How to do this is as varied as the variety of human beings; be on the lookout for opportunities.

Years in Ministry

When it came to interviewing pastors with shorter tenures in ministry, we did not interview any brand-new pastors. We made sure the pastors had served a church for at least three years because we wanted to give them a chance to become burned out (wasn't that kind of us?). We then compared answers from those with three to seven years in ministry with answers from those who had more than seven years in ministry.

When asked directly for insights, pastors didn't tell us anything unexpected. Being newer to ministry was seen as an advantage in terms of having more enthusiasm, having less cynicism, and offering a fresh perspective.

Those same short-tenure pastors said that they were disadvantaged by having less experience overall in facing the multifaceted work of being a pastor, and they pointed out that less experience could bring more stress.

> "I hear some cynical comments here and there, and some dissatisfaction from people who have been around awhile. So I think the fact that I'm in my eighth year of ministry now, being fairly new, does contribute to my well-being."

Pastors with longer tenures quickly pointed to how their years of experience helped their positive mental health, particularly if they accepted their strengths and weaknesses as a pastor, had a sense of competence, and knew how to handle a range of stressful occurrences based on prior experience. However, the pastors we interviewed who had served more than twenty-three years raised some issues that could undermine their well-being. These were difficulties in keeping up with changes in technology and culture and in coping with their own declining physical health.

We only interviewed eleven pastors who had short tenures, so you have to take the next findings with a grain of salt. Nevertheless, we found that short-tenure pastors with low mental health were more likely to report stress due to conflict and issues of fit in their current appointments than were short-tenure pastors with flourishing mental health. The pastors with low mental health also spontaneously said that they lacked close relationships with colleagues and congregants. One pastor reported that the generational gap between him and his much-older congregants made it extremely difficult to build relationships. Once again, emotional support emerged as important.

Young Pastors

In 2008, in addition to our focus groups with female pastors, we held a focus group with young pastors, which we defined as under age thirty-five. Throughout that focus group, we heard the pastors struggle to name who they turned to for emotional support and who they trusted.[13] They grappled with whether they should learn the lessons of ministry on their own or risk seeming inept with their supervisors in order to get support and make the process of becoming a skilled pastor less stressful.

> "Having served the variety of churches from [serving five small churches at once], to a suburban church, to an urban church . . . , I feel like I have lived the United Methodist career plan. And I think I have wisdom and experience that benefits my ministry, benefits my well-being, and benefits my congregation."

I'd like to suggest that expectations here could make a big difference. Clergy supervisors could set up expectations that ministry is difficult and that both struggle and mistakes are normal. No doubt many supervisors already do this, but from our data, it seems that young clergy resist this, perhaps placing on themselves the unrealistic expectation that they should be immediately and immaculately skilled and successful.

It would be wonderful, too, for people to enter the pastorate with close friends, perhaps friends made during seminary training or other ordination processes. I'm imagining friends who knew you before you were a pastor. There also needs to be a way for new pastors to maintain these friendships because let's face it: we are social beings whose lives are sustained by friendships. I think part of the problem is that we hold back from reaching out for support until we are hurting, and by then, we are completely overwhelmed. As humans, we need regular supportive interactions, period.

Church Size

We interviewed pastors serving churches with 50 or fewer parishioners in the pews on Sunday and those serving churches with more than 150 parishioners on Sunday. The pastors serving small churches indicated that their well-being was promoted by the opportunity to have frequent contact with the same parishioners and develop close relationships with them. It may be

---

13. LeGrand et al., "Healthy Leaders."

that pastors experience more meaning by knowing and giving direct pastoral care to individual parishioners, and this may be harder to do in large churches. However, the pastors serving small churches also said that disagreements among parishioners in small churches could lead to monumental rifts that could undermine a pastor's work and cause stress. They further noted that lack of privacy can be difficult when working in a small church.

> "I think it's the ability to know all the people—the intimacy. Yes, it's the people. The people contact. [It's good to be] able to have more people contact than I would in a larger church."

Pastors serving large churches said that having ample financial resources and more staff could benefit pastors' positive mental health by allowing them to direct ministry as they thought best and making it possible to delegate some tasks to staff and lay leaders. At the same time, pastors serving large churches indicated conditions that could detract from their well-being, which included multiple, competing visions for the church, a lack of cohesion among congregants, and exhaustion from attending a large number of activities and engaging with a number of people.

> "I would say that the benefit of it is you have a lot of people and a lot of resources. . . . When something breaks I don't [always] have to figure out how to fix it."

From the 2008 focus groups, we noticed something present only in the group with pastors serving large churches. Those pastors noted the importance of taking sabbaticals while acknowledging that asking for a sabbatical is controversial for many congregations.[14] They also discussed the importance of communicating with their district supervisors and bishops. Compared to other pastors, large church pastors were clearly comfortable with clergy in power, and they thought about how they could influence the denomination as a whole.

African American Clergy

Talking about race is never easy in America. We don't have a solution to problems that are at least four hundred years in the making. But we can report some data and some observations, and we are convinced that silence is more complicit in perpetuating racial inequality than speech is, however difficult.

In 2011, we held focus groups with African American clergy, who named two strategies for maintaining their mental health while facing the challenges of being both a pastor and an ethnic minority. In North Carolina, only

14. LeGrand et al., "Healthy Leaders."

6 percent of UMC pastors are African American.[15] The first mental health strategy African American clergy identified is going to sound familiar: talk with other African American clergy. However, accessing the support of other African American clergy is easier said than done because some areas of the state have relatively few African American UMC clergy. As one pastor shared,

> the saving grace of my current appointment is that there is a number of African American churches and clergy in [this] district, more so than in the other districts, and because of the camaraderie that has been nurtured among the African American pastors . . . I have colleagues that I can share things with, that I can express myself without it being held against me, that I can just let my hair down with. It has been a saving grace, because I have been in those appointments where there are only two or three African American churches and they don't get along. So they don't have any fellowship with one another and it makes you feel like you're out there by yourself.

Simultaneously, African American pastors told us that they sometimes feel the need to isolate themselves emotionally from other African American pastors because they are in competition for a small number of choice church appointments. In theory, pastors can be appointed to any church regardless of the race of the pastor or the racial makeup of the church. However, it is still the case that race is a key determining factor for placement, and for that reason African American pastors may limit the number of peers they turn to for support and what they tell them.

The second mental health strategy we heard from African American clergy distills down to accepting yourself. This strategy is consistent with the burgeoning literature on the benefits of self-acceptance.

African American clergy said it is important to be comfortable with themselves as individuals, including acceptance of their racial identity, in order to cope with discrimination. In the words of participants in two different focus groups,

> so I am what I am by the grace of God. . . . At some point you've got to be OK with you and what God has called you to do, and if you are not comfortable in your skin, then there's no win for you. You're going to be bounded not with others, but with yourself.

> When I was head of [an African American minister caucus] and people used to come in and talk about things that were going on . . . what I always told them

15. Johnson, "Female and Racial/Ethnic United Methodist Clergy," 15.

[was]: "Be who you are." And see, a lot of this stuff we can overcome if we know who we are. Yes . . . we've all been hurt by disappointments and we've all been hurt by not getting the right salary that we should—we were supposed to get, but that's all right too. You can get over it. You can adjust yourself and you can survive. Because why? We're black folk.

Clearly, these respondents acknowledge that the richness of black history provides significant coping resources in dealing with the challenges of being part of a disadvantaged minority.

As I relay these words of wisdom, I also recognize that they fall short of solving larger issues of structural racism and prejudice that continue in the United States. Much more work toward full inclusion is needed at breakneck speed. However, I want to highlight that having close professional relationships is universally important, and also that some African American pastors attribute their positive mental health in part to knowing their history and accepting themselves, even and especially in the face of structures stacked against them.

Ministry and Positive versus Negative Mental Health

I'd like to return to our survey data to give us a different kind of handle on ministry conditions and positive mental health. Using our statewide clergy survey data, we've been able to look at what relates to pastors' negative mental health—things like burnout, depression, and anxiety—and what relates to positive mental health—things like satisfaction with ministry, feelings of personal accomplishment at work, and quality of life (family, friends, neighborhood, hobbies, creativity, learning, etc.). We found some things that relate to *both* pastors' negative and positive mental health, and we found other things that relate only to pastors' positive mental health.[16]

The things that significantly related to both negative and positive mental health were

- social support ("How often do you get the social and emotional support you need?");
- social isolation ("How socially isolated do you feel?");
- financial stress ("How stressful is your current financial situation?"); and
- congregant demands ("During the past year, how often have the people in your congregation made too many demands on you?" or ". . . been critical of you and the things you have done?").

16. Proeschold-Bell et al., "Glory of God."

These relationships went in the directions you would expect. More social support related to better positive mental health and less negative mental health. Conversely, more social isolation and financial stress related to less positive mental health and more negative mental health. Higher congregant demands also related to less positive mental health and more negative mental health. Yet again, this time quantitatively, the importance of supportive relationships and the detriment of social isolation were apparent. Financial stress was also important to both kinds of mental health.

Many studies only measure depression and other kinds of negative mental health. I am glad we also measured some kinds of positive mental health.[17] Had we stuck with only negative mental health measures, we would have missed all the things that only related to positive mental health, which quite possibly serve to promote positive mental health.

One of the three things that related uniquely to more positive mental health was pastors reporting that their current parishioners were willing to change to meet new challenges, accept newcomers, and be a force for positive change in the community.[18] The second thing was pastors believing that their personal strengths and gifts were considered in the process of being appointed to a church (or churches). The third aspect was feeling supported as a person and not just as a pastor (e.g., "How often do people in your congregation make you feel loved and cared for?"). This is a really important point that pastors I've spoken with have brought up anecdotally time and again.

I once received a letter from a recently retired pastor who was reflecting back on his career. He said the most difficult time in his life was when his brother had a stroke. After giving his sermon on Sunday, he asked for prayers for his brother. After the service, no one said anything to him about his brother. A parishioner approached him later that week and asked for prayers for a family member who was having heart issues. The pastor prayed with him and then said, "You know, my brother is going through this too," to which the parishioner responded, "I know, Pastor. You said that earlier." And then he left without a word of kindness for the pastor or his brother. The problem wasn't that just that one parishioner didn't recognize the pastor's pain; it was that no parishioner at that church did, and this was in stark contrast to a church where he had previously served. Pastors appreciate having support for their work, but they can lose their sense of satisfaction

17. To be clear, in this study we did not use the Mental Health Continuum, Short Form, relying instead on other positive mental health measures like ministry satisfaction.
18. Proeschold-Bell et al., "Glory of God."

in ministry if there is not at least a little concern for them when they are experiencing something difficult in their personal life. I think everyone wants to be seen as a whole person, even if the expectation is that support extends from the pastor to the parishioners and generally not from the parishioners to the pastor.

These findings underscore the importance of how parishioners relate to pastors, as well as the church climate and the mindset of the parishioners toward people both within and outside the church. Improving positive mental health is not the responsibility of the pastor alone.

At the same time, from our interview data in the flourishing study, we concluded that there was no one single ministry condition that undermined positive mental health. It may be harder to maintain flourishing mental health when serving more than one church, but we found flourishing pastors who did just that. We did notice, though, that as the number of difficult conditions piled up (e.g., serving multiple churches, caring for a sick loved one, or serving a low-resource church), pastors were less likely to be flourishing.

So positive mental health is distinct from depression and mental illness, and when we start looking for the things that contribute to positive mental health, they seem to be different from the things that likely contribute to mental illness. If we want pastors to be fully alive and to experience the presence of positive mental health, then they—and we—need to attend to their positive mental health. This chapter includes many suggestions, and we hope that at least some of them are helpful. The big takeaway from the flourishers we interviewed was this: flourishers have many different strategies to maintain their positive mental health, and even within a given day, they are flexible in how they attend to their positive mental health.

Flourishers don't assume that anyone else will attend to their mental health. Once flourishers feel their energy drain, they intentionally do something to recharge in order to avoid downward spirals. They would never prescribe to you what you should do—they would tell you to be flexible and intentional and not to wait too long.

And they would say this: they were a creature before they were a pastor. They need to eat, sleep, play, befriend, be outside, exercise. They were a Christian before they were a pastor. Their baptism is the anchor of their identity, not any achievement or job status. And they are good at what they do. Not on their own, but because God has gifted and called them, the church has equipped and ordained them, and their work has borne fruit. Ultimately, that's not why they matter. They matter because God loved them into existence and saves them in Christ.

Parishioners can do a number of things to promote flourishing mental health in their pastors, including the following (suggestions from Jason):

- Pray for your pastor. Most pastors would rather have prayers than a heap of advice any day.
- If your pastor reveals that he or she is going through something difficult, follow up later by asking how he or she is doing.
- Ask your pastor about his or her hobbies, vacation plans, and so forth.
- Hear your pastor out before opposing a new idea. Change is intrinsically hard for humans, and our knee-jerk reaction is to want things to stay the same. Try to keep in mind that any new ideas your pastor has are well-intentioned and may turn out to be great. We all think we're more open to new ideas than we actually are. As an outsider and then a newcomer, your pastor can see things you can't. Listen. And remember: we don't actually fear change. We fear loss.
- Give serious thought to the mission of your church, and talk with your pastor about his or her thoughts on the church's mission and direction. Be sure to listen as well as talk!
- If your church's vision includes welcoming new people, be open to this and think of ways to implement it. Most of us believe we're better at welcoming newcomers than we actually are. At church, hold off talking to friends until you've greeted new people. Always.
- Bring your own skills and leadership to your church and give your pastor responsibility for the things your pastor is uniquely good at and qualified for.

Denominational officials can also take steps to promote the flourishing of the pastors they oversee, including the following:

- Pray for pastors. This is your primary job as you lead them.
- Be transparent about the appointment-making process for any given pastor; the process matters.
- Indicate your awareness of congregations that have become particularly critical or harmful. Support the pastor as needed.
- Provide financial counseling resources to clergy.
- Be aware of how many personal and church-related challenges a pastor is facing at once.* Try not to make appointments that overwhelm any given pastor and be especially cognizant of this with new pastors.

*We found that pastors with low mental health generally had several stressors, including caring for sick relatives, a history of depression, and working in a church that was a poor fit for them.

8

The Lord Bless You and Keep You

You've heard a lot from Jason and me, and we hope you'll remember a few things. We hope you'll remember that pastors need to be given permission on a regular basis to take care of themselves. If you're someone who supports pastors, you need to give them *repeated* permission to attend to their mental and physical health. Because most pastors live into their call so strongly that they prioritize everyone else above themselves, saying something about their health once a year simply won't be enough. If you're a pastor, you need to give yourself grace more often. If you're really tired and wondering whether you should work more or go to bed, don't wonder—just go to bed! Sleep will make you more effective tomorrow, and it will help both your mental and your physical health.

We hope you'll remember that pastors must be proactive in maintaining their weight. With only 21 percent of the pastors we surveyed having a normal weight, every pastor is at risk for being overweight or obese.[1] Proactively protecting your physical health, no matter where you're starting from, can help prevent problems with blood pressure, cholesterol, and diabetes, which are struggles for many pastors. If you're wondering whether you should work more or go for a walk, don't wonder—go for a walk! The evidence about above-average health problems in clergy more than justifies it, and it will help your mental health too.

To be fully alive, cultivate your whole life and not just your ministry life, although the two may overlap in delightful ways. Find what energizes you and

---

1. Proeschold-Bell and LeGrand, "High Rates of Chronic Disease."

build a life such that you can't *not* do it. Spend time in nature, organize and look forward to recurring events with friends, and don't fret about the time spent doing your favorite spiritual activity.

We hope you'll remember that there's no such thing as just "stress." Stress is a process. To handle it, you can seek out further resources (financial or otherwise) to make what's happening more manageable, or you can hone your coping skills. Alternatively, or even simultaneously, you can make an effort to change your viewpoint by deciding that rising to the challenge is so important and will result in so great a reward that the difficult process is worth it. The point of ministry is not to eliminate stress but to be present (without being debilitatingly overwhelmed) in the midst of it.

We hope you'll remember that, unfortunately, a great many pastors will experience depressive symptoms at some point during their ministerial career. Depressive symptoms are something to be concerned about and address, but they shouldn't make you worry whether the pastor (or you) will ever be a great pastor. Also, it's important to attend to your positive mental health. Positive mental health is different from mental illness, and it's universally important to have positive emotions, meaning in life, and close relationships.

We especially hope you'll remember to broaden and build.[2] Fostering positive emotions enhances creative decision-making. It makes you open to new ideas and experiences. It encourages you to spend time with new people. Experiencing positive emotions year in and year out gives you an advantage in building knowledge, skills, and friendships, until you end up blessed with resources to draw on in times of need and resources to share with others. Broadening and building will certainly help pastors maintain their positive mental health; it may also be good for their ministries and churches. You can make it work for you.

Behind the Pulpit
Plan Your Best Day in Ministry

It's instructive to ask folks what a day in the life of a pastor *ought* to look like. We're in the privileged place of getting paid to pray for people. So do it. Talk to God about your parishioners. Rather, talk to God *for* them. Meet with creative types in your community who can expand your ideas of how to be a church. Spend time with the vulnerable and marginalized—Christ is in them, and they will see things you cannot. Read. Not just Scripture but noteworthy books,

2. Fredrickson, "Role of Positive Emotions."

poems, biography, history, sociology—it's all sermon fodder. Go visit the parishioner who can't speak (whether because too young or too old or too sick).
All this will make you more like Jesus and more human, more the pastor you're
called to be. And preach—throw yourself into that work; it will save your ministry and maybe your life.

A friend who is an Anglican bishop lamented to me that many of his priests
think they've done their job when they've visited the nursing home. No, he says,
that's a part (and only a tiny part) of tending the flock. What about growing the
flock? Old school practitioners of homiletics (the art of preaching) used to teach
that preachers should spend an hour in the study for every minute in the pulpit.
Do the math in your faith tradition—how much time would a preacher then be
working on her sermon? Ten hours, twenty hours, forty hours? And then contrast
that with what we actually do. Don't feel guilty! Salvation is all grace. It's just
interesting to pay attention to where our time goes.

Now try this: Think of your best day in ministry. A perfect day. A day when
you were fully alive. A day when everybody was eating what you were cooking.
Linger in that day. What made it so wonderful? Now ask this: What's to stop that
day from coming again? And again?

I know the answer: church work! Eugene Peterson tells of a pastor friend who
lamented that he could never do any ministry "because I have to run this damn
church!"[3] Committee meetings, budgets, reports for the general church, bulletin
preparation, sermon preparation, and, indeed, time spent in the nursing home.
By the time you get to the end of the last sentence, your week is shot and you
may feel you've done none of it well—or worse, that it wouldn't matter even if
you did do any of it well. The perceived inevitability of mainline church decline
hangs over many conversations with pastors. They're often correct, in part. Some
reasons the church is struggling are outside their control.

But we pastors do have some control—more than we think. We can decide
how we spend our time. No one can force your best time and energy go into
soul-draining busywork. What if we prioritize what gives us life as a Christian, as
a person, as a leader called by God for the sake of God's people? I don't mean
the surreptitious pastime that we sneak away from work for; I mean the part of
ministry that God can only ask for from us—because God planted that particular
gift only in us.

Think with me of the future church, envisioned by leading prognosticat-
ing theologians like Elaine Heath, the church that may be coming to wealthier
Western countries in post-Christendom.[4] The church to come will be smaller,

3. Peterson, *Pastor*.
4. See, e.g., Heath, *Mystic Way of Evangelism*.

with fewer tall steeples and more neighborhood gatherings. There will be no career ladder. There will be no guaranteed job or salary level or institutional apparatus. Think of gatherings with friends and neighbors over food, with one another's kids on laps, crackers and cheese and beverages balanced precariously on knees, and Jesus, and little more. Now, look around at those neighbors. They are a lot more diverse than the church was in 1950 (which, granted, is not saying much!). They are from all races, socioeconomic levels, classes, and religious backgrounds. They are here because you built relationships with them. You made a point of connection—"Wait, you care about that? Me too! Let's work together." And the primary thing you care about together is the health of the neighborhood you share.

You see, in the future no one will ask how many people come to your church, because no one will care. What they will ask is what should have been asked about our ministry all along: How is the health of the neighborhood around you? Is it flourishing? Especially for those who are most in need? For creation in ecological peril? For those at the edges of life? You will gather to praise the Lord of the universe with folks with whom you share refrigerator space—not just people with your last name, but friends and strangers with whom you're becoming family in the church. You will not have trained to be a boundary-minding religious professional (ha!) but to be a friend of Jesus. That is, a saint. Which is what all people are called to be once we're most fully alive. How are we going to pay for the mortgage? The pension? The health insurance? No idea. Those aren't the point and never were. But pooling money to give away to bless the poor—that *is* the point. It always was. We just often forget. God's gifts are always Israel-shaped. They're not for us. They're *through* us, for everybody else.

My best days as a pastor were those when I was creating something new. I met with a campus minister because, well, we both cared about the state of students who were trying to be Christians on a secular campus. By the end, we were conspiring on a project to build a trail on the land behind the church that took years and countless volunteer hours and little money but a lot of community buy-in. How did we get there? We got to know one another and realized we shared a sense that ministry is designed to bless a community. I learned about him hiking and building hiking trails, and he learned that the church had dreamed of building a trail on land gifted years ago but had never gotten around to it, and voilà! An idea, a partnership for ministry, a way to bless our town—none of it existed before that meeting, though the pieces were in place. All we needed was already in our midst: a dream, some resources, one another, and a desire to bless our town. That can happen without a pension fund. I promise.

There are other days when you don't get to do what you want. They call it "work" for a reason, and they do have to pay you for it. But those days should get our worst attention. We can do those tasks tired, while on email, at the end of the day, or whenever we're not our best selves. Every pastor knows the children's sermon about the rice, the golf balls, and the jar. Try to put the rice in first and the golf balls won't fit. Put the golf balls in first and the rice will fill in the space around them. The point is that if we put God first in our lives, everything else will fill in. Well, gentle Reverend, isn't it so with your ministry? Prioritize the stuff that matters and patch in the rest.

But the rest *is* my ministry, you may say, trying to "run this damn church!" Agreed—and there are powerful structures conspiring to keep that in place. Conspire back. Do the thing for the church's sake that most gives you and it life. Spend an extravagant amount of time on making that sermon better. Meet with local leaders and artists and provocateurs to learn what God is up to in the neighborhood and dream about how you and the church might join in. Read the book you're longing to read to keep your spirit humming and your mind working. Hatch a way to integrate your exercise with your church's ministry. It can be done! As I shared earlier, we once had a marathon team raise money for a local antipoverty initiative. Or another idea: get college students to teach your elderly parishioners Tai Chi, and you participate too—get healthier and call it ministry all at the same time! Listen to a lecture at a local institution and bring someone along who has no idea their mind needs expanding that way. Ask someone to take up a leadership position who has no idea whether they can do it—and then support them until they do far more than they thought they could. Pray! Prayer runs the universe. Most of the time it doesn't feel like it, but you can demonstrate prayer's effectiveness. It's simple. Fold your hands and bow your head.

The church is the starting point for Jesus's revolution to take back the world and make it the world God intends. This is why you took up pastoral work in the first place. Do it again. The work is still worth doing. And it always will be.

Acknowledgments

From Rae Jean

My professional currency is in journal articles, not books; this is my first. I want to thank David Toole for encouraging me to write this book and for finding for me such an excellent writing partner in Jason Byassee. Jason deserves a world of thanks for making the writing process so much more interesting than it would have been solo. Thank you, Jason, for enriching my understanding immeasurably, giving feedback so kindly, making me laugh during each and every phone call, and sharing in the joy of writing.

I am deeply indebted to the team at the Duke Clergy Health Initiative. Thank you, Kate Rugani, for modeling over the years how to communicate. You are now the permanent parrot on my shoulder while I write, telling me what can be cut and pointing out what is still muddled. Thank you, Carl Weisner, for bringing your curiosity and gift of critical thinking. Thank you, Rachel Meyer, for suggesting creative ways of capturing the reader's imagination, including this book's title and cover image; John James for keeping the conference rolls and Melanie Kolkin for early organization of Spirited Life; and Amanda Wallace for being my memory. Thank you, David Eagle, for analyzing data, reading drafts, and questioning my framing and interpretation until I got it right. Thank you, Jia Yao and Xiang-Fang Li, for your tireless and very precise data analyses; Xin Liu, who contributed analyses to this book; and Liz Turner, who supervised them and explained the stats to me (multiple times) so I could understand. You are the ultimate Clergy Health Initiative crew who have walked this clergy health journey with me in full and for whom I'm extremely thankful. I also thank other readers of draft chapters, including

Glen Milstein, Holly Hough, Celia Hybels, and Cheryl Ann Beals, for making this book much better, and Steve Lindsley, for his contribution to chapter 1.

So much of this book was informed by Spirited Life and what its thirteen wellness advocates learned from the one thousand–plus Spirited Life participants. Even though I didn't know those pastors' names, I learned secondhand from parts of their stories. These wellness advocates—Kelli Sittser, Caren Swanson, Scottie Stamper, LaKeyta Johnson, Lisa MacKenzie, Dwight Tucker, Joel Decker, Tommy Grimm, Katie Huffman, Angela MacDonald, Ellie Poole, and Catherine Wilson—immersed themselves in conversations with pastors, generated creative ideas, dreamed a big program, and actualized it. I'd like to give special thanks to wellness advocate and research coordinator Rachel Blouin, whose consolidation of the literature on stressors, appraisal, and stress symptoms is conveyed in chapter 4, which might not exist without her, and to Monica Rivers for training the Wellness Advocates on health coaching and helping with our program conceptualization. Gary Bennett shaped Spirited Life in more ways than he knows, and I thank Robin Swift, who got me involved in the Clergy Health Initiative in the first place and has been a true friend throughout. Thank you also to Ed Moore for introducing me to the ways of the UMC system and for encouraging the platypus to evolve. I also appreciate insights generated by Cathleen Crain, Niel Tashima, Terry Redding, and Michelle Wilson of LTG Associates.

Several researchers allowed me to include their data and findings in this book, even if not published elsewhere. Many thanks to you, Corey Keyes and Matt Bloom. Thank you, Bill Bacon of The Duke Endowment for being a fabulous thought partner in this work. I would be lost without the quality data collection by Gail Thomas, Crystal MacAllum, Ed Mann, and their team at Westat. Thanks also to the many Spirited Life events staff and their health screening research coordinators, including Holly Hough and Alana Bennett. Several parts of this book were also inspired by clergy, including (the real) Mike Johnson, Karen Howell, and Edie Gleaves.

By now you know I am a believer in positive mental health and the way positive emotions open your mind. I won the cortical lottery, and I thank my parents for the good childhood that seems to have solidified my positive outlook. The constant encouragement I receive from my husband, Scott, and from my colleague and mentor Kate Whetten keep me reaching out and up.

I am grateful for the financial support from the Rural Church Area of The Duke Endowment, which fully funded my and Jason's time to create this book. In particular, I thank Dr. Dennis Campbell, Vice Chair of The Duke Endowment and Chair of the Rural Church Area, for his thoughts and support, and Trustee Constance (Connie) Gray for her unwavering encouragement. Thank you for helping us spread what we've learned among UMC pastors in North Carolina to a wider audience.

From Jason

I am grateful to the Clergy Health Initiative at Duke Divinity School for dialing me into this project. Thanks are due to Carl Weisner and to Rae Jean Proeschold-Bell, who has gone from someone I once admired from afar to a genuine friend whom I admire all the more.

I have done three or four tours of duty at Duke, depending on how one counts: I grew up in the neighborhood when my dad worked at Duke, then studied as a seminary student there, did doctoral work there, and worked for Leadership Education at Duke Divinity when we founded *Faith and Leadership*. I love the place. This opportunity to be back involved in Duke's ministry was a gift. The Duke Endowment's support makes these institutions possible. I love James B. Duke's vision that strong rural churches strengthen rural communities. I owe my ordination to this vision, in fact. I went to Duke to study God. But Duke offered good money for summer internships serving little country churches. I loved those summers and so felt called by God to serve in ministry. I also love his desire to have a world-class university in what was once pine forests and tobacco fields in central North Carolina. If you're going to catch Harvard and Yale, with their three-hundred-year head start, you have to hustle. That hustle makes Duke a place constantly unsatisfied with itself, which is difficult. It also makes Duke the gift it is to the world.

I am also grateful to Boone and Shady Grove United Methodist Churches in North Carolina, where I have served as pastor, and to Valle Crucis, Bethelview, Duke Memorial, Trinity, Winfield, Purley, and New Hope UMCs in North Carolina and Illinois, where my wife, Jaylynn, has served. I have had more unofficial leadership roles at Tenth Church here in Vancouver (where Jaylynn served on staff) and at Gary Memorial and Flowing Grace UMCs in Illinois. These places have cared for us well as we have done ministry together, and they curated the imagination from which these stories came. I am grateful to Jaylynn and to my boys, Jack, Sam, and Will, for trying to be church as a family here in a new place for us, Vancouver, British Columbia. I am grateful to Richard Topping and the Vancouver School of Theology for the opportunity to try life on this coast, in this country, among these new friends.

My staff at Boone Methodist teased me, based on my previous book *The Gifts of the Small Church*, that I would one day write *The Gifts of the Largish University Church in a Small Mountain Town*. I would swear not, but maybe they were right. Many (though not all) of these stories are drawn from my time at Boone UMC, where I served from 2011 to 2015, a place I love and miss terribly. I have altered those stories to protect folks' privacy and the integrity of our relationships, splicing and disguising identities, though trying to tell true stories. None of these folks related to me on the assumption that I would be writing about them. And yet if I have anything to offer this project, it is because of our having gone through the difficult and joyous process of trying to be a church together. I tell a disproportionate number of stories here of challenge—this book is about clergy health and its obstacles, so that was unavoidable—yet not a day goes by when I don't miss that congregation, long for it, pray for it, and wonder what life would be like were I there. What a spectacularly gifted staff and group of lay leaders I was privileged to get to work and plan and pray and play with.

I am grateful to the pastors, Methodist and far beyond, who have shared their troubles as ordained people with me: WJ, JL, PA, LP, KC, HR, WB, and HE especially. These are gifted and well-trained people, magnificent souls, who have struggled mightily in ministry. Any human being would be blessed to have them in their life; any church should be staggered at its fortune to have them as pastors. Human beings are difficult. All God has is sinners to work through, as I often say. And these folks bear scars on their bodies that signify their joining to Jesus and his saving work. Thank you, friends.

I tried to list all the other ministers to whom I'm indebted, friends without whom there is no life worth living, surrogate sisters and brothers, mothers and fathers, and children that I've received through the church. I ran out of time and was sure I was forgetting people.

If the church gives us such people whom we would not have without it, then church is not only worth it; it is beautiful, reflecting beauty itself.

Appendix

Recommendations for Clergy Health Programs

Three Clergy Health Programs

With funding from The Duke Endowment, between 2009 and 2016, the Duke Clergy Health Initiative designed three health programs. The first was a one-year holistic health program that we piloted with eighty-one pastors. Improving on this program, we created Spirited Life, which ran from 2011 to 2016. Over 1,100 UMC clergy in North Carolina participated in Spirited Life, and our rigorous study of it found clinically meaningful improvements for weight, waist circumference, blood pressure, and HDL cholesterol.[1] These physical health results endured across the two-year program, which was impressive because most programs don't sustain results past one year. We were also pleased because most programs target one specific outcome, such as blood pressure, and only enroll people highly motivated to improve it. In contrast, we enrolled all comers and let them pick their health goals, and we still found significant physical health improvements.

Unfortunately, Spirited Life did not improve depression and stress symptoms. Why not? Spirited Life did not address depression directly. We had hoped that by providing health coaching, pastors would identify mental health as a goal and their health coaches would refer them to depression treatment. This happened sometimes, but not often enough. We had also

1. Proeschold-Bell et al., "Two-Year Holistic Health and Stress Intervention."

hoped that improved stress management would decrease depression, but the program did not even decrease stress symptoms. Stress symptoms are difficult to address because of the interplay of stressors, how someone perceives those stressors, and the resources people have available to respond to stressors. That is why we wrote chapter 4, "A Practical Guide to Combating Stress Symptoms."

In a third clergy health program, we wanted to create a church-level program, thinking it might simultaneously strengthen churches and foster lay leader support for pastors. We developed Pastor and Parish, which focuses on staff/pastor parish relations committees—the personnel committees of the UMC. We describe this in more detail below, but briefly, Pastor and Parish is a set of six videos plus workbook exercises that the pastor and the personnel committee do together. We pilot-tested the curriculum with six churches, and an external evaluation company found a year later that all six pastors reported reduced feelings of stress. Since then, at least fifty-four districts in twenty-two UMC conferences have ordered the DVD and workbooks, which are available online.[2]

Lessons and Recommendations

We now share with you candidly the lessons we learned from developing, conducting, and evaluating these three clergy health programs. The sections below are organized into program aspects. For example, in Spirited Life we invited all UMC clergy in North Carolina, targeted holistic health, and across two years offered pastors health screenings, workshops with theological components, health grants, health coaching, a weight-loss program, and stress management programs.[3] Here is what we learned.

Inviting Everyone

We offered Spirited Life to all UMC clergy in North Carolina, regardless of their current health status or readiness to make a behavior change. We simply said, "Come, if not for yourself, then to support your brothers and sisters in ministry." Over 64 percent of invited clergy (1,114) enrolled. We could not serve them all simultaneously, so we created three start times, spaced a year apart, and lost very few pastors as a result of the wait. Some pastors even welcomed having a delay so they could plan ahead to find the time needed.

2. https://clergyhealthinitiative.org; https://pastorandparish.knowclassic.com/.
3. Proeschold-Bell et al., "Randomized Multiple Baseline Design."

We were fortunate that so many pastors engaged in Spirited Life at the same time. We believe they influenced each other for the better and may have created some healthier norms. We recommend seeking high participation among clergy in a limited geographic area to try to change social norms.

Targeting Holistic Health

Through Spirited Life, we wanted to improve mental and physical health, as well as spiritual well-being. For mental health, we sought to decrease depression and stress.[4] For physical health, we sought to decrease metabolic syndrome, which is a cluster of five health indicators linked to heart disease, stroke, and hospitalizations.[5] The indicators are a large waist circumference, high blood pressure, signs of diabetes or pre-diabetes, elevated triglycerides, and not enough high-density lipoprotein (HDL, the "good" cholesterol).[6]

Logistically, targeting holistic health meant offering diverse health programs to meet a variety of health goals. We chose programs that support lifestyle changes, such as changes in how one eats, exercises, relaxes, socializes with others, and prays.[7] Pastors engaged in a variety of these programs. However, this approach made conducting Spirited Life more difficult; we were constantly communicating with participants about program options and with program providers about how to make it easier for pastors to sign up for and participate in those programs.

Despite this extra work, we believe there was great benefit to focusing on holistic health. A major benefit was the lack of stigma attached to participating in Spirited Life. Pastors felt comfortable telling each other that they were in the program. Participating did not by definition convey, for example, that they had mental health problems, and yet they could still address their mental health. A downside to addressing health broadly is that it is harder to find strong improvements in a particular outcome like weight loss across all program participants, since many participants are working on other areas of health. However, we believe this trade-off was worth making. Our focus on holistic health resulted in a larger number of pastors signing up and gave pastors the opportunity to address multiple health goals at once or to segue smoothly to a second or third health goal rather than being limited to one.

---

4. Our understanding of stress evolved while we enacted Spirited Life, and our improved understanding is shared in chap. 4, "A Practical Guide to Combating Stress Symptoms." Today, we would say we wanted to decrease "stress symptoms" and not use the unhelpful word "stress."

5. Isomaa et al., "Cardiovascular Morbidity."

6. Alberti, Zimmet, and Shaw, "Metabolic Syndrome."

7. Walsh, "Lifestyle and Mental Health."

Regular Health Screenings

The first thing pastors did in Spirited Life was attend a health screening event and have their diabetes risk, cholesterol, and blood pressure measured. Mostly for study purposes, we asked pastors to attend a similar health screening one year later and then at six-month intervals for up to two and a half more years. At each event, we gave pastors their results on the spot. Anecdotally, pastors told us that these repeated measures of their health encouraged them to go to the doctor or make behavior changes. We also saw this in our data. One set of Spirited Life participants received health screenings for two years while waiting to join the program. We saw an improvement in their health at their third health screening, *before* they received any programming! Mind you, it seems like it took pastors not just one but two health screenings to make changes, but quite possibly there was a benefit to experiencing repeated health screenings even in the absence of programming. Furthermore, for two sets of Spirited Life participants, we continued health screenings for eighteen months after the end of programming. Some pastors saw their health improvements in blood sugar and triglycerides go away in the six to twelve months after the end of programming, *but then* showed improvements at eighteen months after the end of programming. One explanation we can think of for this worsening-then-improving is that the health screening gave pastors feedback on their health, and when they saw that they were getting worse, they reengaged in the healthy behaviors they had practiced during the program. However, it is impossible for us to be sure what caused the changes we observed.

Theology and Workshops

A couple months after their health screening, Spirited Life participants attended a three-day, two-night workshop. While this was a hardship for some (about 8 percent dropped out because of this requirement; see below for more on our decision to include it), we believed it was essential to begin with a theological grounding given in person. We reasoned that a pastor's call might be getting in the way of tending to the pastor's health in the first place (see chap. 2, "When Work Is Holy"). We addressed this through a rich exploration of Wesleyan theology, with particular attention to theological thinking that emphasized incarnation and how precious the flesh-and-blood body is, given that God chose to send his son in human form. Our theological partner in this was Rev. H. Edgar Moore, who gave sermons on incarnation for each workshop. Reverend Moore assured me that people interested in clergy health programs could find many other pastors to write sermons on incarnation that would work well.

Because Spirited Life was a full two years (see "Program Length" below), we offered workshops at the program's mid- and endpoints. We did this both to reengage pastors who may have stopped making behavior changes and to allow all pastors to reflect on their progress and on what health goals they might want to work on next. We also believe it is essential to repeat health messages; repetition is an important part of learning in general and is positively essential if you want someone to act on what they've learned. So in each workshop, we included messages about theology and health.

The second workshop included one overnight stay. In it, we incorporated worship and communion, which gave pastors a rare chance to be in the pews. We included another, slightly different sermon on incarnation. We made our own videos, interviewing Episcopal priest Claire Wimbush, who has given a lot of thought to theology and physical health as she lives with severe cerebral palsy. (You can find one of these videos on the *Faith and Leadership* website; please use it!)[8] In the workshop, pastors watched the videos and discussed them with each other—they often offered each other wiser insight and counsel than we could have. We also taught skills in these workshops. Sometimes we exposed participants to centering prayer, other times to keeping Sabbath,[9] and other times to psychological stress management techniques.

We made the third and final workshop a time of reflection and celebration. We repeated our theological messages in new ways. For example, Episcopal priest Sam Portaro gave a sermon on what it means to take care, and how you have to *take* care. Pastors also noted what health goals they had achieved and considered the goals they might pursue next. We emphasized that health behaviors are like an ongoing journey; you must press on, no matter how much—or how little—progress you have achieved.

The workshops were well attended. Of the first set of Spirited Life participants, 71 percent attended all three workshops, 20 percent missed one workshop, and 9 percent attended only the required first workshop.

You might be wondering if the workshops needed to include overnight stays. In Spirited Life, we made our first workshop three days long in order to provide both a full stress management program and theological content. However, we now think that the workshop could be much shorter—perhaps just a day. For the final workshops, we experimented with making them just one day and had decent attendance, but attendance was lower than for workshops with

8. "Claire Wimbush: Broken People Walking Toward Wholeness," Faith and Leadership, https://www.faithandleadership.com/multimedia/claire-wimbush-broken-people-walking-toward-wholeness.

9. In partnership with Matthew Sleeth and Nancy Sleeth of Blessed Earth, http://www.blessedearth.org/.

overnight stays. We found that pastors who registered for a one-day workshop were more likely to not show up, perhaps because a single day didn't seem like such a big deal or driving both ways in one day seemed too exhausting when the day arrived, or because they knew we wouldn't lose money on prepaid lodging and didn't feel so bad about canceling.

If we were to do it all again, we would keep the workshops—participants loved them. They loved the fellowship with other clergy and the time away from their churches, including having a private hotel or retreat center room. As people who continually focus on others, pastors loved experiencing this temporary focus on them, as well as being pastored through worship and communion.

Health Grants

At the second workshop, we discussed with pastors the $500 that they could receive a couple months later in January. To do so, they needed to identify a health goal, discuss it with their health coach, and submit a one-page application describing their intended use for the money. Pastors were allowed to fund any activity that fell into eight evidence-based lifestyle activities (described in chap. 7).[10] You won't be shocked to learn that 96 percent of the first group of pastors took advantage of the $500 grants. Over half of the pastors chose to spend money on exercise (gym memberships, equipment, classes), but they also spent money on recreation (kayaks, bikes, gardening), family vacations, and spiritual retreats. Eighteen pastors even bought new clothes for their thinner bodies. If we got to do Spirited Life again, we would still offer a small grant, although we don't know if it needs to be as much as $500. The grant seemed to reengage participants on their core health goals. We believe it was a wise investment that helped them to sustain behavior change and long-term health improvements.

Health Coaching

Following the first workshop, Spirited Life participants were paired with health coaches, whom we called Wellness Advocates. We recommend that any health coach you hire (or contract with) has formal training in health coaching, including an emphasis on motivational interviewing. Motivational interviewing is a set of techniques that keeps motivation alive within the pastor—not within the health coach.[11] Rather than the health coach saying,

10. Walsh, "Lifestyle and Mental Health."
11. Miller, *Motivational Enhancement Therapy*.

"Here are your goals—why aren't you working on them?" the health coach asks
questions like, "What are the pros and cons you see in making this change?"
A motivational interviewing approach acknowledges that behavior change is
hard and can leave a person emotionally conflicted because there are some
aspects of any habit that "work" for you (like eating a box of cookies, which
can feel good even while harming your physical health—see Jason's "Behind
the Pulpit: Agency" in chap. 5).

In Spirited Life, pastors had continual access to health coaching for two
years and could work with their Wellness Advocate on any holistic health
goal; the Wellness Advocate also helped them with the process of setting goals.
They participated in an average of 6.3 health coaching sessions, with a range
of 0 to 20. We suggested that participants schedule monthly health coaching
sessions. We now think sessions should have occurred more frequently at
first, perhaps weekly for six weeks and then tapered to every two weeks and
then monthly. People need more support at the beginning. The coaching was
mostly done by phone, which worked well.

Would we include health coaching if we got to do Spirited Life again?
Health coaching was the program's glue for many participants. Nevertheless,
a large percentage of participants (19 percent) used zero or just one health
coaching session. It may work to contract out health coaching for only the
least healthy or most interested pastors; many companies provide lifestyle
health coaching.

Naturally Slim

In addition to health coaching, following the first workshop, Spirited Life
participants were encouraged to watch the ten weight-loss and healthy eating
videos that comprise Naturally Slim.[12] Each video lasts about an hour, and
the content focuses on noticing when you're hungry, eating a healthy portion
size, and decreasing sugar intake. The program also encourages walking and
suggests writing down what you eat if you aren't meeting your weight goals.

When we started in 2011, we weren't sure if pastors would engage with an
online program, but we found that pastors did indeed log on and watch the
online videos. Among the first set of Spirited Life pastors, 83 percent signed
up for Naturally Slim and 34 percent watched all ten sessions; 28 percent
watched between seven and nine sessions, and only 12 percent did not watch
any sessions. Because so many pastors across the state were in Spirited Life,
we could hear them using the Naturally Slim lingo of "hunger savers" and

12. See https://www.naturallyslim.com/home.

such at clergy gatherings. When pastors got together, they noticed how much weight some of them had lost. The visual improvement was a motivator! What's more, we saw the clergy culture change so that pastors were more aware of physical health and healthy eating. In chapter 5, Jason wrote that "you become like those around you." We were able to leverage this social tendency to benefit pastors.

One decision we had to make was whether we would ask pastors of normal weight to watch the Naturally Slim videos. We decided to do so and are glad we did. It is easier to prevent weight gain in the first place than to lose weight and keep it off, so including everyone was a preventive approach. Also, weight loss and weight maintenance are relevant to all clergy. As covered in chapter 5, only 25 percent of the UMC clergy in North Carolina are at a normal weight,[13] and clergy in other denominations and geographic locations also suffer from high rates of obesity.[14]

Program Length

Spirited Life was unusual in its two-year duration; a more common period for health interventions is six months. Our hope was that with such a long time frame, pastors would have the opportunity to set a health goal, try out a tool or learn a skill, relapse (so to speak), and then be able to return to that tool or skill while still having the support of a health coach.

Overall, pastors participated in some way across the full two-year period. Some disengaged, only to reengage at the midpoint when we offered the $500 grant and required them to discuss their spending plans with their health coach. Spacing the three workshops at regular intervals—beginning, middle, and end—kept pastors engaged and provided an opportunity to reflect on their behavioral progress (even if it was to identify what was *not* working for them).

If we ran Spirited Life again, we would make it slightly shorter. It was innovative to try such a long program, but even our most devoted participants did not use the full two years of health coaching. We think twelve to fifteen months would be long enough to try out behaviors, slip off the bandwagon, and get back on. That said, even after two years many pastors simply did not feel "done." They asked for the option of taking a break and then starting a new health program, which would be another programmatic approach to consider.

13. Proeschold-Bell and LeGrand, "High Rates of Chronic Disease."
14. "Clergy Health Survey," General Board of Pensions and Health Benefits, Center for Health; Halaas, "Ministerial Health and Wellness."

Choice, Engagement, and Reengagement

In Spirited Life, we tried to give pastors choices and let them engage in multiple ways. I noted above that we asked pastors to choose their own health goals and that they could be about the mind, body, spirit, or all three. In addition, we structured the program for pastors to engage in healthy acts often, ideally every week. The structure of many clergy well-being interventions is a weeklong workshop, but in Spirited Life, we spread out the intervention: workshop, health coaching, Naturally Slim, workshop, more health coaching, small grant, and so on. The key to improving health is making several small changes, like giving up one dessert per day or regularly taking a walk. It's my belief that you can't effectively practice regular behavior change while on a retreat. Personally, when I'm on vacation, I'm pretty good at exercising and getting lots of sleep, but I find those things much harder to do while working full-time.

Think back to Jason's piece on agency, where he noted the reasons pastors may feel they have limited choice in their lives. It's possible to get caught up in that thinking and have it generalize across areas of your life, until you stop making even the changes that are clearly in your power. By offering a variety of program options, Spirited Life forced pastors to think about what they most needed—for health but also for life generally. It also forced pastors to figure out where they would find the time to engage in the healthy practices they needed. The Wellness Advocate was available to talk through those choices and help plan.

Stress Management

We tried two stress management programs, and I think it's fair to say that pastors did not like the ones we chose. We chose one that had empathy as a key component and found that pastors felt they were already all too empathetic. The other stress program that we chose, which was online, was perceived as too corporate. And because it was online but lacked Naturally Slim's structure of a weekly one-hour video, pastors did not engage with it, indicating that they were too stressed to spend time online . . . working on their stress. We wonder if finding a way to bolster positive mental health (as conceptualized in chap. 6) would be more fruitful than offering a stress management program.

Broad Recommendations

If you're considering offering a program to improve clergy health, we encourage you to do the following:

- provide pastors with choices in the program to promote their agency;
- find ways for pastors to feel permission to tend to their health and then have this permission-giving message repeated—otherwise pastors' sacred call may take perpetual priority;
- include theological understandings of health;
- destigmatize mental health problems;
- find ways to listen to pastors and offer them confidentiality and unconditional support; and
- engage a critical mass of clergy who already regularly connect and interact with each other (perhaps based on geography or conference), in an effort to impact social norms.

Pastor and Parish: Going beyond Individual Pastors

Spirited Life focused on helping individual clergy make changes. However, it's hard for a pastor to sustain healthy behaviors without friends, family, and parishioners engaging in healthy behaviors. Support for pastors' health also needs to come from their supervisors and denomination officials. The more levels of support you have for health (community, institutions, policies), the more likely it is that individuals can make a health behavior change and stick with it.

The church and its lay leaders have critical influence on a pastor. As we saw in one example from chapter 4, lay leaders can impact pastors by deflecting unwarranted parishioner criticism and making sure warranted criticism is given constructively and kindly. To this end, we worked with longtime UMC pastor and former district superintendent Rev. H. Edgar Moore to develop a curriculum called Pastor and Parish. Pastor and Parish was designed to build better understanding and communication between pastors and church personnel committee members. Better communication could lead to fewer stressful circumstances—something that Spirited Life did not seem to achieve, possibly because it focused on individual pastors—pointing to the need for multilevel programs like this one. In Pastor and Parish, pastors and personnel committee members together watch a series of six videos and go through workbook exercises corresponding to each video. For example, the first session focuses on framing a lay leader's work as a response to their baptism. Another session makes an analogy to a "sacred bundle" to illustrate how parishioners might assume that a pastor knows what's in the church's bundle—its history, including its secrets—when in fact the pastor will not know unless told, setting the pastor up to misstep. The six sessions conclude with the participants creating their own covenant, developed from concepts explored in the earlier sessions, for their work on the committee as a ministry of discipleship and stewardship. Although we can't easily bring Spirited Life to you, you can order the Pastor and Parish DVD and workbooks online.[15]

To Learn More

You can read more about Spirited Life on our website, which includes a report and articles giving more details on the program and the research outcomes. Visit us at www.clergyhealthinitiative.org.

15. See https://clergyhealthinitiative.org and https://pastorandparish.knowclassic.com/.

Bibliography

Adams, C., H. Hough, R. J. Proeschold-Bell, J. Yao, and M. Kolkin. "Clergy Burnout: A Comparison Study with Other Helping Professions." *Pastoral Psychology* 66, no. 2 (2016): 147–75. DOI:10.1007/s11089-016-0722-4.

"Adult Obesity in the United States." Trust for America's Health and Robert Wood Johnson Foundation. 2014. http://stateofobesity.org/adult-obesity/.

Airhart, P. *A Church with the Soul of a Nation: Making and Remaking the United Church of Canada*. Montreal: McGill-Queens, 2013.

Alberti, K. G. M. M., P. Zimmet, and J. Shaw. "Metabolic Syndrome—A New World-Wide Definition: A Consensus Statement from the International Diabetes Federation." *Diabetic Medicine* 23, no. 5 (2006): 469–80.

"Alcohol Facts and Statistics." National Institute of Alcohol Abuse and Alcoholism. February 2017. https://www.niaaa.nih.gov/alcohol-health/overview-alcohol-con sumption/alcohol-facts-and-statistics.

Alloy, L. B., and L. Y. Abramson. "Judgment of Contingency in Depressed and Non-depressed Students: Sadder but Wiser?" *Journal of Experimental Psychology: General* 108 (1979): 441–85.

Althaus, P. *The Theology of Martin Luther*. Minneapolis: Fortress, 1966.

Amano, M., K. Suemaru, R. Cui, Y. Umeda, B. Li, Y. Gomita, H. Kawasaki, and H. Araki. "Effects of Physical and Psychological Stress on 5-HT2A Receptor-Mediated Wet-Dog Shake Responses in Streptozotocin-Induced Diabetic Rats." *Acta Med Okayama* 61, no. 4 (2007): 205–12.

Andrade, L., J. J. Caraveo-Anduaga, P. Berglund, R. V. Bijl, R. DeGraaf, W. Vollebergh, E. Dragomirecka, et al. "The Epidemiology of Major Depressive Episodes: Results from the International Consortium of Psychiatric Epidemiology (ICPE) Surveys." *International Journal of Methods in Psychiatric Research* 12, no. 1 (2003): 3–21.

Associated Press. "Study Shows Average Divorce Rate among Clergy." *Los Angeles Times.* July 1, 1995. http://articles.latimes.com/1995-07-01/local/me-19084_1_divorce-rate.

Baron, R. A. "Environmentally Induced Positive Affect: Its Impact on Self-Efficacy, Task Performance, Negotiation, and Conflict." *Journal of Applied Social Psychology* 20 (1990): 368–84.

Baruth, M., S. Wilcox, and R. Evans. "The Health and Health Behaviors of a Sample of African-American Pastors." *Journal of Health Care for the Poor and Underserved* 25, no. 1 (2014): 229–41.

Bauerschmidt, F. *Holy Teaching: Introducing the* Summa Theologiae *of St. Thomas Aquinas.* Grand Rapids: Brazos, 2005.

Beck, A., A. L. Crain, L. I. Solberg, J. Unützer, R. E. Glasgow, M. V. Maciosek, and R. Whitebird. "Severity of Depression and Magnitude of Productivity Loss." *Annals of Family Medicine* 9, no. 4 (2011): 305–11.

"Behavioral Risk Factor Surveillance System." Centers for Disease Control and Prevention. May 8, 2017. https://www.cdc.gov/brfss/.

Bell, J. C., ed. *Till Victory Is Won: Famous Black Quotations from the NAACP.* New York: Washington Square, 2002.

Bless, H., G. Bohner, N. Schwarz, and F. Strack. "Mood and Persuasion: A Cognitive Response Analysis." *Personality and Social Psychology Bulletin* 16 (1990): 331–45.

Blizzard, S. W. "The Minister's Dilemma." *Christian Century* 73 (1956): 508–10.

Blouin, R., and R. J. Proeschold-Bell. "Measuring Stress in a Clergy Population." *Research in the Social Scientific Study of Religion* 26 (2015): 141–54.

Blumenthal, J. A., M. A. Babyak, P. M. Doraiswamy, L. Watkins, B. M. Hoffman, K. A. Barbour, S. Herman, et al. "Exercise and Pharmacotherapy in the Treatment of Major Depressive Disorder." *Psychosomatic Medicine* 69, no. 7 (2007): 587–96.

Bopp, M., and E. A. Fallon. "Individual and Institutional Influences on Faith-Based Health and Wellness Programming." *Health Education Research* 26, no. 6 (2011): 1107–19.

Burcusa, S. L., and W. G. Iacono. "Risk for Recurrence in Depression." *Clinical Psychology Review* 27, no. 8 (2007): 959–85.

Calvert, G., J. Merling, and C. Burnett. "Ischemic Heart Disease Mortality and Occupation among 16- to 60-Year-Old Males." *Journal of Occupational and Environmental Medicine* 41, no. 11 (1999): 960–66.

Campbell, D. M. "The Call to Ordained Ministry." In *Who Will Go for Us? An Invitation to Ordained Ministry*, 26–59. Nashville: Abingdon, 1994.

Carlson, L. E., and B. C. Thomas. "Development of the Calgary Symptoms of Stress Inventory (C-SOSI)." *International Journal of Behavioral Medicine* 14, no. 4 (2007): 249–56.

Carlson, R. *Don't Sweat the Small Stuff . . . and It's All Small Stuff.* New York: Hyperion, 1997.

Carnevale, P. J. D., and A. M. Isen. "The Influence of Positive Affect and Visual Access on the Discovery of Integrative Solutions in Bilateral Negotiation." *Organizational Behavior and Human Decision Processes* 37 (1986): 1–13.

Carroll, J. W. *God's Potters: Pastoral Leadership and the Shaping of Congregations.* Grand Rapids: Eerdmans, 2006.

Carver, C. S., and S. Vargas. "Coping and Health." In *Handbook of Behavioral Medicine: Methods and Applications.* Edited by A. Steptoe, 199–200. New York: Springer, 2010.

Case, A., R. J. Proeschold-Bell, C. Keyes, K. Huffman, K. Sittser, A. Wallace, P. Khatiwoda, and H. Parnell. "Attitudes and Behaviors That Differentiate Clergy with Positive Mental Health from Those with Burnout." *Journal of Prevention and Intervention in the Community* (forthcoming).

Chaves, M., S. L. Anderson, and A. Eagle. "National Congregations Study." In *Cumulative Data File and Codebook.* Durham, NC: Duke University, Department of Sociology, 2014.

Clay, R. A. "Is Stress Getting to You?" *Monitor on Psychology* 42, no. 1 (January 2011): 58, http://www.apa.org/monitor/2011/01/stress.aspx.

"Clergy." O*NET 20.3 database. 2016. http://www.myplan.com/careers/clergy/description-21-2011.00.html.

"Clergy Health Survey: Report." General Board of Pensions and Health Benefits, Center for Health. June 2015. http://www.gbophb.org/assets/1/7/4785.pdf.

"Clinical Guidelines on the Identification, Evaluation, and Treatment of Overweight and Obesity in Adults." National Institutes of Health. *Obesity Research* 6, supp. 2 (1998): 51S–209S.

Cohen, S. "Contrasting the Hassles Scale and the Perceived Stress Scale: Who's Really Measuring Appraised Stress?" *American Psychologist* 41, no. 6 (1986): 716–18.

Cohen, S., T. Kamarck, and R. Mermelstein. "A Global Measure of Perceived Stress." *Journal of Health and Social Behavior* 24, no. 4 (1983): 385–96.

Cohen, S., and G. M. Williamson. "Perceived Stress in a Probability Sample of the US." In *The Social Psychology of Health: Claremont Symposium on Applied Social Psychology*, edited by S. Spacapam and S. Oskamp, 31–67. Newbury Park, CA: Sage, 1988.

"Conservative Icon Jesse Helms Dead at 86." *WRAL.com.* July 4, 2008. http://www.wral.com/conservative-icon-jesse-helms-dead-at-86/1755723/.

Crawford, E. R., J. A. LePine, and B. L. Rich. "Linking Job Demands and Resources to Employee Engagement and Burnout: A Theoretical Extension and Meta-analytic Test." *Journal of Applied Psychology* 95, no. 5 (2010): 834–48.

Dallman, M. F., N. C. Pecoraro, and S. E. la Fleur. "Chronic Stress and Comfort Foods: Self-Medication and Abdominal Obesity." *Brain, Behavior, and Immunity* 19, no. 4 (2005): 275–80.

Dante. *Inferno*. Translated by Mark Musa. Vol. 1 of *The Divine Comedy*. New York: Penguin, 2003.

Darling, C. A., E. W. Hill, and L. M. McWey. "Understanding Stress and Quality of Life for Clergy and Clergy Spouses." *Stress and Health* 20, no. 5 (2004): 261–77. DOI:10.1002/smi.1031.

Daughters, S. B., A. R. Braun, M. N. Sargeant, E. K. Reynolds, D. R. Hopko, C. Blanco, and C. W. Lejuez. "Effectiveness of a Brief Behavioral Treatment for Inner-City Illicit Drug Users with Elevated Depressive Symptoms: The Life Enhancement Treatment for Substance Abuse (LETS Act!)." *Journal of Clinical Psychiatry* 69 (2008): 122–29.

"Depression." National Institute of Mental Health. Updated October 2016. http://www.nimh.nih.gov/health/topics/depression/index.shtml.

Dewe, P. J. "New Zealand Ministers of Religion: Identifying Sources of Stress and Coping Strategies." *Work and Stress* 1 (1987): 351–63.

Diener, E., R. E. Lucas, and C. Scollon. "Beyond the Hedonic Treadmill: Revising the Adaptation Theory of Well-Being." *American Psychologist* 61 (2006): 305–14.

DiMatteo, M. R., H. S. Lepper, and T. W. Croghan. "Depression Is a Risk Factor for Non-compliance with Medical Treatment." *Archives of Internal Medicine* 160, no. 14 (2000): 2101–7.

Dobson, M. L. *Health as a Virtue: Thomas Aquinas and the Practice of Habits of Health*. Eugene, Oregon: Pickwick, 2014.

Doolittle, B. R. "Burnout and Coping among Parish-Based Clergy." *Mental Health, Religion and Culture* 10, no. 1 (2007): 31–38.

Dostoyevsky, Fyodor. *The Brothers Karamazov*. 12th edition. Translated by Richard Pevear and Larissa Volokhonsky. New York: Farrar, Straus & Giroux, 2002.

Ellison, C. G., and J. S. Levin. "The Religion-Health Connection." *Health Education and Behavior* 24 (1998): 700–720.

Elper, O. W., and S. Handelman, eds. *Torah of the Mothers: Contemporary Jewish Women Read Classical Jewish Texts*. New York: Urim, 2000.

Elsbach, K., and P. Barr. "The Effects of Mood on Individuals' Use of Structured Decision Protocols." *Organization Science* 10 (1999): 181–98.

Erez, A., and A. M. Isen. "The Influence of Positive Affect on the Components of Expectancy Motivation." *Journal of Applied Psychology* 87 (2002): 1055–67.

Eswine, Z. *Spurgeon's Sorrows: Realistic Hope for Those Who Suffer from Depression*. Fearn, UK: Christian Focus, 2015.

Flannelly, K. J., A. J. Weaver, D. B. Larson, and H. G. Koenig. "Rabbis and Health: A Half-Century Review of the Mental and Physical Health Care Literature, 1950–99." *Pastoral Psychology* 54 (2006): 545–54.

———. "A Review of Mortality Research on Clergy and Other Religious Professionals." *Journal of Religion and Health* 41, no. 1 (2002): 57–68.

Flegal, K. M., M. D. Carroll, B. K. Kit, and C. L. Ogden. "Prevalence of Obesity and Trends in the Distribution of Body Mass Index among US Adults, 1999–2010." *Journal of the American Medical Association* 307 (2012): 491–97.

Folkman, S., R. S. Lazarus, C. Dunkel-Schetter, A. DeLongis, and R. J. Gruen. "Dynamics of a Stressful Encounter." *Journal of Personality and Social Psychology* 50, no. 5 (1986): 992–1003.

Frame, M. W., and C. L. Shehan. "Work and Well-Being in the Two-Person Career: Relocation Stress and Coping among Clergy Husbands and Wives." *Family Relations* 43 (1994): 196–205.

Frankl, V. *Man's Search for Meaning*. Boston: Beacon, 1956.

Fredrickson, B. L. "Cultivating Positive Emotions to Optimize Health and Well-Being." *Prevention and Treatment* 3 (March 7, 2000): 001a.

———. *Love 2.0*. New York: Plume, 2013.

———. "Positive Emotions Broaden and Build." In *Advances in Experimental Social Psychology* 47, edited by P. Devine and A. Plant, 1–53. San Diego: Elsevier, 2013.

———. "Role of Positive Emotions in Positive Psychology: The Broaden-and-Build Theory of Positive Emotions." *American Psychologist* 56, no. 3 (2001): 218–26.

———. "Updated Thinking on Positivity Ratios." *American Psychologist* 68, no. 9 (2013): 814–22.

———. "What Good Are Positive Emotions?" *Review of General Psychology* 2, no. 3 (1998): 300–319.

Fredrickson, B. L., and C. Branigan. "Positive Emotions Broaden the Scope of Attention and Thought-Action Repertoires." *Cognition and Emotion* 19, no. 3 (2005): 313–32.

Fredrickson, B. L., and R. W. Levenson. "Positive Emotions Speed Recovery from the Cardiovascular Sequelae of Negative Emotions." *Cognition and Emotion* 12, no. 2 (1998): 191–220.

Fredrickson, B. L., R. A. Mancuso, C. Branigan, and M. M. Tugade. "The Undoing Effect of Positive Emotions." *Motivation and Emotion* 24, no. 4 (2000): 237–58.

"Freedom Has Come to Birmingham." Webisode 14, segment 6 of *Freedom: A History of US*. https://www.pbs.org/wnet/historyofus/web14/segment6_p.html.

Frenk, S., S. A. Mustillo, S. L. Foy, W. D. Arroyave, E. G. Hooten, K. H. Lauderback, and K. G. Meador. "Psychotropic Medication Claims among Religious Clergy." *Psychiatric Quarterly* 4, no. 1 (March 8, 2013): 27–37.

Gable, P., and E. Harmon-Jones. "Approach-Motivated Positive Affect Reduces Breadth of Attention." *Psychological Science* 19, no. 5 (2008): 476–82.

———. "The Blues Broaden, but the Nasty Narrows: Attentional Consequences of Negative Affects Low and High in Motivational Intensity." *Psychological Science* 21, no. 2 (2010): 211–15.

George, L. K., C. G. Ellison, and D. B. Larson. "Explaining the Relationships between Religious Involvement and Health." *Psychological Inquiry* 13, no. 3 (2002): 190–200.

Gleason, John J. "Perception of Stress among Clergy and Their Spouses." *Journal of Pastoral Care* 31, no. 4 (1977): 448–52.

Golder, S. A., and M. W. Macy. "Diurnal and Seasonal Mood Vary with Work, Sleep, and Day Length across Diverse Cultures." *Science* 333 (2011): 1878–81.

Greene-McCreight, K. *Darkness Is My Only Companion: A Christian Response to Mental Illness*. Rev. ed. Grand Rapids: Brazos, 2015.

Haidt, J. *The Happiness Hypothesis: Finding Modern Truth in Ancient Wisdom*. New York: Basic Books, 2006.

Halaas, G. W. "Ministerial Health and Wellness, 2002." Report to the ELCA Division for Ministry. Chicago, 2002. http://www.elca.org/News-and-Events/4542.

Hang-Yue, N., S. Foley, and R. Loi. "Work Role Stressors and Turnover Intentions." *The International Journal of Human Resource Management* 16, no. 11 (2005): 2133–46.

Hauerwas, S. "Speak Christian: An Exhortation to Ministers of the Gospel." *ABC Religion and Ethics*. February 22, 2017. http://www.abc.net.au/religion/articles /2017/02/22/4624681.htm.

Hawkley, L. C., and J. T. Cacioppo. "Loneliness Matters." *Annals of Behavioral Medicine* 40, no. 2 (2010): 218–27.

Headley, B. "The Set-Point Theory of Well-Being." *Social Indicators Research* 85, no. 3 (2008): 389–403.

"Health, United States, 2015: With Special Feature on Racial and Ethnic Health Disparities." National Center for Health Statistics. https://www.cdc.gov/nchs/data /hus/hus15.pdf#019.

"Healthy People 2020: An Opportunity to Address the Societal Determinants of Health in the United States." Secretary's Advisory Committee on Health Promotion and Disease Prevention Objectives for 2020. July 26, 2010. http://www.healthypeople .gov/2010/hp2020/advisory/SocietalDeterminantsHealth.htm.

Heath, E. *The Mystic Way of Evangelism: A Contemplative Vision for Christian Outreach*. Grand Rapids: Baker Academic, 2008.

Hedley, A. A., C. L. Ogden, C. L. Johnson, M. D. Carroll, L. R. Curtin, and K. M. Flegal. "Prevalence of Overweight and Obesity among US Children, Adolescents, and Adults, 1999–2002." *Journal of the American Medical Association* 291, no. 23 (2004): 2847–50.

Heffner, C. L. "Emotion." *AllPsych*. http://allpsych.com/psychology101/emotion.html.

"The History of Antibiotics." Microbiology Society. https://www.microbiologysociety .org/education-outreach/antibiotics-unearthed/antibiotics-and-antibiotic-resist ance/the-history-of-antibiotics.html.

Hoffman, B. M., M. A. Babyak, W. E. Craighead, A. Sherwood, P. M. Doraiswamy, M. J. Coons, and J. A. Blumenthal. "Exercise and Pharmacotherapy in Patients with Major Depression." *Psychosomatic Medicine* 73, no. 2 (2011): 127–33.

Hogg, M. A., and J. Cooper, eds. *The Sage Handbook of Social Psychology.* Thousand Oaks, CA: Sage Publications, 2003.

Holmes, T. H., and R. H. Rahe. "The Social Readjustment Rating Scale." *Journal of Psychosomatic Research* 11, no. 2 (1967): 213–18.

Hom, H., and B. Arbuckle. "Mood Induction Effects upon Goal Setting and Performance in Young Children." *Motivation and Emotion* 12 (1988): 113–22.

Horowitz, M. "Life Events Questionnaires for Measuring Presumptive Stress." *Psychosomatic Medicine* 39, no. 6 (1977): 413–31.

"How Food Can Help Your Stress Levels." Stress Management Society. January 21, 2016. http://www.stress.org.uk/How-food-can-help-your-stress-levels.aspx.

Hummer, R. A., R. G. Rogers, C. B. Nam, and C. G. Ellison. "Religious Involvement and U. S. Mortality." *Demography* 36, no. 2 (1999): 273–85.

Irenaeus. *Against Heresies.* In *Irenaeus of Lyons.* Translated by R. M. Grant. New York: Routledge, 1997.

Isen, A. M. "Success, Failure, Attention and Reaction to Others: The Warm Glow of Success." *Journal of Personality and Social Psychology* 15 (1970): 294–301.

Isen, A. M., K. A. Daubman, and G. P. Nowicki. "Positive Affect Facilitates Creative Problem Solving." *Journal of Personality and Social Psychology* 52, no. 6 (June 1987): 1122–31.

Isomaa, B., P. Almgren, T. Tuomi, B. Forsén, K. Lahti, M. Nissén, M. R. Taskinen, and L. Groop. "Cardiovascular Morbidity and Mortality Associated with the Metabolic Syndrome." *Diabetes Care* 24, no. 4 (2001): 683–89.

Jarmul, D. "A Franklin Celebration." *Duke Today.* June 11, 2009. https://today.duke.edu/2009/06/franklinfolo.html.

Jenson, R. *Systematic Theology.* Vol. 1, *The Triune God.* New York: Oxford University Press, 1997.

John XXIII (Pope). *Overlook Much, Correct a Little: 99 Sayings by John XXIII.* Edited by H.-P. Röthlin. Hyde Park: New City, 2007.

Johnson, E. B. "The State of Female and Racial/Ethnic United Methodist Clergy in the US." 2012. http://s3.amazonaws.com/Website_GCFA/resources/Data_Services/documents/State_of_Female_and_Racial-Ethnic_Clergy.pdf.

Jones, L. G. "Job Description." *Christian Century* 123, no. 1 (January 2006). http://www.christiancentury.org/article/2006-01/job-description.

Kanner, A. D., J. C. Coyne, C. Schaefer, and R. S. Lazarus. "Comparison of Two Modes of Stress Measurement: Daily Hassles and Uplifts versus Major Life Events." *Journal of Behavioral Medicine* 4, no. 1 (1981): 1–38.

Kavanagh, D. J. "Mood, Persistence, and Success." *Australian Journal of Psychology* 39 (1987): 307–18.

Kay, W. K. "Role Conflict and British Pentecostal Ministers." *Journal of Psychology and Theology* 28 (2000): 119–24.

Keyes, C. L. M. "Chronic Physical Conditions and Aging: Is Mental Health a Potential Protective Factor?" *Ageing International* 30 (2005): 88–104.

———. "Mental Health as a Complete State." In *Bridging Occupational, Organizational and Public Health: A Transdisciplinary Approach*, edited by G. F. Bauer and O. Hämmig, 179–92. New York: Springer Science + Business Media, 2014.

———. "The Mental Health Continuum: From Languishing to Flourishing in Life." *Journal of Health and Social Behavior* 43, no. 2 (2002): 207–22.

———. "Mental Illness and/or Mental Health?" *Journal of Consulting and Clinical Psychology* 73, no. 3 (2005): 539–48.

———. "The Nexus of Cardiovascular Disease and Depression Revisited: The Complete Mental Health Perspective and the Moderating Role of Age and Gender." *Aging and Mental Health* 8, no. 3 (2006): 266–74.

———. "Overview of the Mental Health Continuum-Short Form (MHC-SF)." https://www.bttop.org/sites/default/files/public/MHC-SF%20Brief%20Introduction%20 9.22.2014.pdf.

———. "Promoting and Protecting Mental Health as Flourishing: A Complementary Strategy for Improving National Mental Health." *American Psychologist* 62, no. 2 (2007): 95–108.

———. "Social Well-Being." *Social Psychology Quarterly* 61, no. 2 (1998): 121–40.

Keyes, C. L. M., S. S. Dhingra, and E. J. Simoes. "Change in Level of Positive Mental Health as a Predictor of Future Risk of Mental Illness." *American Journal of Public Health* 100, no. 2 (2010): 2366–71.

Keyes, C. L. M., and J. G. Grzywacz. "Health as a Complete State: The Added Value in Work Performance and Healthcare Costs." *Journal of Occupational and Environmental Medicine* 47, no. 5 (2005): 523–32.

Kinderman, P., M. Schwannauer, E. Pontin, and S. Tai. "Psychological Processes Mediate the Impact of Familial Risk, Social Circumstances and Life Events on Mental Health." *PLOS ONE* 8, no. 10 (2013). e76564. DOI:10.1371/journal.pone.0076564.

King, H., and J. C. Bailar III. "The Health of the Clergy." *Demography* 6, no. 1 (1969): 27–43.

King, H., and F. B. Locke. "American White Protestant Clergy as a Low-Risk Population for Mortality Research." *Journal of the National Cancer Institute* 65, no. 5 (1980): 1115–24.

Knox, S., S. G. Virginia, and J. P. Lombardo. "Depression and Anxiety in Roman Catholic Secular Clergy." *Pastoral Psychology* 50, no. 5 (2002): 345–58.

Knox, S., S. G. Virginia, J. Thull, and J. P. Lombardo. "Depression and Contributors to Vocational Satisfaction in Roman Catholic Secular Clergy." *Pastoral Psychology* 54, no. 2 (2005): 139–53.

Koenig, H. G., and H. J. Cohen, eds. *The Link between Religion and Health*. Oxford: Oxford University Press, 2001.

Koenig, H. G., M. E. McCullough, and D. B. Larson. *Handbook of Religion and Health*. New York: Oxford University Press, 2001.

Krause, N., and S. Stryker. "Stress and Well-Being: The Buffering Role of Locus of Control Beliefs." *Social Science and Medicine* 18, no. 9 (1984): 783–90. DOI: 10.1016/0277-9536(84)90105-9.

Kroenke, K., R. L. Spitzer, and J. B. Williams. "The Patient Health Questionnaire-9." *Journal of General Internal Medicine* 16, no. 9 (2001): 606–13.

Kuhne, G. W., and J. F. Donaldson. "Balancing Ministry and Management: An Exploratory Study of Pastoral Work Activities." *Review of Religious Research* 37 (1995): 147–63.

Laitinen, J., E. Ek, and U. Sovio. "Stress-Related Eating and Drinking Behavior and Body Mass Index and Predictors of This Behavior." *Preventative Medicine* 34, no. 1 (2002): 29–39.

Lazarus, R. S. *Psychological Stress and the Coping Process*. New York: McGraw-Hill, 1966.

Lazarus, R. S., and S. Folkman. *Stress, Appraisal, and Coping*. New York: Springer, 1984.

Lee, C., and J. Iverson-Gilbert. "Demand, Support, and Perception in Family-Related Stress among Protestant Clergy." *Family Relations* 52, no. 3 (2003): 249–57. DOI: 10.1111/j.1741-3729.2003.00249.x.

LeGrand, S., R. J. Proeschold-Bell, J. James, and A. Wallace. "Healthy Leaders: Multilevel Health Promotion Considerations for Diverse United Methodist Church Pastors." *Journal of Community Psychology* 41, no. 3 (2013): 303–21.

Lewis, C. S. *A Grief Observed*. San Francisco: HarperOne, 2001.

Lewis, J. Interview by K. Tippett. "Love in Action." *On Being*. Podcast audio. January 26, 2017. https://onbeing.org/programs/john-lewis-love-in-action/.

Lindholm, G., J. Johnston, F. Dong, K. Moore, and E. Ablah. "Clergy Wellness: An Assessment of Perceived Barriers to Achieving Healthier Lifestyles." *Journal of Religion and Health* 55 (2016): 97–109.

Lindsey, M. *Faith in the Halls of Power: How Evangelicals Joined the American Elite*. New York: Oxford, 2008.

Lischer, R. *Stations of the Heart: Parting with a Son*. New York: Knopf, 2013.

Luckhaupt, S. E., M. A. Cohen, J. Li, and G. M. Calvert. "Prevalence of Obesity among U. S. Workers and Associations with Occupational Factors." *American Journal of Preventive Medicine* 46, no. 3 (2014): 237–48.

Luther, M. *Luther's Works: Lectures on Genesis*. Edited by Jaroslav Pelikan. St. Louis: Concordia, 1958.

Lyubomirsky, S., L. King, and E. Diener. "The Benefits of Frequent Positive Affect: Does Happiness Lead to Success?" *Psychological Bulletin* 131 (2005): 803–55.

"Major Depression among Adults." National Institute of Mental Health, 2015. https://www.nimh.nih.gov/health/statistics/prevalence/major-depression-among-adults.shtml.

Marcus, M., M. T. Yasamy, M. van Ommerman, D. Chisholm, and S. Saxena. "Depression: A Global Public Health Concern." 2012. http://www.who.int/mental_health/management/depression/who_paper_depression_wfmh_2012.pdf.

Maslach, C. "Burnout: A Multidimensional Perspective." In *Professional Burnout: Recent Developments in Theory and Research*, edited by W. B. Schaufeli, C. Maslach, and T. Marek, 19–32. Philadelphia: Taylor and Francis, 1993.

Maslach, C., S. E. Jackson, and M. P. Leiter. *Maslach Burnout Inventory Manual*. 3rd ed. Mountain View, CA: CPP, 1996.

Mazzuchelli, T., R. Kane, and C. Rees. "Behavioral Activation Treatments for Depression in Adults." *Clinical Psychology Science and Practice* 16 (2009): 383–411.

McMinn, M. R., R. A. Lish, P. D. Trice, A. M. Root, N. Gilbert, and A. Yap. "Care for Pastors: Learning from Clergy and Their Spouses." *Pastoral Psychology* 53, no. 6 (2005): 563–81.

Meador, K. G., S. A. Mustillo, W. D. Arroyave, and S. M. Frenk. "The Church Benefits Association Survey: Health, Well-Being, Spirituality, and Job Characteristics." http://www.wespath.org/assets/1/7/Church_Benefits_Association_Survey_07-23-07.pdf.

Meek, K. R., M. R. McMinn, C. M. Brower, T. D. Brunett, B. W. McRay, M. L. Ramey, D. W. Swanson, and D. D. Villa. "Maintaining Personal Resiliency: Lessons Learned from Evangelical Protestant Clergy." *Journal of Psychology and Theology* 31, no. 4 (2003): 339–47.

Miles, A., R. J. Proeschold-Bell, and E. Puffer. "Explaining Rural/Non-Rural Disparities in Physical Health-Related Quality of Life: A Study of United Methodist Clergy in North Carolina." *Quality of Life Research* 20, no. 6 (2011): 807–15.

Miller, W. R. *Motivational Enhancement Therapy with Drug Abusers*. Albuquerque: University of New Mexico, 1995.

Monsell, S. "Task Switching." *Trends in Cognitive Sciences* 7, no. 3 (2003): 134–40.

Moss, O., III. *Blue Note Preaching in a Post-Soul World: Finding Hope in an Age of Despair*. Louisville: Westminster, 2015.

Mother Teresa. *Mother Teresa: Come Be My Light; The Private Writings of the Saint of Calcutta*. Edited by B. Kolodiejchuk. New York: Doubleday, 2007.

National Center for Health Statistics. "Prevalence of Current Depression among Persons Aged ≥12 years, by Age Group and Sex—United States, National Health and Nutrition Examination Survey, 2007–10." *Morbidity and Mortality Weekly Report* 60, nos. 51 and 52 (2012): 1747.

National Institute of Mental Health. "Twelve-Month Prevalence of Major Depressive Episode among U. S. Adults (2015)." http://www.nimh.nih.gov/health/statistics/prevalence/major-depression-among-adults.shtml.

"National Survey of Long-Haul Truck Driver Health and Injury." US Department of Transportation. January 14, 2014. https://www.fmcsa.dot.gov/sites/fmcsa.dot.gov /files/docs/National%20Survey%20of%20Long-Haul%20Truck%20Driver%20 Health%20and%20Injury_508CLN.pdf.

Niebuhr, H. R. *The Purpose of the Church and Its Ministry*. New York: Harper and Row, 1957.

Niebuhr, R. *The Irony of American History*. Chicago: University of Chicago Press, 1952.

Nietzsche, F. *The Portable Nietzsche*. Edited and translated by W. Kaufmann. New York: Viking, 1982.

Noller, P. "Clergy Marriages." *Australian Journal of Sex, Marriage and Family* 5 (1984): 187–97.

Nouwen, H. *The Wounded Healer: Ministry in Contemporary Society*. New York: Doubleday, 1979.

Oliver, M. *New and Selected Poems*. Vol. 1. Boston: Beacon, 1994.

Pargament, K. I. *The Psychology of Religion and Coping*. New York: Guilford, 1997.

Pargament, K. I., and A. Mahoney. "Sacred Matters: Sanctification as a Vital Topic for the Psychology of Religion." *International Journal for the Psychology of Religion* 15, no. 3 (2005): 179–98.

Pargament, K. I., B. W. Smith, H. G. Koenig, and L. Perez. "Patterns of Positive and Negative Coping with Major Life Stressors." *Journal for the Scientific Study of Religion* 37, no. 4 (1998): 710–24.

Pascal, B. *Pensées: The Provincial Letters*. New York: Random House, 1941.

Peterson, E. *The Pastor: A Memoir*. New York: HarperCollins, 2011.

———. "Teach Us to Care and Not to Care." In *Subversive Spirituality*, 154–68. Grand Rapids: Eerdmans, 1997.

Podsakoff, N. P., J. A. LePine, and M. A. LePine. "Differential Challenge Stressor-Hindrance Stressor Relationships with Job Attitudes, Turnover Intentions, Turnover, and Withdrawal Behavior: A Meta-Analysis." *Journal of Applied Psychology* 92, no. 2 (2007): 438–54.

Powell, L. H., L. Shahabi, and C. E. Thoresen. "Religion and Spirituality: Linkages to Physical Health." *American Psychologist* 58, no. 1 (2003): 36–52.

Pratt, L. A., and D. J. Brody. "Depression in the United States Household Population, 2005–6." *NCHS Data Brief* 7 (2008): 1–7.

Proeschold-Bell, R. J., and S. LeGrand. "High Rates of Chronic Disease and Obesity among United Methodist Clergy." *Obesity* 18, no. 9 (2010): 1867–70.

———. "Physical Health Functioning among United Methodist Clergy." *Journal of Religion and Health* 51, no. 3 (2012): 734–42. DOI:10.1007/s10943-010-9372-5.

Proeschold-Bell, R. J., S. LeGrand, J. James, A. Wallace, C. Adams, and D. Toole. "A Theoretical Model of the Holistic Health of United Methodist Clergy." *Journal of Religion and Health* 50, no. 3 (2011): 700–720. DOI:10.1007/s10943-009-9250-1.

Proeschold-Bell, R. J., A. Miles, M. Toth, C. Adams, B. Smith, and D. Toole. "Using Effort-Reward Imbalance Theory to Understand High Rates of Depression and Anxiety among Clergy." *Journal of Primary Prevention* 34, no. 6 (2013): 439–53. DOI: 10.1007/s10935-013-0321-4.

Proeschold-Bell, R. J., B. Smith, A. Eisenberg, S. LeGrand, C. Adams, and A. Wilk. "The Glory of God Is a Human Being Fully Alive: Predictors of Positive Versus Negative Mental Health among Clergy." *Journal for the Scientific Study of Religion* 54, no. 4 (2015): 702–21.

Proeschold-Bell, R. J., R. Swift, G. Bennett, H. E. Moore, X. Li, R. Blouin, V. Williams, R. Williams, and D. Toole. "Use of a Randomized Multiple Baseline Design: Rationale and Design of the Spirited Life Holistic Health Intervention Study." *Contemporary Clinical Trials* 35 (2013): 138–52.

Proeschold-Bell, R. J., E. L. Turner, G. G. Bennett, J. Yao, X.-F. Li, D. E. Eagle, R. A. Meyer, R. B. Williams, R. Y. Swift, H. E. Moore. "A Two-Year Holistic Health and Stress Intervention." *American Journal of Preventive Medicine* 53, no. 3 (2017): 290–99.

Redei, E. E., B. M. Andrus, M. J. Kwasny, J. Seok, X. Cai, J. Ho, and D. C. Mohr. "Blood Transcriptomic Biomarkers in Adult Primary Care Patients with Major Depressive Disorder Undergoing Cognitive Behavioral Therapy." *Translational Psychiatry* 16, no. 4 (March 8, 2014): e442.

Rehman, U. S., L. E. Evraire, G. Karimiha, and J. A. Goodnight. "Actor-Partner Effects and the Differential Roles of Depression and Anxiety in Intimate Relationships." *Journal of Clinical Psychology* 71, no. 7 (2015): 715–24.

Reynolds, S. L., and J. M. McIlvane. "The Impact of Obesity and Arthritis on Active Life Expectancy in Older Americans." *Obesity* 17, no. 2 (2009): 363–69.

Rohr, R. *Everything Belongs: The Gift of Contemplative Prayer*. New York: Crossroad, 1999.

———. *On the Threshold of Transformation*. Chicago: Loyola, 2010.

———. "Transforming Our Pain." *Center for Action and Contemplation*. February 26, 2016. https://cac.org/transforming-our-pain-2016-02-26/.

Ross, M. *The Fountain and the Furnace: The Way of Tears and Fire*. Eugene, OR: Wipf and Stock, 2014.

Russell, M. D. *A Thread of Grace*. New York: Ballantine, 2005.

Ryff, C. D. "Happiness Is Everything, or Is It? Explorations on the Meaning of Psychological Well-Being." *Journal of Personality and Social Psychology* 57, no. 6 (1989): 1069–81.

Sarason, I. G., E. H. Potter, and B. R. Sarason. "Recording and Recall of Personal Events." *Journal of Personality and Social Psychology* 2 (1986): 347–56.

Scherer, K. R., A. Shorr, and T. Johnstone, eds. *Appraisal Processes in Emotion: Theory, Methods, Research*. Canary, NC: Oxford University Press, 2001.

Schneiderman, N., G. Ironson, and S. D. Siegle. "Stress and Health." *Annual Review of Clinical Psychology* 1 (2005): 607–28.

Seeman, M. "Personal Control." *Psychosocial Notebook*. University of California San Francisco Research Network on SES and Health. 2008. http://www.macses .ucsf.edu/research/psychosocial/control.php#controlbeliefs.

Siegrist, J. "Adverse Health Effects of High-Effort/Low-Reward Conditions." *Journal of Occupational Health Psychology* 1, no. 1 (1996): 27–41.

Smith, T. W. "Job Satisfaction in the United States." 2007. http://www-news.uchica go.edu/releases/07/pdf/070417.jobs.pdf.

Stewart-Sicking, J. "Subjective Well-Being among Episcopal Priests." *Journal of Prevention and Intervention in the Community* 40, no. 3 (2002): 180–93.

Stone, A. A., J. M. Smyth, T. Pickering, and J. Schwartz. "Daily Mood Variability: Form of Diurnal Patterns and Determinants of Diurnal Patterns." *Journal of Applied Social Psychology* 26, no. 14 (1996): 1286–305.

Stossel, S. "What Makes Us Happy, Revisited: A Look at the Famous Harvard Study of What Makes People Thrive." *The Atlantic*. May 2013. http://www.theatlantic .com/magazine/archive/2013/05/thanks-mom/309287/.

"Stress Management." Mayo Clinic. April 16, 2015. http://www.mayoclinic.org/heal thy-lifestyle/stress-management/in-depth/exercise-and-stress/art-20044469.

Taylor, H. A., S. A. Coady, D. Levy, E. R. Walker, R. S. Vasan, J. Liu, E. L. Akylbekova, R. J. Garrison, and C. Fox. "Relationships of BMI to Cardiovascular Risk Factors Differ by Ethnicity." *Obesity* 18, no. 8 (August 2010): 1638–45. DOI:10.1038/oby.2009.407.

Tice, D. M., and H. Wallace. "Mood and Emotion Control." *Psychological Inquiry* 11, no. 3 (2000): 214–17.

"Trends in Current Cigarette Smoking among High School Students and Adults, 1965–2014." Centers for Disease Control and Prevention. https://www.cdc.gov /tobacco/data_statistics/tables/trends/cig_smoking/.

VanderWeele, T. J. "Religious Communities and Human Flourishing." *Current Directions in Psychological Science* 26, no. 5 (2017): 476–81.

Vaillant, G. E. *Aging Well: Surprising Guideposts to a Happier Life from the Landmark Harvard Study of Adult Development*. Boston: Little, Brown, 2002.

"Vital Statistics of the United States, 1960, Volume 2: Mortality." National Center for Health Statistics. 1963. https://www.cdc.gov/nchs/data/vsus/VSUS_1960_2A.pdf.

Wadlinger, H. A., and D. M. Isaacowitz. "Positive Mood Broadens Visual Attention to Positive Stimuli." *Motivation and Emotion* 30, no. 1 (2006): 87–99.

Wagner, R., and A. Briggs. *The Penultimate Curiosity: How Science Swims in the Slipstream of Ultimate Questions*. New York: Oxford University Press, 2016.

Walsh, R. "Lifestyle and Mental Health." *American Psychologist* 66, no. 7 (2011): 579–92.

Wang, P. S., P. A. Berglund, and R. C. Kessler. "Patterns and Correlates of Contacting Clergy for Mental Disorders in the United States." *Health Services Research* 38, no. 2 (2003): 647–73.

Ware, J. E., M. Kosinski, D. M. Turner-Bowker, and B. Gandek. *SF-12v2: How to Score Version 2 of the SF-12 Health Survey*. Lincoln, RI: QualityMetric Inc., 2002.

Weaver, A., D. Larson, K. Flannelly, C. Stapleton, and H. Koenig. "Mental Health Issues among Clergy and Other Religious Professionals." *The Journal of Pastoral Care and Counseling* 56 (2002): 393–403.

Webb, B. L., M. Bopp, and E. A. Fallon. "Factors Associated with Obesity and Health Behaviors among Clergy." *Health Behaviour and Public Health* 3, no. 1 (2013): 20–28.

Weiten, W., D. S. Dunn, and E. Y. Hammer. *Psychology Applied to Modern Life: Adjustment in the 21st Century*. 9th ed. Boston: Cengage Learning, 2015.

Wells, C., J. Probst, R. McKeown, S. Mitchem, and H. Whiejong. "The Relationship between Work-Related Stress and Boundary-Related Stress within the Clerical Profession." *Journal of Religion and Health* 51, no. 1 (2012): 215–30.

"What Is Stress?" American Institute of Stress. www.stress.org/what-is-stress/.

Winner, Lauren. *Still: Notes on a Mid-Faith Crisis*. New York: HarperOne, 2012.

Wolterstorff, N. *Lament for a Son*. Grand Rapids: Eerdmans, 1987.

Wood, D. "'The Best Life': Eugene Peterson on Pastoral Ministry." *Christian Century* 119, no. 6 (2002): 18–25.

Index

Note: Page numbers in italics refer to figures and tables.